Spirit

Hegel

Spirit

Chapter Six of Hegel's
Phenomenology of Spirit

Edited with Introduction, Notes, and Commentary, by
Daniel E. Shannon

Translation by the Hegel Translation Group,
Trinity College, University of Toronto

Hackett Publishing Company, Inc.
Indianapolis/Cambridge

06 05 04 03 02 01   1 2 3 4 5 6 7

For further information, please address:

Hackett Publishing Company, Inc.
P. O. Box 44937
Indianapolis, Indiana 46244–0937

www.hackettpublishing.com

Cover design by Listenberger Design & Associates

Library of Congress Cataloging-in-Publication Data

Hegel, Georg Wilhelm Friedrich, 1770–1831.
    [Geist. English]
    Spirit: chapter six of Hegel's Phenomenology of spirit / Hegel; edited,
with introduction, notes, and commentary, by Daniel E. Shannon;
translation by the Hegel Translation Group, Trinity College, University
of Toronto.
        p. cm.
    Includes bibliographical references (p.) and index.
    ISBN 0-87220-570-3 (cloth) — ISBN 0-87220-569-X (paper)
    1. Spirit   2. Self (Philosophy)   3. Hegel, Georg Wilhelm Friedrich,
1770–1831. Geist   I. Shannon, Daniel E., 1955–   II. Hegel Translation
Group (Toronto, Ont.)   III. Title.

B2928. E5 H48 2001
193—dc21   00–049868

CONTENTS

INTRODUCTION TO THE
TRANSLATION

In the mid-1980s a group of Hegel scholars gathered at Trinity College at the University of Toronto in order to work on a new translation of Hegel's *Phenomenology of Spirit*. They decided that, given limitations of time and the difficulty of translating by committee, they would take only the most important part of Hegel's work and render it into accurate English. This translation would employ the precise conceptual terminology that corresponds to Hegel's systematic categories. This decision was instigated by H. S. Harris, who argued that both Baille's and A. V. Miller's translations of the *Phenomenology of Spirit* were defective in a number of areas. Even though Baille's translation renders into English every possible permutation of what Hegel's German terms can mean, he does so at the cost of precision, which leaves the reader with a wordy and unwieldy text. Miller's rendition is both more elegant and useful, but often he uses a variety of English expressions to render one German term without ever indicating to the reader that he is doing so. He also makes the mistake of misnumbering the paragraphs of Hegel's text, and on occasion he drops a word or phrase from the German. To illustrate the problem with Miller's translation, we can consider just one instance where he obscures Hegel's meaning by using too great a variety of English terms. The German expression *Sache selbst*, which is an important category in Hegel's definition of Reason, is rendered by Miller as "subject matter," "heart of the matter," and "the thing itself," among others.[1] While the German can mean any one of these when used conventionally, Hegel almost always intends it to des-

---

1. To be quite fair, the Hegel Group also had great difficulty in rendering this category by one English expression. At one time or another we used "Thing," "heart of the matter," "factum," and "subject matter." None of these capture Hegel's meaning accurately. See next note.

ignate the "facticity of individual consciousness;"[2] that is, the condition where consciousness identifies itself through its prudential self-interests and its reflection on worldly values. This term implies, for Hegel at least, a deception that spoils the "true character" of the Self and commits it to personal and moral error. This concept is the key for understanding the dialectic of Spirit, since Spirit's journey in the World is to discover how to overcome the deception latent in the *Sache selbst*. Thus for any accurate translation of Hegel's text it is essential to use as consistently as possible one term for this category, and I have used "facticity itself" accordingly.

The Hegel Group finally finished its work some years later but recognized that this text should not stand alone. The members of the group wanted English-reading students, both the novice and the English-speaking Hegel scholar, to have some guidance on the significance of the main sections and some interpretation on what Hegel's argument truly is. Hegel is an extraordinarily dense writer; both his concepts and complexity of argument leave all but the die-hard enthusiast groping to fathom his meaning. So, at a minimum, a general synopsis of the argument was to be given, and as far as possible the references, sources, and stratagem of his argument should also be presented for the students' use. The editorial notes in the text and the Commentary following the text are meant to be helpful to the nonenthusiast, especially to those who might be familiar with Hegel's text but who nonetheless have difficulty in understanding his meaning.

---

2. Martin Heidegger and Jean-Paul Sartre were the first to use this term, "facticity" (*Faktizität, faciticité*), to indicate both the factual condition of consciousness and the malediction of inauthenticity (for Heidegger) or "bad faith" (for Sartre). Sartre describes the concept as follows: "What am I? A being which is not its own foundation. . . . There is a restlessness, an appeal to conscience . . . , a feeling of guilt. . . . The intuition of our contingency is not identical with the feeling of guilt. Nevertheless it is true that in our own apprehension of ourselves, we appear to ourselves as having the character of an unjustifiable act," *Being and Nothingness*, trans. Hazel Barnes (NY: Simon and Schuster, 1953), p. 128. It seems appropriate to use this expression for Hegel's category of *Sache selbst* as well, since it is both a factual state of self-awareness—I know myself as I am—and as a condition of deception in which I fail to justify my character. In the development of this category Hegel implies that facticity is a practical identification of the Self, which looks to further its self-interests only as a matter of prudence as it turns to the World for validation. Self-consciousness, as this factual being, evaluates itself as the World looks at it, and thus the World's ways become part of self-consciousness's own factual identity. This self-evaluation commits self-consciousness to look to its destiny with others, and thus Hegel begins the chapter on Spirit with how this destiny has unfolded.

I

In the most general terms Hegel's chapter on Spirit is the history of the Concept of Reason in the World. His intention is to show the identification of the historical individual as a universal Self becoming conscious of itself in and through its worldly experiences. This "Self" I will call the "world-historical individual," and we might think of it concretely as both an individual person and a "type" who depicts the religious and/or moral outlook of an epoch. The individuals are supposed to be "singular," that is, actual individuals who act for-themselves and express "existential values." They are people whose factual nature makes them pursue self-satisfaction more often than not over any pursuit of a rightness of action. Their "universality" is seen in that they confront their factual nature involved in a conflict with their substance and self-identity; the pursuit of their true character as forged through this conflict allows them to seek and ultimately attain their own being-for-self (that is, their own self-determination). We all share in this universality; it is part of our "natural" and historical destiny. The result of this is, however, the "good end" where we reach self-satisfaction. This is where we have a true outlook and a good spirit.

The individuals in the chapter depict a conflict inherent in their World, and thus the "substance" of their life—the customs, mores, manners, foundational values, laws, and social systems—is shown within these conflicts to be undergoing a metaphysical change. We see the change, for example, in the upheaval from the time of the ancient World, where the "native spirit," whose substance lies in the family and localized custom, is compelled to sacrifice itself for the sake of human law and the "goods" of civil society. This upheaval leads to the decay and death of that World, and ultimately to the redefinition of Spirit's substance in the "new World," where church, nobility, and burgher ally themselves in a spiritual but also temporal unity. Whereas in the ancient World the substance was aboriginal to familial ties, in the "new World" only a sense of virtue and honor hold society together. Hegel's sense of "change" is not necessarily progressive, however, since the virtue and honor of modernity is easily sold for the highest price or the greatest prize. No matter the direction of the change, Hegel indicates that a change in the Self occurs through violent confrontations among the worldly powers. In each instance, the world-historical individual will recognize that the collision, the violence, and the resulting destruction are all due to a "fault" within its own category of self-identification; that is to say, the conflict is due to a fault lying within the movement of self-determination from which the struggle initiated. In this way the universality of consciousness shows us both the underlying deception that afflicts the facticity of individual consciousness, by which the world-historical individual comes to recognize her "sins," but further that within the conflict, the struggle, and even the destruction of substance, there is also the reality that these individuals have within themselves a spiritual power. Latent within their own self-consciousnesses is the reality of a divinity who is becoming incarnate in the World. This "god" Hegel calls "Spirit."

Although this chapter is historical, it is not concerned with the accidents of history, even though the fortunes of individuals play a prominent role in how the world-historical individual sees herself. Instead, the cohesion of the individual to her social station and the breaking apart of the social cohesion of substance are what interests Hegel most. Hegel's vision is principally religious; for it is religion that attempts to explain the connection between the human and the divine attributes of Self and World. There are many instances of the world-historical individual—for example, Antigone, Elagabalus, Prince de Condé, Rameau, just to name a few. These individuals' drive to overcome self-deception and to be redeemed in a spiritual power is itself due to the reality of this connection. Self-satisfaction never occurs at the individuals' level of existence (what Hegel calls "determinate being" or *Dasein*) without also the recognition and acknowledgment of the effectiveness of religion in explaining our alienation and redemption. The difficulty here, as Hegel shows, is that religion in the conventional sense has been principally the domain of denominations that are themselves afflicted by their own self-estrangement in the World. The "world-weariness" of "pure faith" can never fathom the sacred history of the world-historical individual. Neither can the vanity and pomposity of worldly confessions—what Hegel identifies as "pure insight"—grasp the destiny of such an individual. The religious sentiment that values the prudential self-interest of facticity above all else pushes these confessions to defend the values of a corrupt society, even as they mock them.[3] Much of Hegel's text is an indictment of the weakness of faith to stand up against materialism: a materialism that infects "faith" as if it were a poison. This weakness is due in large measure to the factions within Christianity being proponents of the *ancien régime*. Such so-called unworldly confessions, both Catholic and Protestant, were more concerned with belonging to "good

3. One of the ironies we witness is that the two sides of religious faith and enlightened "freethinking" belong to the same identification of consciousness. They both espouse their own self-interested desires as "pure" and "true," even though neither can acknowledge the truth of the other's viewpoint.

society" and to be a "type" worthy of receiving wealth and honor, than they were with understanding the latent philosophical truth of faith. In terms of the philosophical Concept, religion must be "saved" from its denominations, and the essential task of Hegel's speculative philosophy is shown to redeem religion. The only kind of philosophy that can hope to succeed in this cause, according to Hegel at least, is the "science" of philosophy, which analyzes and describes the experiences of consciousness. The analysis and description serve as a basis of understanding that redemption is not only possible, but has already occurred implicitly in the creation of this very science.

II

The *Phenomenology of Spirit* is the *science of the experience of consciousness.* This is a long expression for Hegel's conviction that the essence of humankind can be discovered in human experience. The "science" that he proposes looks to the formation of concepts that become part of his philosophical system, and they are formed in and through human events and intellectual debates.[4] "Science" equals the articulation and development of the array of the Concept; it focuses on the ongoing struggle to form identity between Self and World. This "science" is both empirical, since it requires observations in order to discover the "shape" of these concepts,[5] and also *a priori,* since the articulation and development of the array is speculative and occurs only in Reason.[6] Hegel's phenomenological science

---

4. Hegel is explicit that "intellectual debates" have a profound effect on forming the Self and its relation to the World. In "Spirit" he is principally concerned with the debate between the freethinkers and the proponents of faith. While there was a political struggle occurring as well, it is the intellectual battle that Hegel is keen on explicating, and that leads first to the collapse of materialism as the source for any genuine self-identification and ultimately to the redemption of religion as having essential value.

5. He speaks of "rational observations," which means that the observations are themselves already directed by a concept. Hegel is an "empiricist" only in the loosest possible sense. We use observations to advance our knowledge, but the observations are not "blind" to the concepts that give us knowledge. Of course, by this description all rationalists are empiricists, since no rationalists ever dismissed the importance of attending to observations and gathering evidence from experience.

6. C. S. Pierce, in a reply to William T. Harris, considered Hegel's "method" to be a method of abstraction, by which he meant that the Concept is informed by observation, but that the Concept is itself independent of the observations, as the term "whiteness" is an abstraction from the quality white. Cf. *Writings of Charles S. Peirce,* ed. Edward C. Moore (Bloomington, IN: Indiana Univ., 1984), II, p. 144ff.

is only the first part of his system.[7] He devised it as an answer to a problem on how the speculative philosopher can introduce and defend systematic philosophy to a nonspeculative and unsystematic philosophical World. This introduction is directed to philosophers, and it is directed both against those who disregard the evidence of history (i.e., the dogmatists) and those who regard the "accidents" of history as the evidence against eternal truth (i.e., the relativists). What makes Hegel's science "transcendental" is his attempt to develop the array of the Concept from observations and descriptions on Self and World. Yet Hegel is not a Kantian; that is, he does not belong to the "party" that championed Kant's philosophy in Germany at the beginning of the nineteenth century. He is a Transcendental Idealist—that is, one who looks back to Leibniz and the Wolffian School for his understanding of speculative Reason.[8] On the one hand, Hegel is defending in his system what Leibniz first proposed in his *Cum Deo!* (1666), namely, that all things are interrelated and have at their center God's Providence. However, Leibniz and his school presented only a static and unverifiable system of concepts: one that was devoid of analyzing the experience of the Self in its development. So, on the other hand, in order to bring speculative Reason into contact with the Self, Hegel defends in his system the principal tenets of Critical Philosophy, as articulated in Fichte's and Schelling's works, which are opposed to metaphysical speculations and express caveats concerning the creations of "pure Reason."

The structure of Hegel's system comes initially from his collaborative work with F. W. J. Schelling.[9] Hegel's early attempts at system building (the Jena systems of 1802–3 and 1804–5) were unsuccessful in reconciling

---

7. To be precise, the *Phenomenology* is the first part of the Jena System of 1805–6. This "system" should not be confused with Hegel's later conceptions of the system. From 1810–12 he radically revised how the system works and how it should be understood. (See notes 11 and 12.) However, he never abandoned the idea that the *Phenomenology* was a philosophical science, and indeed it always remained the "introduction" to systematic philosophy, even as late as the 1830 *Encyclopedia of the Philosophical Sciences*. Cf. *Enzyklopädie der philosophischen Wissenschaften*, hrsg. Eva Moldenhauer u. Karl Michel, Bde., 1–20 (Frankfurt: Suhrkamp, 1971), viii, § 25, p. 91ff.

8. This is most obvious in the *Logic and Metaphysics* of 1804–5, which has overt discussions of monads and a Leibnizian conception of the World. In general, however, Hegel, like Schelling, believed that Critical Philosophy could be reconciled with rationalism. The English translation of this work was the first project of the Hegel Translation Group. Cf. *The Jena System, 1804–5: Logic and Metaphysics*, ed. by John W. Burbidge and George di Giovanni (Kingston-Montreal: McGill-Queens Press, 1986).

9. At least until 1802 Hegel was willing to defend Schelling's system. H. S. Harris has argued convincingly that thereafter Hegel was less interested in working

the rationalistic systems of earlier philosophers and the system of Critical Philosophy that both Schelling and he had been advocating. By 1804, however, even Schelling had given up attempting to build and defend a philosophical system, just as Hegel was about to begin to fashion the system for which the *Phenomenology* was to be written.[10] Schelling's idea of Critical Philosophy abandoned "science" once and for all; instead, he turned to the philosophies of art and mythology as the highest expression of individual self-determination. And by so doing, it was inevitable that Hegel and Schelling would part company, since their respective ideas of Critical Philosophy diverged. The *Phenomenology* was to remain true to the spirit of scientific, rational thought. It was to do what Schelling had first attempted in his *System of Transcendental Idealism* (1800) but what was immediately taken to be a failed enterprise. Hegel was going to begin his system with a work that completed what Schelling failed to do but that would set the philosophical science on a firm foundation.

In the summer of 1805, while he was working both on his lectures concerning the philosophy of history and speculative philosophy, Hegel began to develop an alternative system to his "rationalistic" science, first proposed in the preceding year. This new system would have three parts. The first part was the *Phenomenology of Spirit,* or the "Science of the Experience of Consciousness." The second part should have been "Speculative Philosophy" or the *Logic.* And the final part, which had two independent sections, was to be his "Real Philosophy," or the *Philosophies of Nature and Spirit.* This last project is called by Hegel's critical editors the Third Projection of the Jena System (1805–7), but only the first part, the *Phenomenology of Spirit,* was completed and published. The second part was discarded, or perhaps it was never really started.[11] The third part survives in manuscript form and, later, when Hegel went

his system through Schelling's conceptions. In fact, Hegel, in the academic year 1802–3, began to restructure his metaphysics according to the idea of how the Trinity might become the model for a science of knowledge. Cf. H. S. Harris, *Hegel's Development: Night Thoughts (Jena 1801–1806)* (Oxford: Clarendon Press, 1983), pp. 144ff.

10. Emil Fackenheim puts the point quite succinctly: "Schelling abandoned absolute Idealism in 1804. Hegel, his onetime friend and subsequent rival, did not publish his first major work in absolute Idealism until 1807," *The God Within* (Toronto: Univ. of Toronto, 1997), p. 74.

11. Later in 1810 Hegel will start anew on Speculative Philosophy, which he then takes to be the first part of the System. This "new" work was called the *Science of Logic,* which he did not finish until 1816. Much of the contemporary debate on Hegel's system centers on the relationship between the *Phenomenology of Spirit*

to Berlin, it became the basis for his *Encyclopedia of the Philosophical Sci-ences* (1827). The *Phenomenology of Spirit*, then, plays an important role in Hegel's early thinking of what constitutes a philosophical science as a unity of Reason and history. It was only much later, after he changed his mind in 1810 about the structure of the system, that the *Phenomenology of Spirit* became the introduction to philosophy as science.[12]

The *Phenomenology of Spirit* is itself a controversial work, and the chapter on Spirit is one of the more controversial parts of the treatise. One of the early commentators on Hegel, the scholar Rudolf Haym, found the transition from Chapter 5, "Reason," to Chapter 6, "Spirit," to be the downfall of the entire work. Haym believed that Hegel was con-fused to the point of deranging himself by mixing anthropology, history, and an analysis of cognition together.[13] Chapter 6 is the principal sign of Hegel's so-called derangement. This kind of criticism—that Hegel is confused in his own presentation of the Reason's Concept in the World—will be repeated again by various proponents and critics of Hegel's work. The fact of the matter is, however, that Hegel knew exactly what he was doing, even though the complexity and density of his argument make his presentation obscure. The true meaning of his presentation was given, oddly enough, by one of his most vicious detractors, his old colleague at Jena, F. W. J. Schelling, who, in his *Lectures on Modern Philosophy*, states that for Hegel

> the movement of the Concept is a universal, absolute totality. . . . The Concept here does not have the significance of the simple Con-cept . . . but of *facticity itself,* and, as stated in the Zend [Avista], "the true creator is time," thus . . . the *true* creator is the Concept—with the Concept one has the creator and needs no other outside of it [. . . .] [T]his "prime existence" is however only the occasion and

and the *Science of Logic,* even though they belong to distinct periods of Hegel's thought, and they do not actually belong to the same "idea" of the System.

12. Cf. Hegel's letter to Sinclair, 10 October 1810. Hegel comments in that letter: "I am sending you at last a copy of it [the *Phenomenology of Spirit*], which I did a few years ago. See for yourself what to make of it. It deals with the concrete aspect of Spirit. The science itself is to come only afterward. How will your free, if not anarchical, nature accept the tortuous route of the method within which I allow Spirit to move?" [Letter no. 167]. Hegel has already changed his mind about the nature of the *Phenomenology* as "science."

13. "The *Phenomenology* is a psychology brought into confusion and disorder by means of history, and it is a history brought to derangement by means of psy-chology," *Hegel und seine Zeit* (Berlin, 1857), p. 243.

first stage for the higher potency of interiority or spirituality, to which the subject raises itself in its activity.[14]

Schelling states the point of Hegel's Chapter 6 summarily. The Concept that is being developed in Spirit is "facticity itself," which belongs to an existential-religious conception of the Self. The genesis of this Concept in the World means that it is temporal; time itself (as seen in the sequence of human events) is the creator of it, but the emphasis of Hegel's development is to show "inwardness," or the creation of a spiritual life that transcends the limitations of the historical epochs. What is even odder than Schelling's insight into Hegel—which is "odd" only because Schelling accuses Hegel of stealing the "idea" of the Concept from him and yet it was Schelling who disregarded the idea—is the fact that Hegel developed just this method to be an *antidote* to Schelling's formalized way of conceiving the system.

The placement and role of Spirit in the *Phenomenology of Spirit* is not haphazard. It is to show the truth and vindication of Reason qua Concept. Schelling failed to address the reality of Reason in the World in his Jena writings because for him Reason reached its pinnacle in the individual's creative genius; one does not have to look to history to find "Spirit," especially if your friends are the Schlegels and one of your dinner hosts is Goethe. Schelling's single-minded emphasis on the Concept as embodied in artistic talent is an incomplete and inaccurate picture; it was another of his "friends," the philosopher and mathematician Carl Eschenmayer, who attempted to show the inadequacies inherent to Schelling's idea of the system. Eschenmayer showed that world history is important for the introduction of the idealist's system, and ultimately history is the "proof" of the Concept.

In two separate works, *The Transition from Philosophy to Non-Philosophy* (1803) and *The Orphan and the Hermit* (1805), Eschenmayer made the case that Schelling's "concepts" were hybrids of speculation and experience, but that they were never justified as such. In order to justify them, and thus to show the elevation of spirit to its highest level in religion (not in art as Schelling thought), one had to look at history, especially the development of Christianity out of the ancient World. For Eschenmayer, history could serve as the "proof" for speculative thought that was lacking in Schelling's idea because history supplies the empirical evidence.

---

14. F. W. J. Schelling, *Zur Geschichte der neuen Philosophie*, hrsg. K. F. Schelling, in *Sämmtliche Werke* (Augsburg: J. G. Cotta, 1856–7), Bd. x, pp. 409–11, *passim*. Hereafter these works will be abbreviated as *SW* followed by the volume and page number.

History, Eschenmayer contends, has three epochs: the ancient World of innocence, the early-modern (Christian) World of salvation, and the contemporary World of reconciliation. Schelling, faced with this challenge, simply side-stepped Eschenmayer's criticisms.[15] Instead of looking to history, he defended his conception of religion on the basis of "pure" concepts, and once again he turned to art and mythology. While Schelling never took up Eschenmayer's challenge, Hegel did. And we see this clearly in the chapter on Spirit with its threefold divisions. Hegel alters Eschenmayer's description, however: the ancient World is where and when sin and guilt are recognized; the modern World is a false identification of the Self with wealth and power, which further estranges the individual from herself; and although the contemporary World (the Romantic Moral World-View) offers self-reconciliation, it also presents the *non plus ultra* of self-deception.

Hegel's chapter begins with the ancient World and the fullest recognition of sin as a violation of the nether-worldly gods. In this World there is no chance of redemption, since fate acts against the individual, never for her. The second World is the modern World, and here, unlike Eschenmayer's account, Hegel sees a further estrangement of the Self from her substance—her ethical basis, but unlike the ancient World there is here a recognition of possible redemption. This is a Christian World, and in it even an unhappy consciousness hopes for salvation and holds on to this faith. "Faith," however, is caught in a paradox of sorts. If it is rational, then it must look to Reason and science, and yet the social goods are what offer salvation. In this way profane faith espouses the values of liberty, fraternity, and equality. Or, if it rejects the rational as presenting a false value, that is, a materialistic corruption of religious value, then "faith" itself becomes irrational, a confirmation that it is mere superstition, whose supporters are despots who oppose all human value. In the rational modern World the person of faith is reduced to one who can only declaim that everything is vanity, including herself. There is no salvation realizable within the relationship between Self and World. The last World is Hegel's contemporary community: the World of the German Enlightenment with the dawning age of Romanticism. In this World a genuine reconciliation is advanced by means of "moral salvation," and in it Hegel prepares us for the final revelation (given in Chapter 7, "Religion") that we are already redeemed in the universality of the Self. The "universal Self" is the religious essence of humanity that only appears in the doctrines and practices

---

15. Schelling's reply to Eschenmayer's *From Philosophy to Non-Philosophy* can be found in his essay "Philosophie und Religion" (1804), *SW*, vi, 11–70. But this reply is extremely evasive in terms of answering Eschenmayer's criticisms.

of the Christian religion. So, if Eschenmayer is right that Schelling's system *requires* the history of Reason as the history of salvation, then Hegel has supplied the necessary part of the System in the *Phenomenology of Spirit*. "Spirit" shows the truth of the Concept of Reason as an invincible march through world history.

III

With this background, we should turn toward the text. First, however, there are a couple of additions I should note. I have included in this volume a commentary on the text, a glossary of terms in translation, and a short bibliography that students might find helpful. You will find these in the Commentary and Appendices to the translation.

Finally, this translation was a collaborative venture. It exists only because many people brought their skills, knowledge, and wisdom together. The translation was not an easy affair, and often there had to be compromises made to end debate. In some cases we even had to vote on how to render a passage, the majority having their way. My duties as editor have been mainly to check for inconsistencies, typographical errors, and whenever necessary make corrections or emendations.[16] The product of the work should be considered as collective, however, so I will here list the members of the Hegel Translation Group: first are the core members who are principally responsible for the translation; second are various collaborators who were transitory in the group. Of course, if there are any errors either in the translation or in interpretation of the text they are my responsibility, and none of the contributors should be held accountable for them.

The Hegel Translation Group, Trinity College, University of Toronto

Core Members

John Burbidge, Trent University, emeritus

George di Giovanni, McGill University

H. S. Harris, York University, Glendon College, emeritus

Kem Luther, Sheridan College

David Pfohl

Kenneth L. Schmitz, University of Toronto, Trinity College, emeritus

Daniel E. Shannon, DePauw University

---

16. This was done on the basis of corrected draft pages, after an accident had destroyed much of an original penultimate version.

Collaborators

Rebecca Comay, University of Toronto

Jay Lampert, University of Guelph

Hugh Miller, Loyola University, Chicago

Mark C. E. Peterson, University of Wisconsin Center, Washington County

Acknowledgments

We wish to thank the Provost of Trinity College for the use of the college's facilities. McGill University provided grants to George di Giovanni which enabled him to attend most of our sessions. Finally, I would like to thank John Russon and Barbara Whitehead, who read over parts of the translation and commentary. Their help is most appreciated.

D. E. S.

Greencastle, Ind.

September 1, 2000

NOTE ON THE TRANSLATION

Our translation of Chapter 6, "Spirit," is produced from Hegel's *Phänomenologie des Geistes*, edited by Reinhard Heede and Wolfgang Bonspien (Hamburg: Felix Meiner, 1980). This work presents the new critical edition of Hegel's work. It appears as volume nine in Hegel's *Gesammelte Werke*, edited by the Hegel Commission of the Rheinische-Westphalische Academy of Science, in association with the Hegel Archives. The Hegel Commission is publishing the complete works of Hegel in twenty-one volumes including his lectures and notes. We have included in our translation the page numbers from this critical edition. They appear in square brackets in the text. We have not used their notes but have supplied our own.

For our translation we have retained some of Hegel's original punctuation. You will see, for instance, some sentences beginning with a dash. This is Hegel's way of indicating a break in the argument without his actually starting a new paragraph. We have followed his original word choice and even his spelling. In one instance this actually changes the meaning of a word. In modern editions, where Hegel writes *Principe* the German editors have *Prinzip*. Hegel looks to be referring to a prince, while the so-called corrected word would be referring to a principle.

Where there is more than one possible rendering of a term or phrase we have included alternatives in the notes. In some instances, where there is a tradition of translation that opposes our own, we have cited the other translators—English, French, and Italian—how they rendered the word or phrase, and why we have come to a different conclusion.

We have numbered all the paragraphs. Alongside the beginning of each paragraph we give first the paragraph number from the beginning of the chapter; the second number is the paragraph number from the beginning of the book. The second number corresponds to A. V. Miller's numbering in his translation of the *Phenomenology* (1977), but in one instance in "Spirit" he omitted a paragraph number. We do not know if he omitted other paragraph numbers earlier in the text; so we decided that instead of redoing all the rest of the numbers of the chapter, we would just give, for the bereft paragraph, only its number in the chapter and skip its number from the beginning of the book. In this way we are conforming with Miller's translation, and we hope this will aid the reader if he or she wishes to make comparisons. Miller, however, dropped some phrases and in one case most of a sentence. We have, of course, returned the missing parts.

There are some distinctions that are difficult to mark simply by translating one word for another. For instance, Hegel uses the German terms *reale* and *reelle*, both of which mean "real." Is there a distinction between the two? Most likely, but it certainly is not obvious. H. S. Harris has argued that *reelle, ideelle,* and *formelle* have the meaning of something empirical or conventional, whereas the others, *reale, ideale,* and *formale,* tend to be more abstract and signify a formal concept.[1] But this distinction is not always clear. In any case we are following a convention first used in our translation of *The Jena System, 1804–5* (1986). To indicate in the English that the German word has a double *l* we will use the subscript "$_2$"; for example, we render *ideelle* as "ideal$_2$" but we render *ideale* as "ideal." There are also other conventions that we have used in the earlier translation that we use here. The article *ein,* when used with a neutral adjective or participle, we typically translate as "something;" *das* when used with an adjective is translated as "what is;" for instance, *ein gesetztes* is rendered as "something posited" and *das gesetzte* as "what is posited." We have used nouns for some pronouns, when the pronoun is clearly referring to a preceding noun. We have used parentheses as punctuation, along with frequent dashes and semicolons, to bring order and clarity to the long involved German sentences that Hegel uses. Square brackets indicate insertions in the text, which we believe are required for clear English.

Where we have had to shift from one English word to another in the translation—for instance, if we have been using "determinate being" for *Dasein,* but in some specific case "being there" is required—we indicate the change by placing the German term in angled brackets in a footnote.

---

1. "A Note on Translation" in *System of Ethical Life,* ed. and trans. by H. S. Harris and T. M. Knox (Albany, NY: State Univ. of NY, 1979), pp. 267–8.

VI. SPIRIT[1]

Reason is spirit, since the certainty of being all reality has been raised to 1–438
truth, and it is self-consciously aware of itself as its own world, and the
world as itself. —The immediately preceding movement showed the coming to be of spirit, wherein the object of consciousness—the pure category—raised itself to the concept of reason.[2] In what has been the
observer, reason is this pure unity of the *I* and *being*—of [being] *for-itself*
and of being *in-itself*—is determined as *in-itself* or as *being;* and the consciousness of reason *finds* it.[3] But the truth of the observing is rather the
sublation of this immediately found instinct, of this nonconscious determinate being of reason. The *intuited* category—the *thing found*—enters

---

1. *Geist.* The German means either "mind" or "spirit" in self-reflecting consciousness. In this chapter Hegel will discuss the reflection by self-consciousness
upon its historical experience, beginning with the Greek ethical life and terminat-
ing with the French revolution and its aftermath in the German Romantic era—
die Sturm und Drang period.

2. The reference to the pure category is back to the last section of Chapter 5,
"Individuality Real₂ In and For Itself."

3. *Fürsichseyn.* This German expression is a logical category for Hegel. We
have translated the term as "being-for-itself" when the reference is either to an
object or a concept, and "being-for-self" when it refers to the living subject.
Fürsich is often used by Hegel adjectivally or adverbially; it is the German for *per
se,* and we normally render it as "for-itself." At other times Hegel means by this
term something open to view, in which case we render the term as "explicit."

Ansichseyn. This term is also a logical category for Hegel. We have translated
the term as "being-in-itself" or simply "inherent being" as circumstance
demands. *Ansich* is often used adjectivally or adverbially as well; it is the German
for *in se,* and we normally translate it as "in-itself." At other times Hegel means by
this term something latent or potential, in which case we render the term as
"implicit."

into consciousness as the *being-for-itself* of the *I*, which knows itself now in the objective essence as the *self*. But this determination of the category, as being-for-itself opposite to being-in-itself, is equally one-sided and a moment that sublates itself. Hence, the category becomes determined for consciousness, just as it is in its universal truth, [that is] as an essence subsistent *in-* and *for-itself*. This still *abstract* determination, which constitutes the *facticity itself*, is initially the *spiritual essence*, and its consciousness is a formal[4] knowing of it, which wrestles with its manifold content. In fact, the content of this consciousness is still distinguished from substance as something singular. It either proscribes willful laws or intends the laws (just as they are in and for themselves) having [them] in its knowing as such, and it maintains itself to be the authority of evaluation on them. —Alternatively, considered from the side of substance, this spiritual essence that *subsists in-* and *for-itself* is not yet *consciousness* of its own self. —But the essence *subsisting in-* and *for-itself*, which presents itself at the same time as actual and self-represented consciousness, is *spirit*.

2–439   Its own spiritual *essence* has already been marked out as the *ethical substance;* but spirit is the *ethical actuality*. It is the *self* of actual consciousness over which spirit, or rather self-consciousness, enters as the objective, actual *world*, which, however, has for the self all the significance of something foreign, [239] just as the self has completely lost the significance of something which, whether dependent or independent, is being-for-itself separated from the world. *Substance* and the universal, self-equivalent and enduring essence is the spirit of the solid and undissolved *ground* and *entry-point* of the doing of all, as the *purpose* and *goal*, which is thought of as *inherent*[5] to everyone. —This substance is equally universal *work*, which generates itself through the *doing* of each and everyone, as their unity and identity; for it is the *being-for-self*, [namely] the self and the doing. As *substance*, spirit is the upright and unswerving *selfsame identity;* but as *being-for-self*, substance is the dissolved essence, which graciously sacrifices itself. In it everyone achieves his own work, each tears at the universal being and takes from it his own portion. This dissolution and singularization of the essence is precisely the *moment* of the doing and the self of all; it is the movement and soul of substance and resultant universal essence. Just because of this, substance is the dissolved being in the

---

4. *Formal*. This is one of several terms for which Hegel uses an alternative spelling. The alternative is *formell*, which hereafter will be translated as *formal₂*. The simplest way to distinguish these is that "formal" means pertaining to an abstract form, while "formell" means something conventional, as pertaining to that convention as opposed to content.

5. <*Ansich*>

self: it is not a dead essence, but rather something *actual* and *living*.
Spirit is thereby the self-supporting and absolutely real essence. All 3–440
previous shapes of consciousness are abstractions of it. They exist because
spirit analyzes itself, distinguishes its moments, and dwells on each singular one. This isolation of moments, such as these, has spirit itself as its *presupposition* and its *endurance*, or it exists only in spirit, which is the [true]
existence. In their isolation, they seem as if they [really] *were* so, but the
way they dance forth and step back into their ground and essence, showing them to be only moments or disappearing quantities; this essence is
precisely this movement and dissolution of these moments. At this point,
where spirit, or the reflection of the moments into themselves, has been
posited, we can briefly recall them in our reflection from the present
standpoint: they were consciousness, self-consciousness, and reason.
Spirit, then, is *consciousness* in general—comprehending Sense-Certainty,
Perception, and Understanding within itself; as far as it holds fast to the
other moment of the analysis (that its object is its own *being-for- itself*), it
is self-consciousness.[6] But, as the immediate consciousness of what it is *in*
and *for itself*, as the unity of consciousness and self-consciousness, spirit is
the consciousness that *has reason*. This consciousness, as the "having"
indicates, has its object determined *implicitly* by reason (or by the value of
the category), but in such a way that spirit still does not have for that consciousness the value of the category. This spirit is the consciousness that
we have just considered [in "Reason"]. When this reason, which spirit
has, is finally intuited by spirit as reason that *is* reason or as reason that is
actual in it, and becomes its world, then spirit exists in its truth: it *is*
spirit, it is the *actual, ethical* essence.

[240] Insofar as it *is* the *immediate truth*, spirit is the *ethical life*[7] *of a* 4–441
people; the individual that is a world. It must advance beyond what it

---

6. *Bewußtseyn, Selbstbewußtseyn, Vernunft,* and *Geist.* These are four main sections of the *Phenomenology.* In the first three chapters, the subject of the dialectic
was *consciousness (Bewußtseyn),* in particular the consciousness of "sound human
understanding" *(gesund Menschenverstand).* In Chapter 4 the subject changes to
self-consciousness (Selbstbewußtseyn), whose object is its own self, namely, as one
who seeks self-certainty, first as a being of natural appetite, then as a social being
under domination by another, and finally as a religious being, who suffers from
unhappiness. Consciousness and Self-consciousness are implicitly united in *Reason (Vernunft),* and in it consciousness has the dominant aspect. Finally, in this
chapter on *Spirit (Geist)* the union has become explicit, or the category of unity
has become actual, and in it self-consciousness discovers its essence to be Reason.

7. This is the only time that Hegel uses the phrase "das *sittliche Leben*"—*the
ethical life. Die Sittlichkeit* is synonymous with this phrase and will be translated
throughout the rest of the text as "the ethical life."

immediately is for consciousness; it must sublate the beautiful ethical life; and through a series of shapes attain to the knowledge of itself. But these shapes differ from those that went before, because they are real[8] spirits and proper actualities; instead of [being] merely shapes of consciousness, they are shapes of a world.

5–442   The *living ethical* world is spirit in its *truth.* As it first comes to the abstract *knowledge* of its essence, ethical life perishes in the formal universality of legal right. Spirit, which from this point on is inwardly divided, describes one of its worlds, the *realm of culture,* in the rigid actuality of its objective element; and against it in the element of thought, it describes the *world of faith,* or the *realm of essence.* But when they are grasped *conceptually* by spirit, which goes into itself from this loss of itself, both worlds are confounded and revolutionized by *insight* and its diffusion—that is, the *Enlightenment;* and the realm that has been divided up and spread out into "this world" and "the beyond" returns to self-consciousness. In *morality* self-consciousness now grasps itself as what is essential; it grasps the essence as the actual self, which no longer sets its *world* and the *ground* of it outside itself, but lets everything fade away into itself. As *conscience* it is the spirit that is *certain of its own self.*

6–443   Thus the ethical world—the world that is torn into this world and the one beyond—and the moral world-view are the spirits whose movement and return into the simple, self-subsistent self of spirit are now to be developed. What will emerge as their goal and result is the actual self-consciousness of the absolute spirit.

A. TRUE SPIRIT, THE ETHICAL LIFE

7–444   In its simple truth, spirit is consciousness and strikes its moments apart. *Action* separates it into substance and the consciousness of substance; it separates substance no less than it does consciousness. As universal *essence* and *purpose,* substance confronts itself as the *singularized* actuality; the infinite middle term is self-consciousness, which [241] is *implicitly* the

---

8. *Real.* Hegel has an alternative spelling for this word too, namely, *reelle.* There is also a difference in meaning. *Real* is a speculative term that refers to something theoretically real, e.g., God, or to physical necessity; while *reelle* is an empirical term that refers to something practically real, i.e., what is demonstratively existent but also transitory. See H. S. Harris, "A Note on Translation" in *System of Ethical Life,* ed. and trans. by H. S. Harris and T. M. Knox (Albany, NY: State Univ. of New York, 1979), pp. 267–8. In order to avoid ambiguity *reelle* will be translated as *real$_2$.*

unity of itself with the substance, and now becomes that unity *explicitly* and unites the universal essence with its singularized actuality; it raises the latter to the former, and acts ethically. It brings the universal essence down to the singularized actuality; it fulfills the purpose—the substance that resides only in thought; it brings forth the unity of its own self with the substance as *its own work,* and hence as *actuality.*

In this setting apart of consciousness, the simple substance has, on the one hand, remained in antithesis to self-consciousness; but, on the other hand, along with this antithesis, as a world articulated into masses, it displays the nature of consciousness, or inward self-differentiation, in itself just as much. In this way substance splits itself into a differentiated ethical essence: into human and divine law. And in the same way, the self-consciousness that confronts it allots itself to one or another of these powers according to its essence; self-consciousness, as knowledge, divides into both the unknowing of what it is doing and the knowing of it, which, for this reason, is a deceived knowing. As a result, self-consciousness experiences in its own deed both the contradiction of *those powers,* in which substance divided itself, and their reciprocal destruction; it experiences this contradiction along with the contradiction between its own knowledge of the ethical life of its action and what is ethical in and for itself, and so finds *its own* downfall. But in fact, the ethical substance has become *actual self-consciousness* through this movement, or *this* self has become subsistent *in* and *for itself;* and in that movement, ethical life itself has perished. 8–445

a. The Ethical World, Human and Divine Law, Man and Woman

The simple substance of spirit separates itself as consciousness. In other words, just as the consciousness of abstract or sensible being passes over into perception, so too does the immediate certainty of real ethical being; and just as simple being becomes for self-perception a thing of many properties, so too any case of action becomes for ethical perception an actuality of many ethical connections. But for sense-perception the useless multiplicity of properties is drawn together into the essential antithesis of singularity and universality; likewise for ethical perception, which is the purified substantial consciousness, the multiplicity of ethical moments becomes the duality of one law of singularity and one of universality. Each of these masses of substance remains, however, wholly spirit; and whereas things have no other substance in sense-perception than the [242] two determinations of singularity and universality, so in the present 9–446 case the determinations express only the superficial antithesis of both sides as opposed to each other.

10–447   For the essence that we consider here, singularity has the significance of *self-consciousness* in general, and not that of a singular, accidental consciousness.[9] Therefore, in this determination, ethical substance is *actual* substance, that is, absolute spirit *realized* in the multiplicity of [qualitative] existent *consciousness[es]*: it is the *common essence*,[10] which was the absolute essence *for us* upon entering into the practical shaping of reason in general. It has now entered into truth *for its own* self, namely, both as conscious, ethical essence and as the *essence for the* consciousness, which we have for an object. The common essence is spirit, which is both *for itself,* since it preserves itself in the counter-show[11] of individuals, and is substance, since it preserves the individuals within itself. As *actual substance,* spirit is *one people;* as *actual consciousness,* it is the *citizenry* of the people. This consciousness has its essence in simple spirit, and the certainty of itself in the *actuality* of that spirit, that is, the whole people; and immediately therein it has its *truth,* therefore, not in something that is not actual, but in one spirit that *exists* and *is valid.*

11–448   This spirit can be called human law, because spirit is essentially in the form of the *actuality that is conscious of itself.* In the form of universality, spirit is *familiar* law and *present* custom; in the form of singularity, it is the actual certainty of its own self in the *individual* in general, and as government it has its own certainty as *simple individuality.* Spirit's truth is the open *validity* that lies open in the light of day; it is an *existence* that

---

9. The singularity of self-consciousness belongs to one who identifies himself with the common essence. This could be the male citizen who identifies himself with the state, or it could be woman who identifies herself with the gods and the family and not with the state. In contrast to them, the singular, accidental consciousness does not see itself identified with an essence. It is only the "perceiving consciousness."

10. *Gemeinwesen.* This German expression can mean either "common essence" or "community." Hegel plays on both senses of the term.

11. *Gegenschein.* The previous translators (English, French, and Italian) take this term to mean "shining back" or "reflection." However, there is a stronger sense of opposition than simple reflection. The reference is to the ancient conception of the "beautiful public life," wherein all singular elements are set against the common essence: they are *positive* elements vis-à-vis the negativity of the community. Hegel says of this conception in his Jena manuscripts: "The family of the prince is the solely positive element, the others are to be left behind. These other *individuals are valued as something external,* as cultivated *by what they have made of themselves;* the whole, or the common essence, is as little bound to one as to the other: it is the self-sustaining divisible body . . ." *The Philosophy of Spirit* (1805–6), *GW,* viii, p. 264, lines 11–15.

emerges for immediate certainty in the form of the determinate being that is set free.[12]

But another power, namely, the *divine law*, confronts this ethical power 12–449 and its open public presence. For, as the *movement* of self-*conscious doing*, the ethical *state power* has its antithesis in the *simple* and *immediate essence* of ethical life; as *actual universality*, ethical state power is a violence against individual being-for-self; and as actuality in general, it has in the *inner* essence something that is still other than it is.[13]

It has already been mentioned that each of the opposite ways in which 13–450 ethical substance exists contains the entire substance with all of the moments of its content. So, if the common essence is substance qua actual self-conscious doing, then the other side has the form of immediate, or subsisting, substance. This, then, is on the one hand the inward concept or the universal possibility of ethical life in general; but on the other hand, it has the moment of self-consciousness in it too. This self-

---

12. *freyentlassen.* Jean Hyppolite takes this term to indicate that individuals are set free by the human law; thus the lawgiver by promulgating the laws of the city frees humans from nature. See Hyppolite, *Genèse et Structure de Phénoménologie de l'esprit de Hegel*, t. 2 (Paris: Montaigne, 1946), p. 324ff. and cf. 328–32. In fact, Hegel probably means that the prince is the one who is set free from the "familiar law and present customs," since only the prince "has his certainty as *simple individuality.*" Hyppolite is thinking of Greece in the Golden Age as understood by Plato and Aristotle, but Hegel is thinking of Thebes, in the pre-Dorian age, as portrayed by Sophocles, where life was short, brutish, and seemingly ruled by fate and chance. Hegel's image reflects on Oedipus in *Oedipus the King* and not on Solon or Lycurgus, who exemplify Aristotle's lawgiver. (In Hölderlin's translation of Sophocles' play Oedipus is a "tyrant," the only "free" being in the play. Hegel is developing the idea that in the ancient world only the prince is truly free.)

13. The divine law belongs to the ethical substance itself—the custom (*nomos*) of its ethical life governs and maintains the family. Hegel understands this law to be associated with kinship and the individual's passions for recognition. The law's coercive authority is fury and revenge. Human law, on the contrary, is a *positive law* of the actual state, which favors no one so that it may favor all. It is based upon a general compact among the (male) community members. Its purpose is to preserve the whole, even at the expense of the individual. Hegel sees this law as both rational and universal. Its coercive authority is judicial and unimpassioned. —According to the ancient and medieval authorities (Aristotle, Cicero, Isidore, and Aquinas), human law has in its core the eternal law—a law that has a divine source and that is a imprinted on the hearts and minds of humankind. From this eternal law positive law ought to flourish in us and in the state. In the last line of this paragraph Hegel agrees that the inner essence of the human law is the eternal, divine law, but the latter is incommensurate with the former and instead of flourishing in us, it stands in opposition to the authority and violence of the state power.

conscious moment, which expresses ethical life in the element of *immediacy* or of *being*, or is an *immediate* consciousness of itself—equally as essence and as this self in some [243] other—that is, a *natural ethical community*: this moment is the *family*. As the *unconscious*, still inward concept, the family stands opposed to its self-conscious actuality; as the *element* of the actuality of the people, it stands opposed to the ethical life that cultivates and preserves itself by *laboring* for the universal: the Penates stand opposed to universal spirit.[14]

14–451   However, although the *ethical being* of the family is determined by what is *immediate*, the family is within itself *ethical* essence *insofar* as it does not have the relationship *of nature* among its members, or their connection is not an *immediate, singular,* and *actual* one.[15] For the ethical is inherently *universal;* likewise this relationship of nature is essentially spirit, and only as spiritual essence is it ethical. What constitutes its peculiar ethical life is now to be shown. —To begin with, because the ethical is inherently universal, the ethical connection of the family members is not the connection of feeling or the relationship of love.[16] It seems, then, that the ethical must lie in the relationship of the *single* family member to the

---

14. The Penates are the household gods who protect the family from sickness, infertility, crop failure, etc. Hegel refers to them by their Latin name, and perhaps he has in mind the Lares, the guardian spirits of deceased ancestors.

15. The "relationship of nature" that Hegel refers to is that of the irrational animal and the primitive human. In this connection self-satisfaction is dominant and is measured in terms of food, sex, and drink (cf. "Self-Certainty" in Chapter 4 of the *Phenomenology*); the right of possessions; and the power of strength. The family's connection is *ethical*; it is as much for one self as it is for the other family member.

16. Hegel's point initially should strike us as queer. His contention is that there are no "real" individualities (*Individualitäten*) in the primitive state, hence there is no mutual recognition of the other self in my self—that is to say, there is no love. Hegel understands "love" as the spiritual dissolution of one individual into another, which is consummated when the other reciprocates in kind. The paradigm of genuine love is the marriage relationship. In marriage the two selves still remain, but their separate natures have blended into one. In ¶19–456 a reciprocal recognition does occur, and it is there that "love" first enters the scene. However, here the affections of the singular beings are erotic, but also familial and dutiful. Such an ethical recognition does not concern the selves' autonomy, since they do not have to love each other, but the senses of obligations to the other affect their substance as natural beings. Nature is subsumed under ethical obligations. One last point: Hegel's concept of love is drawn from the Pauline conception of *agape*, but we should not consider Hegel's concept as either especially Greek or "ethical"; it is a religious concept and appears at the end of this chapter. Cf. Hegel's essay "On Love" in *The Early Theological Writings*, trans. by T. M. Knox (Chicago: Univ. of Chicago, 1948), pp. 302–8.

whole family qua substance, so that its conduct or actuality has only the family as [its] purpose and content. But the conscious purpose that the *conduct* of this whole has, insofar as the purpose merges with the whole itself, is itself the single member. The acquisition and maintenance of power and wealth is concerned only in part with need, and pertains to desire; in part they become only something mediated in their higher determination. This determination does not fall within the family itself, but concerns the true universal, the common essence. It is, rather, something negative vis-à-vis the family and consists precisely in the removal of the single member from the family, the subjugation of the member's naturalness and singularity; it draws the family member toward *virtue,* toward life in and for the universal. The *positive* purpose, which is peculiar to the family, is the single member as such. And in order for this connection to be ethical, neither the member who acts nor the one to whom the action refers should enter upon the scene *accidentally,* as happens sometimes in rendering assistance or performing service.[17] —The content of ethical action must be substantial, that is whole and universal; hence, the action can only refer to the *entire* single [member], or to him qua universal. Again, this is not something that might merely be *represented,* a *rendering of service* that promotes his entire fortune;[18] whereas the service rendered is actual and immediate action, it only makes something singular in him— not even when the action qua education in a *series* of endeavors actually has the entire single member for its object and brings him forth as its work; for apart from the negative purpose vis-à-vis the family, the *actual action* has only a restricted content.[19] Finally, it matters little that the

---

17. The "positive purpose" is the self-preservation of a single being, which is opposed to the civic purpose of serving the community or the common essence. The latter is public virtue, the original source for Aristotle's sense of *arete.* Virtue draws the singular family member away from his familial essence (his blood, his life) toward death. In order for the positive purpose of self-preservation to be ethical in respect to the family, the actions performed must be tied to the preservation of it. Thus for the family there are no "accidental" relations that concern its preservation; they are all substantial and, therefore, all significant actions are those that pertain to the family's essence, to its self-preservation qua individual entity, and consequently to the preservation of its members and its wealth. Thus in the case of Oedipus, his parents Jocasta and Laius were quite within their "family rights" to expose the child who threatened the family; just as it was Oedipus' ethical duty to flee Corinth when the Oracle informed him that he would kill his father and marry his mother.

18. <Glück>

19. The *service rendered* is the action of raising the children to be members of the family. There are "ethical" obligations involved here, but they are quite

action is a needed rescue, through which the entire, single member is truly saved; [244] for the needed rescue is itself a completely accidental deed, of which the occasion is a common actuality that may occur or may not. Thus the action embraces the whole existence of the blood-kinsman and has him (not the citizen, for he does not belong to the family, nor the one who is to become a citizen and *ceases* then to be valued as *this single* [member]), but just *this* single one who belongs to the family—[the action] has him as a *universal* essence, as its object and content, which has been relieved from the sensible, i.e., singular, actuality. This action no longer concerns the *living* but the *dead,* one who is brought together out of the long succession of his dispersed being into *one* completed shape[20], and is raised from the unrest of accidental life to the rest of simple universality.[21] —So, because he is only *actual* and *substantial* as a citizen, the single [individual], as one who belongs to the family and is not a citizen, is just a *nonactual,* pithless shade.

15–452   This universality to which the single [individual] attains as *such,* is *pure being* or *death;* it is the immediate, *natural state of having been,* not the *deed* of a *consciousness.* Hence, it is the duty of the family member to add on this aspect, so that even his ultimate *being,* this *universal* being, shall not belong solely to nature and remain something irrational, but shall be

---

restricted in content; e.g., in *Alcestis* Admetus rebukes his father for not dying in his place and threatens not to perform the obsequies for the father when he dies. Pheres, his father, is quite rightly indignant at this son's dishonor, and tells him a little truth about Greek law. He says, "I begot and raised you to be master of this house, but I am not obliged to die for you. I did not inherit this as a family custom [*nomon*], fathers dying for sons, nor as a Greek custom either. Your are fortunate [*eutuches*] or unfortunate for yourself alone. What you should have in justice received from me you have: you rule over many subjects, and I shall leave you many acres of land. . . ." (681–8). Again, we see that the ethical conduct concerns the continuation of the house but not the "good fortune" of any singular member, except for what is necessary for their life. The father's responsibility to his son is not an act of virtue (*arete*) but of familial law (*nomos*). Cf. Euripides, *Alcestis,* ed. and trans. by David Kovacs (Cambridge, MA: Harvard University, 1994).

20. <Gestaltung>

21. The family serves the dead and they expect the "dead one" to serve the family as one of the Lares. With the death of any member the family remains, and the dead member is only preserved in remembrance and religious devotion. A living family member is expected to die for the honor of the family. This is his ethical obligation. Hegel has in mind the death of Oedipus at Colonus. His death repudiates the state-power of his home city, Thebes; his death, although for himself, also satisfies the divine law and fulfills his family obligation, because it supposedly ends the curse. His daughter, Antigone, seeing her father's death, praises him, not simply because of her natural attachment to him, but because she as the

something that has been *done,* and the right of consciousness shall be asserted in it. Or the sense of the action is, rather, that because the rest and universality of its own self-conscious essence does not belong to nature, the show of nature, appropriating that sort of deed to itself, shall fall away, and the truth shall be established. —What nature does to him [the self-conscious essence] constitutes the aspect from which its coming to the universal is displayed as the movement of a *subsistent being.* Of course, this movement itself falls within the ethical community, and has the community as its purpose; death is the fulfillment and highest labor that the individual as such undertakes for the community. However, insofar as the individual is something essentially *singular,* it is an accident that his death was immediately linked with his labor for the universal and was a result of it; for if his death was partially the result of labor, it is still the *natural* negativity and movement of the singular [individual] as a *subsistent being* in which consciousness does not return into itself and becomes *self-consciousness.* In other words, because the movement of the *subsistent being* is the movement that becomes sublated and attains to *being-for-self,* death is the aspect of separation in which the being-for-self, which is attained, is something other than the subsistent being that emerged in the movement. —Since the ethical life of spirit is in its *immediate* truth, the aspects into which its consciousness steps apart also fall into this form of *immediacy,* and singularity crosses over into this *abstract* negativity, which, being devoid *in its own self* of consolation and reconciliation, must accept them *essentially* through an *actual* and *external* action. —So, the blood-kin completes [245] the abstract, natural movement by adding on the movement of consciousness; it interrupts the work of nature, and saves the blood relation from destruction, or better, since its destruction—its coming to pure being—is necessary, the kin takes the activity of destruction upon

---

custodian of divine law realizes it has been satisfied—the blood line may now be purified. In contrast to Oedipus' death, the death of his citizen son, Eteocles, who fights for the city, expresses the true universality of ethical action as something beyond family obligation. He has the virtue of courage and stands for the civic good. Indeed, the death of any citizen, even the ruler, is a mere contingency in respect to the common essence or the community. But unlike the death of the family member, the death of the citizen overcomes nature, because it serves in promoting and representing the true universal, namely, the city. All the same, the citizen attains only a being-for-self (independence and self-esteem), which immediately vanishes in death. It is the family member who is preserved as a shade. This preservation occurs only because the family remembers its obligations. It performs the rites of death and burial. In the *rite of burial,* then, which aids in the destruction of the body, the singularity of the family member is protected. By being wedded to the earth, the dead individual is protected from elemental forces. The city cannot protect this singularity; only the family can.

itself. In this way, it may come to pass that the *dead,* or universal *being,* also becomes something that returns into itself, a *being-for-self;* to wit, the *single* singularity, powerless and pure, is raised to *universal individuality.* Because he has freed his *being* from his *doing* or negative unity, the dead man is empty singularity, merely a passive *being for another,* surrendered to every base and irrational individuality and to the forces of abstract matter, both of which are now more powerful than he: "individuality" on account of the life it has, "matter" on account of its negative nature. The family wards off from the dead man this action of unconscious desires and abstract essences that dishonors him. It puts its own action there instead, and weds the kinsman to the womb of the earth, to elementary, imperishable individuality.[22] By this action it makes him a partner in a community, which, moreover, overpowers and restricts the forces of singular matter and of the baser living things that wanted to act freely against him and destroy him.

16–453   Thus, this ultimate duty constitutes the fulfillment of the *divine* law, namely, the positive *ethical* action vis-à-vis the single [individual]. Every other relationship toward him that does not abide in love, but is ethical, belongs to human law and has the negative significance of raising the single [member] above his confinement within the natural community, to which as an *actual being* he belongs. But now, even though human right has for its content and power the actual, ethical substance that is conscious of itself, namely, the whole people, while divine right and law has for its content and power the single [member] who is beyond actuality, still the individual is not without power. His power is the *abstract,* pure *universal:* the *elementary* individual, which, as the ground of the individuality that tears itself free from the element and constitutes the self-conscious actuality of the people, equally snatches its essence back into the pure abstraction. —How this power is displayed in the people itself will be developed further.

17–454   In both laws, the one as much as the other, there are also *distinctions* and *levels.* For, since both essences have the moment of consciousness in them, the distinction unfolds itself within them. This unfolding constitutes their movement and peculiar life. The consideration of these distinctions points to the modes of *operation* and of *self-consciousness* for both

---

22. Namely, by religious practice, especially the performance of death rites, which for the family is a "divine" right. The dead are thought to require this recollection in order, first, to preserve themselves in the beyond, and, secondly, to obtain *ethical standing* there. If the dead are to be preserved as individuals, they must be returned to the earth from which their seed sprung. (The myth of Cadmus, founder of Thebes, is that he sowed seeds from which the Thebans sprung.)

the two *universal essences* of the ethical world, as well as their *cohesion* and their *transition* into one another.

The *community*, the higher and open law that is valid in the light of day, has its actual vitality in *government*, that in which it is an individual. [246] Government is *actual* spirit *reflected into itself*, the simple *self* of the whole ethical substance. This simple force in fact allows the [common] essence to spread itself into its articulations, and gives subsistence and a proper being-for-self to each part. In this articulation spirit has its *reality* or its *determinate being*, and the family is the *element* of this reality. But, at the same time, spirit is the force of the whole that reintegrates the parts into a negative unity, gives to them the feeling that they lack independence, and sustains them in the consciousness that their life is only in the whole. Thus, the community can, on one side, organize itself into systems of personal independence and ownership, of personal and property rights, just as it can articulate the modes of labor (initially directed toward the singular purposes of profit and pleasure) into associations of their own and make them independent. The spirit of universal association is the *simplicity* and the *negative* essence of these self-isolating systems. In order not to let them take root and become fixed in this isolation, with a result that the whole is allowed to fall apart and the spirit to flee, government has to shake them to the core[23] from time to time by means of wars, so as to damage and confuse their established order and their right to independence. But the individuals who let themselves be absorbed in these associations, so that they tear themselves loose from the whole and strive after an invincible *being-for-self* and personal assurance, are given in the government's imposed labor a feeling for their lord, Death. Through this dissolution of the form of subsistence, spirit wards off [its own] sinking out of the ethical into natural determinate being and preserves the self of its consciousness; it raises this self to *freedom* and to its [own] *strength*. —The negative essence shows itself to be the authentic *power* of the community and the *strength* of its self-preservation; thus the truth and confirmation of the power of the community is in the essence of the divine law and in the *nether kingdom*. 18–455

In the same way, the divine law that holds sway in the family has, on its side, distinctions in itself, and their connection makes up the living movement of its actuality. But among the three relationships of husband and wife, of parents and children, and of siblings as brother and sister, that *relationship* between *husband* and *wife*, first of all, is the *immediate* self-cognition of one consciousness in the other and the cognition of reciprocal recognition. Because self-cognition is *natural* and not ethical, 19–456

---

23. <in ihrem Innern>

it is only the *representation* and *image* of spirit, but not the actual spirit itself. —The representation or image, however, has its actuality in something other than what it is; hence this relationship [of husband and wife] has its actuality not in itself but in the child (in another whose becoming it is, and in which the relationship itself disappears; this change of successive generations has its continuity in the people). The devotion of husband and wife to one another is thus mixed with natural [247] attachment[24] and sentiment, and their relationship does not have in itself its return to itself. This is also the case with the second relationship, the *devotion* of *parents* and *children* to each other. The devotion between parents and children is affected by just this one emotion [of having] the consciousness of its actuality in the other, and of seeing being-for-self arising in the other without holding it back; but the actuality of the other remains something foreign. Conversely, the devotion of the children to their parents is affected by the emotion [of having] their genesis or [being] in-itself in another who is disappearing, and of achieving their being-for-self and their own self-consciousness only through the separation from their source: a separation in which the source dries up.

20–457   These two relationships remain within the transition and non-identity of the two sides that are allotted to them. —The unmixed relationship occurs, however, between *brother* and *sister*.[25] They are of the same blood, but in them it has come into its *calm* and *equilibrium*. Hence, they do not desire one another, and neither one has given being-for-self to the other nor received it; rather, each is a free individuality with respect to the

---

24. <Beziehung>

25. If the reference is to Oedipus' family, then what has been overcome is the "natural" sin of the mixed blood relation, i.e., the fruit of the incest between Oedipus and Jocasta. Hegel's point must be that the blood relation yields to the ethical relationship of the universal. The "unmixed relationship" is not a matter of having the same blood but of having a recognition that the other is your equal and your other self for whom you have carnal desire. So what Antigone recognizes in her brothers is that they are part of her own being, but, unlike her parents, she has no "natural desire" for them. She is free of the curse latent in nature itself. It is not clear to me, however, that Hegel has the family of Oedipus in mind here. Hegel might well be thinking of the *Oresteia* and related plays, where the *pure relationship* between brother, Orestes, and his sisters, Electra and Iphigenia, are made quite apparent. The true ethical connection appears in the siblings and not in the parents. One sister, Iphigenia, offers her life for the father's pride and thus shows greater virtue than either father or mother. The other sister, Electra, appears as both conscience and judge, when her mother murders her father. She excites revenge in her brother, who as the avenger fulfills the ethical duty that his sister calls him to. Here the sins of the parents are not conveyed to the children. And even when the Furies attack Orestes for matricide, he successfully defends

other. Thus it is as sister that the female principle has its highest *presentiment* of the ethical essence; it does not come to *consciousness* and actuality of this essence, because the law of the family is the essence that subsists *in itself* and is *inward*. It is not exposed to the light of consciousness, but remains an inward feeling—the divine that is exempt from actuality. The female principle is bound to these Penates, and beholds in them partly its own universal substance, but partly its singularity; yet in such a way that this attachment to singularity is, at the same time, not the natural one of pleasure. —As *daughter* the woman must watch the passing of her parents with natural emotion[26] and ethical calm; for it is only at the expense of this relationship that she arrives at the being-for-self of which she is capable. In her parents, therefore, she does not behold her being-for-self in a positive way. —The relations between *mother* and *wife*, however, have singularity in part as something natural, which pertains to pleasure, in part as something negative, which in those relations glimpses only its passing, and just because of that, it is in part something contingent that can be replaced by another. In the house of the ethical life, what matters is not the husband or this child, but *a husband* or *children in general*—not the sentiment, but the universal on which these relationships of the woman are grounded. The distinction of her ethical life from that of the man consists precisely in the fact that she remains immediately universal in her determination for singularity, and in her pleasure, and foreign to the singularity of desiring. In the man, on the contrary, these two sides go asunder; since he possesses as citizen the *self-conscious* strength of *universality*, he thereby acquires for himself the right of desire and, at the same time, preserves for himself freedom from it. And, since singularity is mingled with the [248] wife's relationship, its ethical life is not pure. But insofar as it is pure, singularity is *indifferent*, and the wife lacks the moment in which she [re]cognizes herself as *this* self in another. —However, the brother is, for his sister, the calm and similar essence in general—

---

himself against them by appealing to the ethical commands of the god Apollo and to the wisdom of Athena.

Several commentators (Kaufmann, Wiedmann, Solomon, Derrida) propose that Hegel has his own family in mind, especially his relationship to his sister Christiana. This is just a fanciful suggestion that can be entertained only if one reads Freud into this passage. But if one forces the Freudian suggestion, which is absurd, then one will miss Hegel's "ethical" point that the protection and preservation of the family and its ways passes on to the children by tradition. It is a "natural" law that children take over the character of the parents. Hegel is attempting to show that in the ethical life the unnatural component of this inheritance is overcome, since the children transcend the envy and lusts of their elders.

26. <Bewegung>

her recognition in him is pure and not mixed with natural attachment. So, the indifference of singularity and its ethical contingency are not present in this relationship; rather, the moment of the *singular self,* both as recognizing and recognized, can here assert its rights, since it is bound up with the equilibrium of blood and with an attachment that is free from desire. Hence the loss of a brother is irreplaceable for the sister, and her duty toward him is the highest.

21–458   This relationship is also the limit at which the family, which is closed in upon itself, dissolves and goes outside of itself. The brother is the side where the spirit of the family comes to the individuality that turns itself toward others and passes over into the consciousness of universality. The brother abandons this *immediate, elementary,* and, therefore, truly negative ethical life of the family in order to acquire and bring forth the actual ethical self-consciousness of it.

22–459   He goes out of the sphere of divine law, in which he was living, over to human law. But the sister becomes, or the wife remains, the manager of the house and the guardian of the divine law. In this way both sexes overcome their natural essence and come forth in their ethical significance, as diversities that share between them two distinctions produced by the ethical substance. These two *universal* essences of the ethical world have their determinate *individuality,* therefore, in *naturally* distinguished self-consciousnesses, because the ethical spirit is the *immediate* unity of substance and self-consciousness—an *immediacy* that therefore appears, at the same time, as the existence[27] of a natural distinction on the side of reality and distinction. —This is the side that showed itself in the shape of individuality, which is real for itself, to be the *original determined nature* in the concept of spiritual essence.[28] This moment here loses the indeterminacy that it still has there, and the contingent diversity of dispositions and capacities. At this point there is a definite antithesis of the two sexes, the naturalness of which at the same time contains the significance of their ethical determination.

23–460   Nevertheless, the distinction of the sexes and of their ethical content still remains within the unity of substance, and the movement of the content is just the abiding coming to be of the substance. The husband is sent forth from the family spirit to the communal essence, where he finds his self-conscious essence. Just as the family has in this way its universal substance and persistence in him, so conversely, the community has the formal element of its actuality in the family, and its strength and preservation in the divine law. Neither of them is on its own in and for itself. [249] The

---

27. <Daseyn>

28. Reference is to Chapter 5, c. "Individuality that is Real₂ in and for Itself."

human law proceeds into its living movement from the divine, the law that holds on earth [proceeds] from that of the nether world, consciousness from that that lacks consciousness, mediation from immediacy; and equally each returns to the place from which it went forth. Contrariwise, the nether worldly power has its *actuality* on earth; through consciousness it becomes determinate being and activity.

Thus the universal ethical essences are the substance as universal and as singular consciousness. They have the people and the family as their universal actuality, but man and woman as their natural self and activating individuality. In this content of the ethical world we see the purposes accomplished that the preceding nonsubstantial shapes of consciousness set for themselves. What reason grasped only as object has become self-consciousness, and what the latter has only in itself is present as true actuality. —What observation knew as something *already found*, in which the self had no part, is here custom already found, but [as] an actuality that is, at the same time, the deed and work of him who finds it. —The singular [individual], seeking the pleasure of the *enjoyment of his singularity*, finds it in the family; and the necessity in which the pleasure perishes is his own self-consciousness as a citizen of his people; or it is his knowing *the law of the heart* as the law of all hearts and knowing the consciousness of the *self* as the recognized universal order; it is *virtue* that enjoys the fruits of its sacrifice. Virtue brings to fruition what it sets out to do, namely, to elevate essence to the actually present, and its enjoyment is this universal life. —And finally, the consciousness *of the facticity itself* is satisfied in the real substance, which contains and maintains the abstract moments of that empty category in a positive way.[29] In the ethical powers it has a genuine content that has taken the place of those nonsubstantial commands that sound reason wanted to give and to know—and in this way it equally receives a criterion for testing; full of content and determinate in itself, not for the laws, but for what is done.[30]

24–461

---

29. The universal ethical essence gives *substance* to the moments of reason. Hegel here refers back to the "Realization of Rational Self-Consciousness" and its shapes (see *Phenomenology of Spirit*, *GW*, ix, pp. 193–214). Those shapes were "Pleasure and Necessity," "the Law of the Heart and the Frenzy of Self-Deceit," and "Virtue and the Way of the World." And finally, the reference to facticity itself, like the references to law giving and law testing, goes back to "Individuality Real₂ In and For Itself" at the end of Chapter 5.

30. Previously in the chapter on Reason, virtue could not bring to pass what it set out to do because the way of the world was set against it. In other words, "virtue" was *fated* under an external order. Likewise, at the end of "Reason," in the section called "Individuality Real₂ In and For Itself" (*GW*, ix, pp. 214–37), facticity itself was not satisfied in any real substance but sought satisfaction in its ideals

25–462   The whole is a stable equilibrium of all parts, and each part is a native
spirit that does not seek its satisfaction beyond itself, but has that satisfaction within itself precisely because it is in equilibrium with the whole.
Of course, the equilibrium can be alive only because inequality arises in
it and is brought back to equality by *justice*. Justice, however, is neither
some foreign essence that is to be found in the beyond, nor the actuality
of something unworthy [to the spirit of the people], [such as] a malice
that responds to malice, treachery to treachery, ingratitude to ingratitude, and so forth, that passes judgment in the manner of a thoughtless
accident, an unconceived interrelation, a nonconscious deed or omis-
sion. [250] Rather, as the justice of the *human* right that brings the
being-for-self that departs from the equilibrium (that is, the independence of the estates and individuals) back to the universal, it is the government of the people. This is the individuality of universal essence
present to itself, and the genuine self-conscious will of all. —But the
justice that restores the universal to equilibrium, when it becomes too
powerful against the singular, is precisely the simple spirit of him who
suffers the injustice; it is not broken in spirit, into one who suffers and
an essence beyond.[31] The sufferer himself is the nether worldly power,
and the essence is *his* Fury that wreaks vengeance; for his individuality—his blood—lives on in his house. His substance has a lasting actuality. The injustice that can be imputed to the singular in the realm of
ethical life is only the fact that something simply *happens* to him.[32]

---

and moral maxims. But now in "True Spirit" the situation has changed. "Virtue"
is united with both the custom of the community and with the state power; it has
been reconciled to the real world of the universal, and this gives substance to facticity, namely, the virtue of having identity with the community's law. Hegel's idea
comes from Plato, who, according to Hegel at least, realized the actuality of the
Greek political life in order to show it to be rational: "Plato did not set up the
ideal, but he grasped the state of his time from within": *The Philosophy of Spirit*
(1805–6), *GW,* viii, p. 263, lines 24–5. Plato establishes the principle of the "beautiful accord," which Hegel refers to in this section.

31. There are two justices: one of human right, which is the justice of the city,
and one of the individual right, which is the justice of the clan and its ethical obligations. They are supposed to be reconciled in the "beautiful accord" between
individual and the state.

32. The "injustice" is simply the accidents of life that make us unhappy,
especially the "accident" of death. Hegel is recalling the wisdom of Hercules,
who tells us in *Alcestis*, "For each man there comes a time when he must die, and
there's no one living who can know whether he will be living when the next day
comes. Where the train of chance will make its way is unclear. There's no way to
learn it; it can't be learned by skill" (782–6). But the "train of *tuche*" is also fate.

Nature is the power that perpetrates upon consciousness the injustice of making it into a pure thing. Consciousness is universality, not of the *community,* but the *abstract* universality of *being.* And in the resolution of the injustice that it has suffered, the singularity does not turn itself against the *community* (for it has not suffered at its hands), but against abstract being. As we have seen, the consciousness of the blood-kinship of the individual resolves this injustice in such a way that what has *happened* becomes *work* instead, with the result that *being,* the *ultimate,* is something *willed* and hence joyful.

In this way the ethical realm is, in its *subsistence,* a world that is un- 26–463 stained and unsoiled by discord. Similarly, its movement is a tranquil passage[33] from one of its powers to the other, so that each of them contains the other and brings it forth. To be sure, we see it divide into two essences with their respective actualities. But this antithesis is really the confirmation of the one through the other, where they immediately touch each other as actual essences; their means, and [common] element, is the immediate interpenetration of the essences. The one extreme, the universal, self-conscious spirit, comes to be linked with its other extreme, its force and its element, the *nonconscious* spirit, by means of the *individuality* of the *man.* On the other hand, the *divine* law has its individuation in the woman, that is, the nonconscious spirit of the singular has its determinate being in her: through her as the *middle* [or *means*], the nonconscious spirit steps forth out of its nonactuality into actuality, out of its not knowing and not being known into the conscious realm. The unification of man and woman constitutes both the active middle of the whole, and the [common] element that, even though divided into the extremes of divine and human law, is their immediate unification. This unification makes the two initial syllogisms into the same syllogism; and the opposite movements of actuality going down toward nonactuality, [i.e.,] of the human law, which organized itself [251] into independent members, falling down into the danger and trial of death, and of the nether worldly law that goes up toward the actuality of the day and to conscious determinate being, are united into one. The first movement is the lot of man, and the second, the lot of woman.

The direction of fate is unclear, but it seems to embrace a series of "thoughtless accidents" that will doom the individual and his house, e.g., Oedipus' own activity of killing his father, marrying his mother, all of which are "nonconscious deeds." Hegel is attempting to show that Plato's rational concept of the state has not grasped the whole truth.

33. <Werden>

b. The Ethical Action, Human and
Divine Knowledge, Guilt and Destiny

27–464   The antithesis is so constituted in this realm, however, that self-consciousness has not yet come forth in its right as *singular individuality;* on
the one side, individuality counts in this realm only a *universal will,* on
the other side, as the *blood* of the family; *the singular individual* counts
only as the *inactual shade.* —*No deed* has *yet* been done, yet the deed is
the *actual self.* —The deed disturbs the peaceful organization and
movement of the ethical world. What appears in this world as the order
and harmony of both, its essence—each of which confirms and completes the other—becomes through the deed a transition of *opposites* in
which each proves itself to be the nullity, rather than the confirmation of
itself and of the other. It becomes the negative movement or eternal
necessity of fearsome *destiny,* which swallows up in the abyss of its simplicity the divine and human laws alike, as well as the two self-consciousnesses in which these powers have their determinate being. It
passes over for us into the *absolute being-for-self* of the purely singular
self-consciousness.

28–465   The *ground* from which this movement proceeds and upon which it
takes its course is the realm of ethical life; but the *activity* of this movement is self-consciousness. As *ethical* consciousness, self-consciousness
is the *simple, pure orientation* to the ethical essentiality, or *duty.* Neither
arbitrariness, nor even struggle, nor indecisiveness is present in it; for
the giving and testing of laws has been relinquished. Instead, the ethical
essentiality is for it what is immediate, unwavering, and without contradiction. Hence, neither the wretched spectacle of a collision between
passion and duty nor the comedy of a collision between duty and duty
can occur. According to its content, the latter is the same as that
between passion and duty. For [252] passion can just as well be represented as duty, because, as consciousness withdraws into itself out of its
immediate substantial essentiality, duty becomes the formal$_2$ universal
into which every content fits equally well (as was shown above).[34] Yet
the collision of duties is comic because it expresses contradiction,
namely, that of an *absolute in opposition:* therefore [the contradiction
expresses] the absolute and immediately the nullity of this so-called
absolute or duty. —But the ethical consciousness knows what it has to
do and is committed to belong either to the divine or the human law.
This immediacy of its commitment is a *being-in-itself* and, therefore, (as

---

34. The reference is to Chapter 5, c. "Reason as Law Tester" (*GW,* ix, pp.
232–7).

we saw)[35] it has the significance of a natural being as well. Nature, not the contingency of circumstance or choice, allots one sex to one law and the other to the other; or conversely, the two ethical powers give themselves their individual being and realization in the two sexes.

Now, since on the one hand ethical life consists essentially of this   29–466 immediate *commitment* (and consequently only the one law is the essence for consciousness), [and since] on the other hand the ethical powers are actual in the *self* of consciousness, these powers acquire the significance of *excluding* themselves and of being self-*opposed:* they are *explicitly* in self-consciousness just what they are only *implicitly* in the *realm* of ethical life. The ethical consciousness is essentially *character,* because it is *committed* to one of these powers; the two of them do not have for it the same *essentiality.* For this reason the antithesis appears as an *unhappy* collision of duty simply with an *actuality* that has no rights. The ethical consciousness is in this antithesis as self-consciousness. As such, it sets out at once [either] to subject this opposed actuality to the law to which it belongs by violence, or to deceive it. Since each ethical consciousness sees right only on its own side and injustice on the other, the one that belongs to the divine law perceives on the other side the capricious *violence* of men, but the one that is allotted to the human law perceives in the other the obstinacy and the *disobedience* of being-for-self. For the ordinances of government form the universal and public sense that is open in the light of day; but the will of the other law is the subterranean sense that is locked up within—the sense that appears in its determinate being as the will of singularity, and which, when it contradicts the first [law], is an outrage.

Thus there arises in consciousness the antithesis of the *known* and the   30–467 *unknown,* just as the antithesis of the *conscious* and the *unconscious* [253] arises in substance, and the absolute *right* of *self-consciousness* comes into conflict with the divine *right* of *essence.* For self-consciousness qua consciousness, the objective actuality as such has essence; but, in its substance, self-consciousness is the unity of itself and this opposite, and the ethical self-consciousness is the consciousness of substance; so the object, in its opposition to self-consciousness, has entirely lost the significance of having an essence for itself. Just as the spheres in which it is merely a *thing* have long since disappeared, so too have disappeared the spheres in which consciousness fixes something from itself and makes a singular moment into the essence.[36] Against such one-sidedness, actuality has a force of its

---

35. The reference is to ¶22–459.

36. In the chapter on perception the object was just a thing, while throughout the chapter on Reason consciousness was always posited as something essential, which it is not.

own; it stands united with the truth against consciousness and simply shows consciousness what the truth is. But from the chalice of the absolute substance, ethical consciousness has drunk the obliviousness of every one-sidedness, everything that pertains to being-for-self, to its purposes and to its own peculiar concepts; and so consciousness has drowned everything at once in this Stygian water: all the essentiality proper to objective actuality with its independent significance.[37] Hence, it is the absolute right of ethical consciousness, when it behaves in accordance with the ethical law, to find in this realization nothing but the sheer accomplishment of this law itself, and to show that the deed is nothing else than ethical conduct. —The ethical, as both the absolute *essence* and the absolute *power* at once, cannot endure any inversion of its content. If it were only absolute *essence* without power, then it could experience inversion at the hands of individuality; but as ethical consciousness, individuality has renounced this inverting. For the sake of this unity, individuality is the pure form of the substance that is its content, and conduct is the transition out of thought into actuality, simply as the movement of an antithesis that has no essence; the moments of which have no particular content or essentiality distinct from one another. Therefore, the absolute right of the ethical consciousness is that the *deed* (namely, the *shape* of its *actuality*) shall be nothing other than what it *knows*.

31–468   But the ethical essence has split itself into two laws, and consciousness, with its unambiguous stance[38] toward the law, is allotted only to one. Just as this *simple* consciousness takes its stand[39] on the absolute right that, as ethical consciousness, the essence has appeared to it as it is *in itself,* so this essence takes its stand upon the right of its *reality,* or upon the right to be replicated there. But, at the same time, this right of essence does not stand opposed to self-consciousness, as though it were somewhere else; it is rather the very essence of self-consciousness [254] and in this alone does it have its determinate being and its power; its antithesis is the *deed* of *self-consciousness.* Just because self- consciousness is a self to itself, and advances to the deed, it raises itself out of *simple immediacy* and posits the *division* itself. Through this deed it surrenders the determinateness of ethical life, gives up being the simple certainty of immediate truth, and

---

37. There are references here to one of the rivers of Hell. By drinking of the waters of the Lethe, the souls forget their former lives. This is necessary in order to transmigrate to their new bodies (see *Republic,* X, 621a–b). Hegel calls this "Stygian water" because the waters of the Styx (the river of Hell that surrounds Dis, Hell's capital) are the source of the Lethe.

38. <Verhalten>

39. <besteht>

posits the separation of its own self into itself (as agent) and into what stands opposite to it an actuality that is negative for it. Hence by virtue of this deed it comes to *guilt*. For the deed is its own *doing*, and the doing is its own most essence; and *guilt* obtains the significance of *crime*, too, for as simple ethical consciousness, self-consciousness has appealed to the one law but has renounced the other and violated it through its deed. —*Guilt* is not an indifferent, ambiguous essence such that the deed, as it *actually* is in the light of day, could be or not be the *conduct* of a guilty self, as if something external and contingent could be connected with the doing, something that did not belong to it, so that from that point of view the conduct would therefore be innocent. On the contrary, the doing is precisely this division, the positing of itself for itself, and of a foreign external actuality opposed to it: that there is such an actuality belongs to conduct itself and comes to be because of it. Only the absence of conduct is without guilt, like the being of a stone, but not even like that of a child. —But according to its content, ethical *action* has the moment of crime in it, because it does not sublate the *natural* distribution of the two laws to the two sexes. On the contrary, being the unambiguous orientation to the law, it remains within *natural immediacy*, and, as conduct, it makes this one-sidedness into the guilt of seizing only one of the sides of essence and of behaving negatively toward the other; that is, it violates it. Where guilt and crime, conduct and action fit in universal ethical life will be made more explicit later on. So much is immediately evident: it is not *the singular* individual who acts and is guilty, for as *this* self he is merely the inactual shade; that is, he is only the universal self. Individuality is purely the *formal* moment of *conduct* in general, the content of which is laws and customs determined for the singular individual by his station. He is the substance as genus, which does indeed become species through its determinateness, though, at the same time, the species remains the universal of the genus. Self-consciousness descends within the people from the universal only as far as particularity, not as far as singular individuality that posits in its conduct an excluding self, an actuality that is negative toward itself. On the contrary, a sure trust in the whole lies at the foundation of its action; nothing foreign interferes with it, neither fear nor hostility.

[255] The developed nature of the *effective* act is what the ethical self-consciousness now experiences in its deed, both when it submits to the divine law and when it submits to the human. The law revealed to it is linked in its essence with the opposite one. The essence is the unity of both, but the deed has only developed the one against the other. Being linked in the essence with the other, however, the fulfillment of the one calls forth the other as a violated and now hostile essence seeking revenge, which is what the deed made it. Only one side of the resolution as a whole 32–469

lies open in the light of day for the action; but *in itself* the resolution is the negative that opposes another to it, something foreign to the resolution, which is knowledge. So actuality keeps the other side, which is foreign to knowledge, hidden within itself, and does not show itself to consciousness in the way that it is in and for itself: to the son it does not show the father in the assailant whom he slays, nor the mother in the queen whom he takes to wife.[40] In this way, a power that shuns the daylight lies in wait for the ethical self-consciousness, and only sallies out and catches it red-handed when the deed is done; for the accomplished deed is the sublated antithesis of the knowing self and the actuality confronting it. The agent cannot disown the crime and his guilt. The deed is this: to move the unmoved and bring forth the unconscious with the conscious, nonbeing with being. Thus in this truth the deed steps into the sunlight as a thing in which a conscious side is bound up with an unconscious one, one's own side with a foreign one; [and it steps into the sunlight] as the divided essence, whose other side consciousness experiences, and experiences as its own, too, though as the power it has violated and provoked it to hostility.

33–470   It may be that the right, lying in ambush does not have its own proper shape for the acting *consciousness,* but is present only *implicitly* in the inner guilt of decision and of action. But the ethical consciousness is more complete, its guilt is purer, where it is *already acquainted* with the law and the power that it confronts, where it takes these to be violence and injustice, something ethically arbitrary, and, like Antigone, it commits the crime knowingly. The accomplished deed inverts the perspective of ethical substance; the *accomplishment* itself proclaims it: what is *ethical* must be *actual,* for the *actuality* of the purpose is the purpose of the activity. Action expresses precisely the *unity* of *actuality* and *substance;* it declares that actuality is not accidental for the essence, but rather that, being in bonds with the essence, actuality is not granted to any right that is not the true one. Ethical consciousness must recognize its opposite as its own actuality for the sake of this actuality and of its own action. It must recognize its guilt: [256] "Because we suffer, we recognize that we have erred."[41]

---

40. This is an obvious reference to Oedipus in the play *Oedipus the King.*

41. Sophocles' *Antigone,* 926. Hegel renders the passage differently from the way it appears in Sophocles. Antigone says, "But if, indeed, these things be fair in the gods' eyes / Then, having suffered, I would acknowledge that I have erred" (925–6). Hegel is influenced by Friedrich Hölderlin's adaptation and translation of Sophocles' play. Hölderlin numbers the lines differently from what appears in the original Greek; he also offers a slightly different version of her words. As a result the "guilt" is shifted from her to the people and ruler of Thebes. Hölderlin renders these verses as, "If this truly has now come before the gods, then *we* suffer

This recognition expresses the sublated dissension of the ethical *pur-*   34–471
pose with *actuality;* it expresses the return to the ethical *sentiment* that
knows that nothing counts but the right. But therein the agent gives up
his *character* and the *actuality* of his self, and has perished. His *being* is
this: to belong to his ethical law as to his substance; with the recognition
of the opposite, however, the law has ceased to be substance for him and,
instead of actuality, has attained nonactuality—to a disposition. —Of
course, the substance appears *in* individuality as its *pathos,* and individuality as that that animates it and hence stands above it; but the substance is
a pathos that is at the same time the agent's character. Ethical individuality is immediate, and is in itself one with this universal; it has its existence
only in this universal and cannot survive the downfall that this ethical
power suffers at the hands of its opposite.

But ethical individuality possesses thereby the certainty that individ-   35–472
uality, whose pathos is the opposite power, "suffers no more ill than it
has inflicted."[42] The movement of the ethical powers against one
another, and the movement of the individualities that put them into life
and action, have only reached their *true end* when both sides experience
the same downfall.[43] For neither power has any precedence over the
other, so as to be the *more essential* moment of substance. The equal
essentiality and the indifferent subsistence of the two beside one
another means their being without a self. They exist as the essential self
in the *deed,* but it is a diverse one that contradicts the unity of the self
and constitutes its lack of right and its inevitable downfall. So, too, the
character in part (according to its pathos or substance) belongs just to
the one power; and in part (from the side of the knowing) the one character, like the other, is split into a conscious and an unconscious aspect.
Now, since each character itself calls forth this antithesis, and, through
the deed, this not-knowing, too, is its work, each brings upon itself the

---

and ask to be forgiven our past sins. But if this is an error, then *you* should not
suffer any greater misfortune than what you have made openly against me" (961–
5). Cf. Friedrich Hölderlin, *Sämtliche Werke,* hrsg. von Friedrich Beissner, Bd. I5:
Übersetzungen (Stuttgart: W. Kohlhammer, 1952), p. 243. (emphasis added).

42. *Antigone,* 927. The line actually goes "But if it is he [Creon, who has
sinned], may he not suffer more ill than he has inflicted on me." In Sophocles the
line refers to Creon, but in Hölderlin's adaptation the reference seems to be to the
gods' infliction of suffering on "us" citizens.

43. The two powers are the divine and human laws. Creon orders the death of
Antigone. Her suffering shows the triumph of human over divine law. But his
decree also has the effect that he will lose his spouse and child, and ultimately,
through a divine command, his kingdom as well. His suffering is the triumph of
divine over human law.

guilt that consumes it. The victory of the one power and of its character, and the submission of the other side would therefore be only a part, the uncompleted work that marches irresistibly forward toward the equilibrium of both. Only in the equal overthrow of both sides is absolute right fulfilled; ethical substance has emerged as the negative power that engulfs both sides: the almighty and righteous *Destiny* has made its entrance.

36–473   If both powers are taken according to their determinate content and its individualization, then what presents itself is the image of their patterned conflict which, on its [257] formal₂ side, presents itself as the conflict of ethical life and self-consciousness against nature, which lacks consciousness, and a contingency that is present on account of it. This contingency has a right against self-consciousness, because the latter is only *true* spirit, only in *immediate* unity with its substance. And, on the side of its content, the image of the conflict presents itself as the split between the divine and human law. —The youth leaves the nonconscious essence, leaves the family spirit, and becomes the individuality of the community. But that he still belongs to nature, from which he has torn himself away, is shown by the fact that he emerges in the contingent form of two brothers who take power over the community with equal right. *For them*, since they are entering the ethical essence, the inequality of earlier and later birth, being a distinction of nature, has no significance. But as the simple soul or self of the people's spirit, the government does not tolerate a duality of the individuality; and over against the ethical necessity of this unity nature steps in as the accidental condition of plurality. Hence, the two brothers come to be at odds, and their equal right to the power of the state brings them both to ruin; for they are equally in the wrong. Seen in the human way, the brother who has committed the crime is the one who, not being *in possession* [of the state-power], attacks the community, at whose pinnacle the other stood. On the other hand, the brother who has the right on his side is the one who knew how to apprehend the other merely as something *singular*, detached from the community, and drove him out, being in this state of impotence. He has laid hand only on the individual as such, not on the community, not on the essence of human right. The community, attacked and defended by empty singularity, preserves itself, and the two brothers meet their downfall together at each other's hands; for the individuality that ties the peril of the whole to its *being-for-self* has expelled itself from the community, and is itself undone. The community, however, will honor the one found to be on its side; but the government—the restored simplicity of the communal self—will, on the contrary, deprive of his last rites the other one, who proclaimed the laying waste of the community at its very walls.[44] He who violated the highest spirit of consciousness, the spirit of the community, must be stripped of the honor that belongs to the departed spirit, the honor of his essence, entire and complete.

However, if the universe thus lightly casts off the pure pinnacle of its 37-474 pyramid and achieves *victory* over the self-enraging principle of singularity, namely, the family, then it has thereby let itself be drawn into *struggle* with the divine law, [i.e.,] it is only self-conscious spirit letting itself be drawn into *struggle* with the nonconscious; for the nonconscious spirit is the other essential power, and for that reason is not destroyed by that other power, but is only abused by it. But against the law that has authority in the daylight, the nonconscious spirit has only the bloodless shade to help it to its *actual* fulfillment. As the law of the weak and of darkness, therefore, it succumbs at first to the law [258] of the daylight and of force, for its power rules under the earth, not upon it. But in depriving the inward of its honor and might, the actual has thereby consumed its own essence. The revealed spirit has the root of its force in the underworld; the *certainty* of the people, self- assured and self-assuring, possesses the *truth* of the oath that binds all into one only in the nonconscious and speechless substance of all, in the waters of forgetfulness. The fulfillment of the revealed spirit is thereby changed into its opposite, and spirit experiences the fact that its highest right is the highest unrighteousness, its victory is rather its own downfall. The dead man, whose right is injured, knows on that account how to find tools for his revenge that have just as much actuality and force as the power that injured him. These powers are other communities, whose altars the dogs and birds befouled with the corpse, for the corpse has not received its due,[45] since it has not returned to the elementary individual and so has not been raised to nonconscious universality. Instead, it has remained above the earth in the realm of actuality, and as the force of the divine law it now obtains a self-conscious actual universality. These powers turn hostile and destroy the community that has dishonored and shattered its power, the piety of the family.[46]

---

44. The reference is to one of the following: either Aeschylus' *Seven against Thebes*, 631–52 or to Sophocles' *Oedipus at Colonus*, 1254–1446, or again simply to *Antigone*, 29–37. Each of these plays refers to the event Hegel is describing in this passage.

45. *Antigone*, 998–1032.

46. The reference is to Euripides' *The Suppliant Women*. The other communities are Argos and Athens. The "force of divine law" is expressed in Athena's speech at the end of the play. She says, "To the children of the Argive champions I say this: when you come to manhood, you will sack the city of Ismenus and exact vengeance for the blood of your fathers slain. . . . No sooner have your beards grown in than you must march the bronze-clad army to the seven gated city of

38–475   In the representation the movement of human and divine law expresses its necessity in individuals, in whom the universal appears as a *pathos* and the activity of the movement as their *individual* doing; and this gives the show of contingency to the necessity of the two laws. But individuality and its deed constitute the principle of singularity in general, the principle that in its pure universality was called the inner divine law. As the moment of the revealed community, the inner law does not just have that netherwordly efficacy, which, in the law's determinate being, is external. On the contrary, it has an actual determinate being and movement that is equally revealed to the actual people. Taken in this form, what was represented as the simple movement of individualized pathos takes on another aspect; both the crime and the destruction of the community brought about through it take on the proper form of their determinate being. —The human law—which in its universal determinate being is thus the community, in its activity, generally the male principle, and in its actual conduct, the government—*is, moves,* and *maintains* itself by digesting the dismemberment within itself of the Penates (or the independent singularizing into families over which the female principle is manager) and by preserving them dissolved in the continuity of its fluidity.[47] But, in general, the family is at the same time the element of human law—the singular consciousness is the universal activating ground. Since the community [259] establishes itself only through the disturbance of family happiness and the dissolution of self-consciousness in the universal, it creates its own inner enemy in what it suppresses and what is at the same time essential to it, [namely] the female principle in general. This principle—the eternal irony of the community—changes the universal of the government into a private purpose through intrigue, transforms the universal activity of government into the work of some definite individual, and inverts the universal property of the state into the possession and adornment of a family.[48] In this way, the earnest wisdom of ripe old age,

---

Cadmeans. Unwelcome will you be to them as you arrive, lion cubs now full grown, sackers of the city. It cannot be otherwise" (1213–24). Euripides, *The Suppliant Women*, ed. and trans. by David Kovacs (Cambridge, MA: Harvard University, 1998).

47. This sentence characterizes human law in recognizable Aristotelian terms. Cf. *Politics*, Bk. I, ch. 2, 1252a25–1253a39.

48. Hegel's remark appears to be highly chauvinistic and even derogatory toward the "female principle," but we must remember that he is expressing the situation of the Greek (and later Roman) political life. Even in the Greek plays that are "pro" female, it is quite clear that it is the women who counsel war, seek revenge, and push their husbands to action. Even in *The Suppliant Women*, which is a decidedly "pro" female play, Theseus would not have gone to war were it not

which, being dead to singularity—to pleasures and enjoyments, as well as to any active role—thinks and cares only for the universal, is made by the female principle into a laughingstock for the mischievous immaturity of youth, an object of contempt for their enthusiasm.[49] The female principle in general raises the strength of youth to what has value: that of the son, master of the mother who bore him; that of the brother, in whom the sister has a man who is her equal; that of the young man, through whom the daughter loses her dependence and achieves the enjoyment and dignity of wifehood. —The community can maintain itself, however, only through the oppression of this spirit of singularity, and, because that spirit is an essential moment, the community really engenders it as well. In fact, by its oppressive attitude toward the spirit of singularity, it engenders it as a hostile principle. But since this principle is merely evil and inwardly null when it cuts itself off from the universal purpose, it would be completely powerless were it not that the community itself recognizes, as the *force* of the whole, the strength of youth—the male principle that, not being mature, still remains within its singularity. For the community is one people, it is itself an individuality; it is essentially individual for *itself* only because there are *other individualities for it*—because it *excludes* them from itself and knows itself to be independent of them. The negative side of

for his mother, Aethra, and the other mothers who persuade him that war is the gods' command. Hegel's reference to the intrigue and abuse of the universal for an individual's particular want as belonging to the female principle reflects not only on the bad character of a murderous Clytemnestra or the illicit pleasures of Jocasta but anticipates the dispositions of the mothers and wives of the Roman despots. Hegel knows the stories of how, for example, Caligula and Nero came to power. It was through their mothers' contrivances, even to the point of poisoning their husbands, as alleged in the case of Claudius' death. So it is not that Hegel is being overtly chauvinistic with these remarks. He is indicating an ethical character belonging to womankind as recorded in the ancient world. This conception shows *female facticity*, which itself shows us the nature of guilt.

49. Cf. the "possession" of Cadmus and Tiresias is by the female spirit of the Bacchante; they are made to look foolish and act even more foolishly. Of course, the irony is that these old men are not fools, rather they recognize the female principle to be stronger than the rational (male) principle (*Bacchae*, 200–9). When the male principle in the person of King Pentheus attempts to subdue the female Bacchae, it will be torn apart by their feminine frenzy; his own mother and sister kill him. The female principle is considered stronger than the male principle because it belongs to the spirited part of the soul, while the male principle belongs to the rational (and ineffective) part. Hegel is attempting to show us how our social self emerges from the natural self, and in this context passion and appetite are stronger, more vital powers than rationality. That reason is "superior" to these other powers occurs only through the suppression of the female principle.

community, *inwardly* oppressing the singularization[50] of the individuals, but outwardly active as a self,[51] has its weapons in individuality. War is the spirit and form in which the essential moment of the ethical substance—the absolute *freedom* of the ethical *self* from all determinate being—is present in the actuality and the confirmation of the substance. For while, on the one hand, the singular *systems* of property and personal independence—like singular *personality* itself—feel the force of the negative; on the other hand, it is just this negative essence that elevates itself in war[52] as the preserver of the whole. The brave youth for whom the female principle has desire, the oppressed principle of destruction, comes into the daylight and is what has value. It is now natural force and that that appears as the accident of luck that decide between the determinate being of the ethical essence and spiritual necessity. But since the determinate being of the ethical [260] essence and spiritual necessity rest upon strength and luck, it is thus *already decided* that it has perished. —Just as previously merely the Penates perished within the spirit of the people, so now because of their individuality the *living* spirits of the people perish within a *universal* community, whose *simple universality* is spiritless and dead, and whose life principle is the *singular* individual as singular. The ethical shape of spirit has disappeared, and another one takes its place.

39–476   Thus this downfall of ethical substance and its passing over into another shape is determined by the fact that ethical consciousness is directed toward the law in an essentially *immediate* fashion. What is involved in this determination of immediacy is that nature in general enters within the activity of ethical life. Its actuality reveals only the contradiction and the seed of destruction that the beautiful concord and restful equilibrium of the ethical spirit have precisely in their rest and beauty. For immediacy has the contradictory significance of being the nonconscious rest of nature and the self-conscious restless rest of spirit. —Because of this naturalness the ethical people is in principle an individuality that is determined by nature and hence restricted; and, therefore, it finds its sublation in another. This determinacy is [called] restriction when posited in its determinate being, but equally it is the negative in general and the self of the individuality. But since it disappears, the life of spirit and this substance, which is self-conscious in all of its [determinacy], is lost. It emerges in them as a *formal₂ universality*, [i.e.,] it no

---

50. \<Vereinzelung\>

51. \<selbst-tätig\>

52. *in ihm*. We take this to refer back to *der Krieg* (war) in the preceding sentence, but grammatically it is possible to refer it back to *Eigentum* in the preceding clause.

longer dwells in them as living spirit; instead the simple solidity of its individuality is shattered into a multitude of points.

c. The Condition of Right

The universal unity, into which the living immediate unity of individuality   40–477
and substance returns, is the spiritless community that has ceased to be the unselfconscious substance of individuals, and in which they now count as essential selves and substances in virtue of their singular being-for-self. This dead spirit, the universal—the universal split up into the atoms of absolutely many individuals—is an *equality* in which *everyone* counts as *each* one, that is, as *persons*. —What would be called [261] the hidden divine law in the world of ethical life had, in the deed, issued from its inner [state] into actuality; in that world the *singular* counted and was actual from the aspect of the universal *blood-kinship* of the *family*. As *this* singular, he was the *departed* spirit, *without a self;* but now he has come out of his nonactuality.[53] Because ethical substance is only the *true* spirit, spirit goes back into the *certainty* of itself; spirit is that substance as the *positive* universal, but its actuality is to be *negative* universal *self*. —We saw the powers and shapes of the ethical world in the simple necessity of empty *destiny*. This power of the ethical world is substance reflecting itself into simplicity; but the absolute essence that reflects, that very necessity of empty destiny into itself, is nothing other than the *I* of self-consciousness.

From now on this *I* counts as an essence that subsists *in and for itself;*   41–478
this *being recognized* is its substantiality; but the substantiality is *abstract universality*, because its content is *this rigid self*, and not the self that is dissolved substance.

Here, then, the personality has emerged from the life of ethical sub-   42–479
stance; it is the *actually valid* independence of consciousness. As *nonactual thought* that came to be through the *renunciation* of *actuality*, this independence occurred previously as *stoic* self-consciousness; and just as that issued from lordship and bondage, which was the immediate determinate being of *self-consciousness*, so too personality has issued from the immediate *spirit*, which is the universally sovereign will of all, and equally their sub-

---

53. The dead have arisen and take on the form of the "rigid self." What Hegel means by this is that in Greek life the dead were beyond the living and stood as the guardians of divine law who protected the dwelling place. In Roman life the guardians who protect the dwelling are the tribunes, consuls, censors, etc., that is, the guardians of Roman law. The Lares and the Penates are just "goods" of possession, and the essential self is not the pithless shade but the "citizen." Yet for all this there is no ethical life in Rome: there is only the dead abstraction of self and the material personal atoms in a void.

servient obedience. What was *implicitly* for Stoicism, [existing] only in *abstraction*, is here an *actual world*. Stoicism is nothing other than the consciousness that brings the principle of the condition of right, spiritless independence, to its abstract form; through its flight from *actuality*, consciousness arrived only at the thought of independence; it is absolutely for-*itself* because it does not tie its essence to some determinate being or other, but has given up every determinate being and posits its essence solely in the unity of pure thought. In the same way, the right of the person is neither tied to a richer or more powerful determinate being of the individual as such, nor even to a universal living spirit, but rather to the pure one of abstract actuality; that is, to that one as self-consciousness in general.

43–480   Now just as the *abstract* independence of Stoicism displayed its realization, so, too, this latest independence will repeat the movement of the earlier one. The abstract independence passes over into the skeptical confusion of consciousness, into a babble of the negative, which strays aimlessly[54] from one contingency of being and of thought to [262] another. Indeed, it dissolves the contingencies in its absolute independence, but engenders them again just as much; and, in fact, it is only the contradiction of the independence and dependence of consciousness. —Similarly, the personal independence of *right* is rather this same universal confusion and mutual dissolution. For what counts as the absolute essence is self-consciousness as the purely *empty one[ness]* of the person. In contrast to this empty universality, substance has the form of *fulfillment* and of *content*, and this content is now set free completely in disorder; for the spirit that subjugated it and held it together in its unity is no longer present. — Hence this empty one[ness] of the person is in its *reality* an accidental determinate being—an essenceless moving and doing that comes to no enduring state. Thus, like skepticism, the formalism of right exists by virtue of its concept without a content of its own; it finds a manifold subsistence, a possession, and, like skepticism, impresses upon it the same abstract universality by which it is called *property*. But, although actuality determined in that way in skepticism is called *show* in general and has only a negative value, in [the sphere of] right it has positive value. The negative value consists in the fact that the actual has the significance of the self qua thinking, as the *implicit* universal, but the positive value consists in the fact that the actual is *mine* in the significance of the category, with a validity that is *recognized* and *actual*. —But both are the same *abstract universal;* the actual content or *determinacy* of being mine is not contained in this empty form and does not concern it—be it the determinacy of some external possession or again, of an inner richness or poverty

---

54. <gestaltlos>

of spirit and character. So the content belongs to a *power of its own* that is other than the formal universal (which is the power that is chance and is arbitrary). —Hence, in its actual validity the consciousness of right experiences rather its complete inessentiality and the loss of its reality; and to designate an individual as a *person* is an expression of contempt.

The free power of the content so determines itself that, through the 44–481 nature of this determinacy, the dispersion into absolute *multiplicity* of the personal atoms is, at the same time, collected into *one* point that is alien to them and is equally devoid of spirit. On the one hand, this point, like the rigidity of their personality, is a pure singular actuality; but in its antithesis to their empty singularity, it also has for them the significance of all the content, and hence of the real essence; and as against their actuality that is supposed to be absolute, though it is in itself without essence, this point is the universal power and absolute actuality. In this way this Lord of the World[55] is himself the absolute person encompassing within himself all determinate being at once, for whose consciousness no higher spirit exists. He is a person, but the solitary person who has confronted *all* [others]; all [of these others] [263] constitute the valid universality of the person, for the singular as such is true qua singular only as the universal multiplicity of singularity. Cut off from this, the solitary self is, in fact, the inactual impotent self. —At the same time, the singular is the consciousness of that content, which has confronted that universal personality. But this content, liberated by its negative power, is the chaos of the spiritual powers that, unfettered as elemental essences, move against each other in a wild orgy of mad destruction; being impotent, their self-consciousness is the powerless wrapping and the field of their tumult.[56] Knowing himself thus as the sum-total[57] of all actual powers, this Lord of the World is the monstrous self-consciousness that knows itself as the actual god; but since he is only the formal self, which is unable to curb them, his movement and self-enjoyment are that equally monstrous orgy.[58]

---

55. The epithet "Lord of the World" is first used by Gibbon to describe Commodus, who styled himself the "Roman Hercules." Edward Gibbon, *Decline and Fall of the Roman Empire* (NY: Modern Library, n.d.), Vol. I, p. 83.

56. The wrapping is the emperor's mantle, which becomes a prize on the field of tumult, i.e., on the battlefield. The allusion is to how most Roman emperors were killed either in battles or in palace coups.

57. <Inbegriff>

58. Although many of the emperors could reasonably be described here, two stand out in Gibbon's treatment of Rome's decline. The first is Commodus. Gibbon remarks, "every sentiment of virtue and humanity was extinct in the mind of Commodus. Whilst he thus abandoned the reins of empire to these unworthy favorites, he valued nothing in sovereign power, except the unbounded licence of

34 VI. A. True Spirit, The Ethical Life

45–482   The Lord of the World has actual consciousness of what he is—of the universal power of actuality—in the destructive authority that he exercises against the self of his subjects who stand against him. For his power is not the *unitedness* of spirit in which the persons would recognize their own self-consciousness; they are rather persons for-themselves and exclude continuity with others from the absolute rigidity of their point-like being; thus just as they are in a merely negative relation to one another, likewise they are to him who is their connection or continuity. As this continuity, he is the essence and content of their formalism. But their content is foreign, and their essence, a hostile one, which, moreover, sublates just what counts for them as their essence, that is, the being-for-self that is void of content. And as the continuity of their personality, he destroys precisely that [essence]. Thus, the legal[59] personality experiences its own lack of substance inasmuch as the content that is foreign to it asserts its validity in its, and the Lord of the World asserts himself in [other] persons because he is their reality.[60] The destructive grubbing in this soil without essence acquires the consciousness of its own overall lordship. But this self is mere devastation; it is therefore outside of itself, and further it is the casting away of its self-consciousness.

46–483   This is how the side in which self-consciousness is actual as absolute essence is constituted. But the *consciousness* that is *driven back into itself* out of this actuality makes this inessentiality that belongs to it an object of thought. Earlier we saw the stoic independence of pure thought pass through skepticism to find its truth in the unhappy consciousness—the

---

indulging his sensual appetites. His hours were spent in seraglio of three hundred beautiful women, and as many boys, of every rank, of every province; and, wherever the arts of seduction proved ineffectual, the brutal lover had recourse to violence" (p. 81). The emperor who actually thought himself to be a god was Bassianus Antonious who called himself, after the Syrian sun god, Elagabalus (or Heliogabalus). Gibbon says, "A long train of concubines, and a rapid succession of wives, among whom was a vestal virgin, ravished by force from her sacred asylum, were insufficient to satisfy the impotence of his passions. The master of the Roman world affected to copy the dress and manners of the female sex, preferring the distaff to the sceptre, and dishonoured the principal dignities of the empire by distributing them among his numerous lovers; one of whom was publicly invested with the title and authority of the emperor's, or, as he more properly styled himself, of the empress's husband" (p. 128). This "monarch of the world" also married both his mother and sister and, like Caligula before him, raised his horse to the rank of senator.

59. <rechtliche>

60. The Lord of the World who sees himself in others is Marcus Aurelius, the Stoic. The Stoical consciousness is the paradigmatic "legal personality."

truth of the situation concerning its being in and for itself.[61] But at that time, this knowledge appeared only as the one-sided view of consciousness as such, whereas now its *actual* truth has made its entrance. It consists in the fact that the *universal* [264] *validity* of self-consciousness is its own estranged reality. This *validity* is the universal actuality of the self; but the actuality is immediately inversion just as much—the loss of the self's essence. —The actuality of the self that was not to be found in the ethical world has been gained through the return of the actuality into the *person;* what was there united comes now on the scene, developed but self-estranged.

B. SELF-ESTRANGED SPIRIT; CULTURE

The ethical substance kept the antithesis enclosed within its simple con- 47–484
sciousness, and kept consciousness in immediate unity with its essence. Hence the essence has for consciousness the simple determinacy of *being*. Consciousness is directed to this being immediately; it is its custom. Consciousness does not value itself as *this exclusive self,* nor does substance have the significance of a determinate being excluded from consciousness, with which it would have to unite itself only by means of self-estrangement while, at the same time, producing the substance. This spirit, however, whose self is what is absolutely discrete, has its content facing it as an equally hard actuality; here the world has the determination of being something external—the negative of self-consciousness. But this world is spiritual essence; it is implicitly the interpenetration of being and individuality. The determinate being that belongs to it is the *work* of self-consciousness, but it is just as much an actuality that is immediately present and foreign to it. This world has a being of its own in which self-consciousness does not recognize itself. It is the external essence and the free content of [the world of] Right. But this external actuality, which the Lord of the World of Right embraces within himself, is not only the elemental essence that is accidentally present to the self; it is furthermore the labor of the self—though not its positive labor but its negative labor.[62] The

---

61. A reference back to Chapter 4 of the *Phenomenology*. Stoicism was there only an abstraction—a formal determination of self-consciousness—while here we see its actualization in the world.

62. Hegel is recalling the lessons of "Truth of Self-Certainty" Chapter 4 of the *Phenomenology*. It is the servant (*Knecht*) who does the work and is estranged from his labor. The self-consciousness of servitude is the prerequisite for freedom, and Hegel sees the shift from the Roman World to the Christian World as the justification of this consciousness. The servant is now anyone bonded to this

actuality preserves its determinate being through self-consciousness's *own* externalization and abandonment of essence, which, in the devastation that rules in the world of Right, appears to self-consciousness to be brought about by the external violence[63] of the elements let loose. By themselves these elements are just pure devastation and their own dissolution. But this dissolution—this negative essence that they have—is precisely the self; the self is their subject, their doing and becoming. But this doing and becoming, whereby the substance becomes actual, is the estrangement of personality, since the self that counts *immediately* in and for itself (that is, [265] *without estrangement*) is without substance: it is the play of those raging elements. *Its* substance, therefore, is just its externalization, and the externalization is the substance, that is, the spiritual powers arraying themselves into a world, and preserving themselves thereby.

48–485   In this way substance is *spirit:* the self-conscious *unity* of self and essence, though both [self and essence] have also the significance of mutual estrangement. Spirit is the *consciousness* of an actuality that stands freely for itself as object. This consciousness, however, is confronted by that unity of self and essence: the *actual consciousness* [faced] by the *pure* one. On the one hand, through its externalization, actual self-consciousness issues into the actual world, and what is actual returns to self-consciousness. On the other hand, however, this very actuality—both the person and the objectification equally well—is sublated. Both are purely universal. Their estranged being is *pure consciousness* or *essence.* The present has its opposite immediately in its *beyond,* which is its thinking and its having been thought—just as the beyond has its opposite on this side, which is its actuality estranged from it.

49–486   Hence spirit cultivates not just *one* world but a double [sided] one—a world that is separated and set against itself.[64] —The world of ethical spirit is its own *presence;* hence, each of its powers stands in this unity, and insofar as they are mutually distinct, each stands in equilibrium with the whole. There is nothing that has the significance of being the negative of self-consciousness; even the departed spirit is present in the *blood* of the clan, in the *self* of the family, and the universal *power* of the government is the Will, or the self of the people. Here, however, what presence signifies is only the objective *actuality* that has its consciousness in the beyond.

World and separated from God's grace. The spiritual attitude of this kingdom should remind us of Thomas à Kempis's *Imitation of Christ.*

63. <Gewalt>

64. The two-sided World has one side consisting of God's kingdom, which is identified as the Church triumphant, and one side identifiable as the temporal kingdom of monarchical rule.

Each single moment, as *essence,* receives this [consciousness], and along with it actuality from some other; and inasmuch as consciousness is actual, its essence is something other than its actuality. Nothing [in consciousness] has a spirit grounded and dwelling within it but is outside of itself in something foreign. The equilibrium of the whole is neither the self-abiding unity nor the tranquility of its having returned to itself, but it rests rather on the estrangement of its opposite.[65] Hence the whole is a self-estranged reality similar to each singular moment: it falls apart into one realm in which *self-consciousness* is *actual*—both itself and its object— and another that is the realm of *pure* consciousness, which, being beyond the first realm, does not have an actual object but has its being in *faith.* Now, just as in the separation of the divine and human laws and in their [respective] shapes, the ethical world returns to its destiny (back to the *self* [266] that is the *negative power* of this antithesis), and just as its consciousness returns from the separation into knowledge and unconsciousness,[66] so these two realms of self-estranged spirit will return to the *self* as well. But whereas the former was the initial immediately valued *self,* [that is,] the singular *person,* this second self will be the self returning to itself from its externalization, [that is,] the *universal self,* which is consciousness that has hold of the *concept.*[67] As the self that *gets* hold of itself, pure insight brings culture to completion. It grasps nothing but the self and everything as the self; that is, it *conceives* everything, effaces all objectivity, and transforms everything that has being *in-itself* into something that is being *for-itself.* When it turns against faith, which is the foreign realm of *essence*—the realm that lies beyond—pure insight is the *Enlightenment.*[68]

---

65. The World of God's kingdom and the World of the temporal powers are estranged from each other, even as they mutually support each other. Hegel is expressing the distinction and opposition that Augustine claims is necessary in his *City of God.*

66. <Bewußtlosigkeit>

67. Hegel is anticipating later developments of the Concept. Throughout this entire section there is a struggle for validation. One side will develop along the path of materialism: believing that the higher power of Reason lies either in social status or in nature. The other side will develop along the path of piety: believing that the higher power lies in faith and a rejection of the present World. In fact, according to Hegel, both sides are moving toward a rational insight on the importance of the Self, that its identity and unity qua self-consciousness is essential. What both sides are working toward is the notion of Cartesian identity between Self and World within the bipolarity of the Concept.

68. Hegel is referring to the French Enlightenment (c. 1701–89) with its emphasis on personal liberty, material pleasures, the culture of wit, and social utility. The champion for this vision is Denis Diderot and his satirical visions of

The Enlightenment completes the estrangement in the realm of essence as well, where the estranged spirit finds its salvation in the consciousness of resting identity with itself. The Enlightenment disturbs the domestic arrangement that spirit maintains there by bringing in the instrument of the world on this side; and spirit cannot disclaim this as its own possession, since spirit's consciousness belongs to this world as well. —In this negative transaction, pure insight realizes itself at the same time; it brings forth its own object: the unknowable *absolute essence* and the *useful*. In this way actuality loses all substantiality and there is nothing more *inherently* in it, whereas just as the realm of faith is overthrown, so too is the real world. This revolution brings forth *absolute freedom* whereby the previously estranged spirit returns to itself completely.[69] It forsakes the land of culture and passes into another land: to the land of *moral consciousness.*[70]

I. The World of Self-Estranged Spirit

50–487   The world of this spirit falls apart into two. The first world is that of actuality or its own estrangement, but the other is the world that spirit, elevating itself above the first, builds for itself in the ether of pure consciousness. Although it is *opposed* to the estrangement of the first world, this other world is not free of it, precisely because it is opposed to the first one. Instead, it is only the other form of the estrangement, which consists exactly in having consciousness in two different worlds and encompasses them both. Hence, what is being considered here is not the self-consciousness of the absolute essence as the latter is *in* and *for itself;* that is, not religion but *faith,* inasmuch as it is a flight from the actual world and is, therefore, not *in* and *for-itself.* Thus this flight [267] from the realm of the present is in its self immediately a doubled one. Pure consciousness is

---

society. Diderot is the champion of atheism, even to the point of disparaging Voltaire and D'Alembert for their notions of a God beyond nature. It is important to note that Hegel sees a valid position for the atheist, since this "religious" society is hypocritical and presents a "false" value.

69. The "revolution" is the French Revolution of 1789.

70. "Moral consciousness" belongs to the final stage of Spirit in the World. It marks a shift away from the values and beliefs of the French Enlightenment to the German conception of "moral enlightenment." Therein the inward movement of the Concept, which develops the Self as an autonomous thinking thing, is completed, and thus the Self becomes an autonomous giver and tester of laws. It is also the move to a thoroughly isolated Self, whose feelings and passions are in conflict with its autonomous rational will and intellect. This isolated, autonomous Self, while attaining the pinnacle of self-identity and self-certainty, is also a rigid "bloodless" being. Morality must embrace a religious attitude in order to overcome its own isolation and rigidity.

the element of *faith* but also of the concept. Thus the two make their entrance together at the same time, and faith only comes into consideration in antithesis to the concept.

a. Culture and Its Realm of Actuality

The spirit of the world is the spiritual *essence* permeated by a *self-*   51–488
consciousness that knows itself to be immediately present as *this subsistence for itself,* and knows *essence* as an actuality confronting it. But the determinate being of this world—like the actuality of self-consciousness—depends on the movement by which this [self-consciousness] externalizes itself from its personality, and thereby brings forth a world of its own and behaves toward it as something foreign, so that from then on it gains power over it. But the renouncing of its being-for-self is itself the generation of actuality, and, therefore, through this renunciation this self-consciousness gets power immediately over actuality. —In other words, self-consciousness only is *something;*[71] it only has *reality* inasmuch as it is self-estranged. In this way, it posits itself as universal, and this universality constitutes its worth and actuality. This *equality* with everything is not, therefore, the previous equality of Right—not that immediate recognition and worth of self-consciousness simply because *it is;* rather, that it should have worth is due to the estranging mediation of having made itself conform to the universal. The spiritless universality of Right takes every natural mode of character, as well as of determinate being into itself, and justifies it. But the universality that counts here is one that has *come to be,* and that is why it is *actual.*

Thus it is *culture* by which the individual acquires worth and actuality.   52–489
The individual's true *original nature* and substance is the spirit of the *estrangement* of *natural* being.[72] This externalization, therefore, is equally his *purpose* and his *determinate being.* At the same time, it is the *means,* or the *transition,* of the *conceived substance* into *actuality* and, conversely, of the *determinate individuality* into *essentiality.* This individuality cultivates itself into what it is *in itself,* and by this culturation it *is* for the first time *in itself* and has actual determinate being. It has as much actuality and power as it has culture. Although the self actually knows itself here as *this* [self], nonetheless its actuality consists solely in the sublating of the natural self. The originally *determinate* nature is reduced to the *inessential* distinction of quantity, to a greater or lesser energy of the will. The goal and content

---

71. <*Etwas*>

72. The view that one's worth comes from Culture and social division, which is the original state of our natural being, comes from Rousseau and his second discourse, *On the Origin of Inequality* (1755).

of the will, [268] however, belong solely to the universal substance itself and can only be something universal. The particularity of a nature that becomes the purpose and content is something *impotent and nonactual:* it is a *kind* that strains ludicrously and in vain to put itself to work. It is the contradiction of giving to the particular the actuality that is immediately universal. Hence, if individuality is posited in a mistaken way in the *particularity* of nature and of character, still, no individualities or characters are to be found in the real world. Instead, the individuals have a similar determinate being for each other; the individuality that is assumed is the determinate being that is *intended*—it has no subsistence in this world where only what externalizes itself and, consequently, only what is universal achieves actuality. —For this reason, *what is intended* counts for what is, for a kind. "Kind" is not quite the same as *espèce,* "which of all the nicknames is the most dreadful, for it signifies the highest degree of contempt."[73] "To be a *kind* and to be *good in its kind*"[74] is, however, a German expression that adds to the meaning of *espèce* a respectable air; as if nothing at all bad were meant by this term, or as if in fact it did not still involve the consciousness of what "kind," "culture," and "actuality" are.[75]

---

73. A line from Diderot's satire, *Rameau's Nephew* (c. 1762). Hegel had access only to Goethe's translation of 1805. Hegel employs this line as a description of the entire age. Cf. Goethe's *Gedenkausgabe der Werke, Briefe und Gespräche,* hrsg. Ernst Beutler, Bd. 15 (Zürich: Artemis Verlag, 1953), p. 1006. The context for the quotation is important, since it shows us that Hegel has in mind Diderot's doctrine of the "paternal molecule" (*väterliche Faser*), which accounts for why a son will be like his father. In more general terms Diderot believed that biological connections were part of greater material connection among peoples, what he calls in the dialog the *Urfaser,* or original molecule, which accounts for the national character of a people. Even the political organization of the state is due to the kind of underlying material connections that spring from the nature of people. Hegel is adopting Diderot's materialism throughout this entire section. For a good account of this dialog, how it came to be translated by Goethe, and Hegel's use of it, see Margaret Stoliar, "The Musician's Madness: Goethe and Hegel on 'Le Neveu de Rameau,'" *Australian Journal of French Studies,* 24 (1987), 309–32.

74. <*Art* und in *seiner Art* gut sein>

75. Hegel is contrasting the meaning of *espèce* with the German *Art,* even though they denote the same thing, a "natural kind." He is pointing out that *espèce* is used ironically while *Art* is not. Hegel is certainly right that Diderot uses the word ironically. In the eighteenth century, and even later, the word was used to signify someone who was supposedly a member of the *bonne société.* According to the commentator Jean Fabre, "the word *espèce,* as a spoken word, appears in the jargon of a so-called good society, from which Diderot has disassociated himself. The word was in use since 1740. '*L'espèce,*' says Duclos, '[is] a new term that has the sense of someone who is just, as opposed to a man of means; *l'espèce* is one who having no longer merit from his station lends himself only to degradation. . . .'

What appears in connection with the singular *individual* as his culture 53–490
is the essential moment of *substance,* namely, the immediate transition of
its conceived universality into actuality, or the simple soul of substance,
whereby the *in-itself* is *determinate being* and *something recognized.* Hence,
the movement of the self-cultivating individuality is immediately its coming to be its universal objective essence, that is, the coming to be of the
actual world. Although this world has come to be through individuality,
for self-consciousness it is something immediately estranged, and it has
for it the form of an actuality that is not disturbed. But, at the same time,
certain that the world is its substance, self-consciousness seeks power over
it. Self-consciousness gains this power over the world through culture;
from this point of view, culture appears as self-consciousness that makes
itself in accordance with actuality, to the extent that the energy of its original character and talent permit. What appears here as the dominion[76] of
the individual, which substance comes under, and, thereby, becomes sublated, is what constitutes the actualization of substance. For the individual's power consists in his making himself according to that actualization;
that is to say, he externalizes his own self and therefore posits himself as
the objective existing substance. Henceforth, his culture and his own
actuality is the actualization of substance itself.[77]

The self is actual for itself only as something *sublated.* Hence, its sub- 54–491
lated being does not constitute for it the unity of the *consciousness* of itself
and of the object; rather, the object is for the self its negative. —So substance is cultivated in its moments by means of the self as soul, in such a
way that each opposite [269] animates the other. Through its own
estrangement each moment gives subsistence to the other and equally
receives it. At the same time, each moment has its determinacy as an

---

Hegel, in *Phenomenology of Spirit,* returns to this word and uses it ingeniously but
taking it in a contrary sense [to its historical use]," *Le neveu de Rameau* (Geneve:
Libraire Droz, 1950), p. 267ff.

76. <Gewalt>

77. In this paragraph "Culture" is defined as the soul of the World whose in-
itself is the individual. The individual is self-consciousness moving from the universality defined by the *espèce,* to an actuality defined by its equality of thought.
Self-consciousness has the equality of thought that produces actual consciousness. But that consciousness, the substance produced, is alien to its World.
Hegel's conception is rooted in Rousseau's idea that the individual's reason produces the Self, but in a given society that product is fabricated along social divisions. Hegel is also following Diderot's view in *Rameau's Nephew* that such
individuals who "fabricate" themselves are *verrückt,* disturbed, in their own Self
because they lack identity with the dominant social divisions: they are not members of the so-called good society.

incontestable worth, and a solid actuality against the other. Thinking fixes this difference in the most general way through the absolute opposition between *good* and *bad,* which, shunning each other, can in no way become the same. Yet, this firm being has the immediate transition into its opposite as its soul. Indeed, its determinate being is the inversion of every determinacy into its opposite, and only this estrangement is the essence and maintenance of the whole. This actualizing movement and animating of the moments is now to be considered. The estrangement will estrange itself, and through estrangement the whole will withdraw into its concepts.

55–492   First, then, the simple substance itself is to be considered in the immediate organization of its extant, not yet animated, moments. —Just as nature displays itself in its universal elements, so the inner essence, or simple spirit of self-conscious actuality, displays itself as a world in just such universal, yet spiritual, masses. [Among nature's universal elements] air is the *abiding* purely universal, transparent essence—while water is the essence that is forever *sacrificed—fire* is the *ensouled* unity of the elements, the unity that perpetually dissolves their antithesis just as it perpetually divides their simplicity into antithesis—and finally, the *earth* is the *solid knot* of this membership, and the *subject* of these essences, as also of their process, their departure and return.[78] [Similarly, the inner essence or simple spirit displays itself] in the *first* mass [as] the *universal in-itself,* the *self-equivalent* spiritual essence; in the second mass, [it is] the essence *existing for itself,* the one which having become internally *unequal, offers* itself *up* and *abandons* itself; in the *third* [it is] subject as self-consciousness, and has the force of fire immediately within it. In the first essence, the subject is conscious of itself as *being-in-itself,* but in the second it becomes a *being-for-self* through the offering up of the universal. But the spirit itself is the being *in* and *for itself* of the whole, which *splits apart* into subsisting substance and the offering of self's own substance; and equally, spirit *takes*

---

78. The four elements enter into a sortie. These elements when in balance represent a stability of mind and body; they constitute the *mentis compos* of the human being. They may appear as "humors," which when kept in balance mean that the mind is sound. Hegel will show that the composition of the elements both in the "good society" of France and in the mind of singular individuals (namely, Rameau's nephew) are out of balance, and thus both the society and the individual's mind become "torn" into virtual madness. Hegel's theory that there is a material cohesion to both society and in the individual comes from Diderot, who offers the theory of "the molecule," first in *Rameau's Nephew* and later in *D'Alembert's Dream* (c. 1769). The theory of the humors comes from Galen, but they were popular in the late seventeenth century as well. The four are sanguine, phlegmatic, choleric, and melancholy humors.

substance *back* again into its own unity, both as the flame erupting from substance and consuming it, and as its subsisting shape. —We see that these essences correspond to the community and the family of the ethical world, but without possessing the domestic spirit that they had; but whereas destiny is alien to that spirit, in this case self-consciousness is and knows itself as the actual power of these essences.[79]

These members are to be considered both as they are initially repre-   56–493
sented within pure consciousness, [that is] as *thoughts* or as beings *in themselves,* and also as they are represented in actual consciousness as *objective* essences. —In the form of the simplicity of pure consciousness, the first immediate and alterable *essence* of all consciousness, being *self-equivalent,* is the *good*—the independent spiritual [270] power of the *in-itself,* beside which the movement of consciousness, which is being-for-itself, is only a by-play. In contrast, the other essence is the *passive* spiritual one, or the universal so far as it prostitutes itself and lets individuals take to themselves the consciousness of their own singularity with respect to it: it is their null essence—the bad. —This absolute dissolution of essence is itself what persists; just as the first essence is the foundation,

---

79. We have just seen that nature is both opposite and "negative" to the actual substance of self-consciousness. But it is the Spirit of this World that is produced from nature, not from the actual movement of self-consciousness. Hegel first discusses the elements of nature: air, fire, water, and earth. These "living" elements generate the soul of this world (noted at the end of Hegel's chapter "Force and Understanding"), the elements of which are the four estates. The element of the earth—the solid knot of this membership—is the peasant class. This class is the only one that does not count in the social organization. The three other classes— Church, nobility, and bourgeoisie—are all members of the universal and play the role of other natural elements. Initially, we can say that the church is the element of air, that which abides in the spiritual ether; the nobility is water, which offers itself in service and "good work"; the bourgeoisie is the element of fire, or the element that consumes by buying and selling, which shifts sides, and which unites the others economically but also divides them by its demands for state power. As the Concept develops, the social elements will shift their roles because they are out of balance (see preceding note). The state has absorbed the facticity of the individual, which only means that the state's attempt to form spiritual unity within itself is hopeless. Hegel likens it to one suffering from an internal tearing of the *mentis compos.* Only the peasants, who are not enfranchised, remain the same. Their labor keeps them united to the earth, and they retain an immediacy of self-certainty. Hegel's "materialistic" vision of society seems to come not simply from Diderot but from the natural theology of the period. His metaphor of the elements as the "spiritual essences" reflects upon and presents a late seventeenth- and early eighteenth-century religious conception of physical nature. Cf. Thomas Burnet, *The Sacred Theology of the Earth* (1680) and Fabricius, *The Theology of Water* (1726).

point of departure, and result of the individuals (and they are in it in a purely universal way), so too by contrast the second essence is, on the one hand, the *sacrificing* of self [as] *being for another;* and hence it is, on the other hand, the individuals' continual return to their own selves as *singulars* and their persistent coming to be *for-themselves.*

57–494   At the same time these simple *thoughts* of good and bad are, however, immediately self- estranged. They are *actual* and exist in actual consciousness as *objective* moments. Thus the first essence is the *state power,* while the second is *wealth.* —Just as the state power is simple *substance,* so it is universal *work*—that is, the absolute *facticity itself,* in which their *essence* is expressed for the individuals, and their singularity is simply and solely consciousness of their *universality.* State power is both the work and the simple *result.* In this result the fact that it originates from their doing vanishes, and it remains the absolute foundation and subsistence of all their doing. —This *simple* ethical substance of their life is *being,* in virtue of the determination of their unalterable self-identity; therefore, it is only *being for another.* Hence, substance is in itself immediately the opposite of itself, or *wealth.* Although it is the passive or null essence, wealth is nevertheless a universal spiritual being; just as it is the *result* of the *labor* and *doing of all,* so too it dissolves once more into everyone's *enjoyment.* In this enjoyment individuality does indeed come to be *for itself* or is *singular;* but this *enjoyment* is itself the result of the universal doing, just as, in its turn, the doing brings forth the universal labor and enjoyment of all. The *actual* has simply the spiritual significance of being immediately universal within this moment. Every singular [being] really intends to act *selfishly;* for it is the moment in which he acquires the consciousness of his own being, and for this reason he does not take it to be something spiritual. But even from a merely external perspective, it is evident that in his enjoyment there is occasion for everyone to receive enjoyment; in his labor, he labors as much for everyone as for himself, and everyone labors for him. Hence his being *for himself* is in itself *universal,* and the selfishness is only something intended, which cannot become actual as intended, namely, to do something that is not for the good of everyone.

58–495   So, in both of these spiritual powers self-consciousness is aware of its substance, content, and purpose. In them it intuits its dual essence: in one [271] its *being-in-itself,* and in the other its *being-for-self.* —But, at the same time, self-consciousness, as spirit, is the negative *unity* of their subsistence and the separation of individuality from the universal, or of actuality from self. Hence, lordship and wealth are present to the individual as objects, that is, as things he knows that he is *free* from, and he thinks that he can choose between them, or even choose neither. As this free and *pure* consciousness, the individual confronts essence as something which is

only *for* him. Consequently, he has essence as the *essence* within himself.
—In this pure consciousness the moments of substance are for him neither state power nor wealth but the thoughts of *good* and *bad*. —But further, self-consciousness is the connection of its pure with its actual
consciousness, of what is thought with objective essence: it is essentially
judgment. Of course, for the two sides of the actual essence their immediate determinations have already settled which is good and which is bad;
the good is state power, while the bad is wealth. But this initial judgment
cannot be viewed as a spiritual judgment; for in it one side has been determined only as what exists *in itself*, or as positive, and the other is only what
exists *for itself* and is negative. All the same, they are spiritual essences—
each of them the penetration of both moments, and hence they are not
exhausted in these determinations—and the self-consciousness that is
connected with them is *in* and *for itself*; hence it must be connected with
each of them in a double way, so that their nature (which is to be self-
estranged determinations) will come forth.[80]

For self-consciousness at this stage, the object in which it finds itself is   59–496
both *good* and *in itself*, while that in which it finds the antithesis of itself is
bad. The *good* is the *identity* of objective reality with self-consciousness,
but the *bad* is their *nonidentity*. At the same time, what is good and bad for
self-consciousness is good and bad *in itself*; for self- consciousness is precisely that in which these two moments of being *in itself* and being *for
itself* are the same. It is the actual spirit of the objective essences, and the
judgment is the demonstration of its power in them—the power that
makes them what they are *in themselves*. It is not the way they are immediately in themselves *equal* or *unequal* (that is, the abstract being in-self or
for-self) that is their criterion and their truth, but rather what they are in
the connection of spirit with them: their identity or nonidentity with it is
their criterion and truth. This *connection* with the essences (which are

---

80. There are three moments of self-consciousness that emerge from the sortie in "Self-Estranged Spirit." The first is "pure consciousness," which has the
thoughts of the good and bad. The second is that of "judgment," which takes the
good to be state power and the bad to be wealth. The third is the unity of pure
consciousness and judgment, which is a spiritual connection, and this is the *position of religious consciousness*. What makes this position religious is that it subsists
through its connection to what lies beyond it. It is a Catholic consciousness, however, so it looks to the state and the Church as the objective relata that sustains
unity. "Religion" is then the middle term, or true essence, of self-consciousness.
So, what we are witnessing is that from the spiritual elements and the social
classes come the three forms of consciousness. (Again, the fourth form is not discussed since it has no status in this world; yet it alone retains the simplicity of self-
certainty.)

originally posited as *objects*, but come through *self-consciousness* to be what is *in-itself)* becomes, at the same time, their *reflection* into self; through this they obtain actual spiritual being, and that which is *their spirit* emerges. But just as their first *immediate determination* is differentiated from spirit's *connection* with them, so too the third [moment], the spirit that belongs to them, is differentiated from the second. —At first, this *second in-itself,* which emerges by virtue of [272] spirit's connection with them, must turn out already to be something other than the *immediate* one; for this *mediation* of spirit is rather what moves the immediate determinacy and makes it into something else.[81]

60–497   Accordingly, the consciousness that exists *in* and *for itself* finds now in *state power* its *simple essence* and *subsistence* in general, but not its *individuality* as such—only its being *in itself,* not its being *for self.* Instead, it finds there that conduct is denied as singular conduct and is subjugated to obedience. Faced with this power, therefore, the individual reflects himself into himself. For him the power is the oppressive essence and the *bad;* instead of being equal to individuality, power is absolutely unequal to it. —*Wealth,* on the contrary, is the *good;* it leads to universal enjoyment, it prostitutes itself, and it procures for everyone the consciousness of their self. *In itself* it is universal beneficence, and if it denies some benefit and does not satisfy every need this is an accident that does not damage its universal and necessary essence, which is to share itself with every singular [being] and to be a thousand-handed donor.[82]

---

81. The third moment of self-consciousness has unity and self-identity. It has three phases as well. The first is the actual Spirit of this World. It is a universal will that has an understanding of its essence. This Will = Understanding is the Spirit of Law reflected in the customs and mores of the people (as articulated in Montesquieu's and D'Argenson's essays on the origin of French government). Each actual self-conscious Spirit, therefore, recognizes itself through law and the history of the Estates General. The second phase is just the self-conscious recognition that there is a connection between the individual and his social status under law. The third phase is the law itself, or the mediation between the Understanding and its social condition. Eventually, this becomes the Self-Certainty of a "Moral World-View."

82. Actual self-consciousness is religious, but by the mediation of the Spirit of Law, which has defined its social status, this self-consciousness recognizes that what is bad—that is, wealth—is now good. It inverts its position because social status grants it both the satisfaction of enjoyment and the ability to do good work. Wealth becomes the "natural good," since by it pure consciousness can do religious work. Voltaire in his *History of the Paris Parlement* (1769) thinks that this shift occurs with the Jesuits' entrance into France. They and other "new" religious orders appealed directly to "base" tendencies of both the bourgeoisie and the court: "They [the Jesuits] had established superstition with the boureoisie,

Both of these judgments give to the thoughts of good and bad a   61–498
content that is opposite to what they were for us. —But, at first, self-
consciousness was only connected with its objects incompletely, to wit,
only according to the standard of *being-for-self*. But consciousness is the
essence that has being *in itself* as well, and it must likewise make this side
the standard. Only in this way is the spiritual judgment perfected. From
this side, *state power* declares its essence to consciousness; it is in part
tranquil law and in part government and command that regulates the singular movements of universal conduct. The one is the simple substance
itself; the other is its conduct that quickens and preserves itself and everyone else. Thus the individual finds here his own ground and essence
expressed, organized, and activated. —Through the enjoyment of *wealth*,
on the contrary, the individual does not experience his universal essence
but obtains only *transitory* consciousness and the enjoyment of himself as
a *singularity* existing for itself, as well as the enjoyment of the *nonidentity*
with his essence. —Thus, the concepts of good and bad here receive the
opposite content to the one they had before.[83]

Each of these two modes of judgment finds an *identity* and a *noniden-*   62–499
tity. The original judging consciousness finds state power to be *unequal* to
it but the enjoyment of wealth to be *equal;* the second, on the other hand,
finds state power equal to it but the enjoyment of wealth *unequal*.[84] An
opposite connection with the two real essentialities is present—a twofold
finding of equality and a twofold *finding of inequality*. —We must appraise
this divergent judging; we have to apply the established standard to it.
Accordingly, the *connection* in consciousness that *finds equality* is the *good*
and that that [273] finds inequality is the *bad;* and henceforth both of
these modes of connection are themselves held fast as *divergent shapes of
consciousness*. By thus behaving in a divergent way, consciousness itself

---

and their debauchery conserved it; their celebrations began with a procession in
which the portrait of a grotesque image of a saint was mounted on a pole; later
they would get drunk, and the fury of their drunkenness would redouble that of
the faction" *Oeuvres Complètes de Voltaire* (Paris: Baudouin Frères, 1828), t. 34, p.
142. Hegel seems to agree with Voltaire's position that this is the beginning of the
destruction of the ethical bond of the old regime.

83. Wealth no longer becomes a means to an end but the end itself. The
"good" is the enjoyment that wealth brings; the "bad" is the state power that
keeps us from having more wealth. The Spirit of Law is what dominates and
oppresses it. This is the consummate bourgeois consciousness. Hegel's logical
point is that the *in-itself*, which was earlier rooted in a social nature, now is indifferent to that nature.

84. The difference is between the lower, bourgeois consciousness and the
upper, privileged classes of the nobility and the Church.

comes under the determination of the diversity of being good or bad, and
not because it has either *being-for-self* or pure *being in itself* as its principle;
for both of them are equally essential moments. The double judgment,
previously considered, presented the principles separately and hence contained only *abstract* modes of *judging*. Actual consciousness has both principles in it, and the difference falls solely within its *essence*—namely, in
the *connection* of itself with the real.

63–500   The mode of this connection is one of opposition: on the one side,
there is the relation to state power and wealth as to something *equal*, and
on the other side, [the relation to them] as to *something unequal*. —The
consciousness of the connection that finds equality is the *noble-minded*
one. In the public authority it sees what is equal with it: that it has its *simple essence* and its activity within this power, and it remains in service to
the essence as much through inner respect as through actual obedience.
Similarly with respect to wealth: that wealth provides for it consciousness
of its other essential side, that is, *being-for-self.* Hence, the noble-minded
consciousness sees wealth, in connection with itself, as the *essence* as well;
it recognizes the one from whom enjoyment comes as a benefactor and
holds itself under an obligation of gratitude.[85]

64–501   In contrast [to this first consciousness], the consciousness of the other
connection is the *contemptuous* one, which holds fast to the *nonidentity*
within both essentialities. So, in the lordly power it sees a fetter, an
oppression of its *being-for-self;* and hence it hates the lordly, obeys only
with malice, and stands always on the brink of revolt.[86] Similarly, in the
wealth through which it gains the enjoyment of its being-for-self, this
consciousness sees only inequality, that is, the inequality with the subsisting *essence.* For only through wealth does the contemptuous consciousness come to the consciousness of singularity and of transitory
enjoyment—it loves yet despises it—and with the disappearance of the
enjoyment (something that intrinsically disappears), it regards its relation
to the wealthy as having disappeared as well.

65–502   Only now do the connections express the *judgment*, the determination
of what both essences are as *objects* for consciousness, but not yet what

---

85. Hegel is now considering the second estate, the nobility, which was established as a military class. Its code is honor, not wealth, but wealth is still valued as
a reward of service to the state power. As such, this class identifies itself with the
state.

86. This refers to the bourgeoisie who are not raised to privilege and also to
the lesser nobility who are resentful that their powers are being diminished. The
"lesser" nobility do not have the honor of the "nobility of the sword" but only
"nobility of the robe."

they are *in* and *for* themselves. On the one hand, the reflection presented in the judgment is initially *for us* a positing of one determination as well as the other, and hence an equal sublating of both, which is not yet their reflection for consciousness itself. On the other hand, they *are* immediately *essence* to begin with; they have neither *become* it nor do they have *self*-consciousness. The consciousness for which they exist is not yet what gives them life—[274] they are predicates that are not yet themselves subject.[87] And on account of this separation, the whole of the spiritual judgment still falls apart into two consciousnesses, each of them coming under a one-sided determination. —Now, just as at first the *indifference* of the two sides of the estrangement (one being the *in-itself* of pure consciousness, namely, the determinate *thoughts* of good and bad, and the other their *determinate being* as state power and wealth) were raised to a connection of the two, [that is] to a judgment; so too, this external connection must raise itself up to an inward unity—that is, as the connection of thought to actuality, and the spirit of both shapes of the judgment must emerge. This happens when *judgment* becomes *syllogism,* [that is] it becomes the mediating movement wherein the necessity and the middle term of both sides of the judgment emerge.[88]

In judgment the noble consciousness thus finds itself over against   66–503
state power in such a way that, indeed, state power is not yet a self but only the universal substance in which this noble consciousness is aware of itself as its own *essence,* aware of its goal and absolute content. In connecting with the substance positively, noble consciousness behaves negatively toward its own goals, its particular content and determinate being; it allows them to disappear.[89] It is the heroism of *service,* the *virtue* that

---

87. The actual spirit of the underprivileged is without a constitution in this new-found Spirit of Law. It cannot govern itself, nor can it abide the dominion of those who stand above it. The resentment leads to haughtiness and insurrection. Hegel is leading up to that period in French history called the Fronde (1648–52). This was when the Paris *parlement* and contemptuous nobility revolted against the boy king, Louis XIV.

88. The syllogism is the actual relationship among the estates. The Estates General becomes the dominant theme wherein the upper and lower classes are connected. What actually united them in the *ancien régime* was the king, who identifies himself with the state: *per* Louis XIV.

89. The nobility, as it comes to conform to the king's honor and to seek wealth, titles, and privileges, loses its identity and self-defining unity in action. But here it still believes that it remains true to its *code of honor* and is still willing to sacrifice material goods for the sake of honor and universal service. This is the "nobility of the sword" versus the lesser nobility who come to privilege only by purchasing their offices from the state power.

sacrifices the singular being to the universal, and thereby brings the universal into existence[90]—the *person* who voluntarily renounces possessions and enjoyment, who acts for the present power and is effective.[91]

67–504   Through this movement, the universal becomes linked with determinate being in general, just as the existent consciousness forms itself by means of this externalization into essentiality.[92] On account of this estrangement in its service, consciousness sinks into determinate being. But the self-estranged *being* is the *in itself;* hence it receives respect in its own eyes and in the eyes of others through this formation. —The state power, however, which was at first only the universal *as thought*—the *in-itself*—comes through this very movement to be the *subsistent* universal or the actual power. This is only in the actual obedience, which the state power achieves through the *judgment* of self-consciousness, that the state power is the *essence* through the free sacrifice of self-consciousness. This act, which links the essence with the self, produces a *dual* actuality, namely, itself as that which has *true* actuality and the state power as the *true,* or that which *counts.*

68–505   Nevertheless, through this estrangement, the state power is not yet a self-consciousness that knows itself to be state power; only its *law,* or its *in-itself,* counts. It still does not have a *particular will.* For the self-consciousness in service has not yet externalized its pure self, nor has it breathed life into the state power with it but only with its being; it has sacrificed to the state power only its *determinate being* and not its [275] *being-in-itself.* —This self-consciousness counts as one that conforms to the *essence;* it is recognized on account of its *being-in-itself.* The others find their *essence* activated in it but not their being-for-self; their thinking or pure consciousness comes to fulfillment, not their individuality. It counts, therefore, in their *thoughts* and enjoys their *honor.* It is the *haughty* vassal

---

90. <Daseyn>

91. The heroism of service is no longer on the battlefield, but in the Paris *parlement* and the royal palace. The "noble" class is now the administrator and courtier. "Nobility" is secured as the *noblesse de robe,* which is a reward for status and wealth, not for honorable sacrifice.

92. "Determinate being in general" is the government, in particular the monarchy. The monarchy historically emerges as government in three steps: the establishment of the Bourbons as the royal house, which did not actually take place until Louis the Pious invaded and defeated the house of Toulouse during the Albigensian heresy; the convening of the Estates General in 1302, which gave France a constitution under Philip the Fair, at which time the rights of the third estate were recognized; and finally, the recognition of the absolute monarchy under Louis XIV in whose absolute power all "determinate being" was encompassed. Hegel is only concerned with the last period.

who is active on behalf of the state power to the extent that the state power is not a private but the *essential* will; and he counts only in this honor, only in the way he is *essentially* represented by common opinion, not in the *gratitude* of individuality, since it has not helped [him] to achieve his *being-for-self.*[93] His *speech*, were he to have a relation with the private will of the state power (a will that has not yet emerged), would be *counsel*, which he would tender for the common good.[94]

Thus the state power still lacks will when confronted by counsel and is 69–506 indecisive with respect to the diverse opinions concerning the common good. It is not yet *government*, and hence not yet actual state power in truth. —The *being-for-self*, the *will*, which, as will, has not yet been sacrificed, is the inner departed spirit of the estates, which reserves for itself its *particular* good in contrast with its speaking of the *common* good; and it is disposed to make this prattle of universal good into a surrogate for action. The sacrifice of determinate being, which takes place in service, is indeed complete if it is pursued to the point of death. But the perpetual risk of death itself, which one survives, leaves behind a determinate existence[95] and, therefore, a *particular* [being] *for itself*, which makes the counsel of what is for the common good duplicitous and suspect. It, indeed, reserves to itself its own intention and particular will against the state's authority. Hence it does not behave now as something equivalent to that authority and falls under the determination of the contemptuous consciousness: of always standing on the edge of revolt.[96]

---

93. The "haughty vassal" is most likely Prince de Condé, who fought for the crown against the people in the first battles of the Fronde (1649), but then demanded rewards for his service that were finally refused to him by Cardinal Mazarin. Condé turned thereafter against the monarch. Voltaire's account seems to be Hegel's source. Voltaire writes, "Le prince de Condé *demanda hautement le prix des ses services*. Le cardinal [Mazarin] trouva le prix trop exorbitant; et, pour réponse à ses griefs, il le fit mettre en prison à Vincennes . . ." *Histoire du Parlement de Paris*, in *Oeuvres Complètes*, t. 34 (Paris: Baudouin Frères, 1878), p. 313 (emphasis added). The French says, "Prince de Condé asked haughtily a price for his service. The cardinal found the price too exorbitant, and as a response to the prince's grievance placed him in the prison at Vincennes."

94. This is another indication that Hegel is referring to the Fronde. Louis XIV is a juvenile and the regency belongs to his mother. The "battle" is over who will control him. The rebellious nobility, led by Condé, want to keep Louis to themselves and not allow his mother and Cardinal Mazarin to govern him. When Louis comes to the age of majority, his private will becomes the state's will.

95. <bestimmtes Dasein>

96. With the emergence of the absolute despot, the nobility becomes divided between those at court and those in the provinces. The petty nobles in the provinces lose the actual privilege of their position. They may still have honor, but

70–507   This contradiction, which has to be sublated, contains in this form—
[that is,] in the inequality of *being-for-self* that stands against the universality of state power—at once the further form: that the externalization of
determinate being, since it completes itself, namely, in death, is something existing and not something that returns to consciousness—that the
consciousness does not survive the externalization and is not *in* and *for
itself* but simply passes over into its unreconciled opposite. The only true
sacrifice of *being-for-self* is therefore the one in which it gives itself up
completely as in death, but maintains itself just as much in this externalization. Thereby, it comes to be actually what it is in itself, its self-identical unity and self-opposition. Because the inner, departed spirit, the self
as such, steps forward and estranges itself, the state power is at the same
time raised to a private self; similarly, [276] without this estrangement the
deeds of honor and the counsels of insight, given by the noble consciousness, would remain duplicitous, because they still retain the departed
reserve of a particular interest and of willfulness.[97]

71–508   It is only in *speech*, however, that this estrangement occurs. Speech here
emerges in its proper significance. —As *law* and *command* in the world of
ethical life, as *counsel* initially in the world of actuality, speech has the
essence [of these worlds] for its content and is this form. But here it
acquires the form that is itself its own content and is valid [simply] as
speech. It has the force of speaking as something that accomplishes what is
to be accomplished. For it is the *determinate* being of the pure self as self; in
speech *singularity that exists for itself,* which belongs to self-consciousness
as such, enters into existence, so that it is *for others.* Otherwise, the *I,* as
this *pure I,* is just not *there.* In every other externalization, it is embedded
in an actuality and in a shape from which it can withdraw. From its action,
as from its physiognomic expression, it is reflected into itself and leaves
every incomplete determinate being for dead, in which there is always too
much just as there is also not enough. Speech, however, contains the *I* in
its purity; it alone expresses the *I* itself.[98] Simply as *determinate being,* the

---

honor counts for nothing; rather what counts is one's position at court. The court
nobles have no honor; they have only words, not deeds, that win them victories.

97. Cf. "Virtue and the Way of the World" in *Phenomenology of Spirit, GW,* ix,
p. 211ff. The sense is that the particular interest and willfulness of the noblemen
are always lying in wait to be sprung against either the essential will of the state or
the common interests of the estates. The offer of duty, fidelity, and honor is not a
selfless surrender of free will: the offer is given only for a reward.

98. In the manner of Louis XIV whose *voice* was absolute. Voltaire writes of a
specific example in which even his greatest opponents hushed their voices: "It was
parlement that protested to him [Louis XIV] that it would conduct itself by the
very remonstrances [i.e., legal documents that could suspend the king's decree]

determinate being of speech is an objectivity that has in it the *I*'s true nature. The *I* is *this I*—but equally [it is] *universal;* its appearing is just the immediate externalizing and disappearing of *this I,* and thus its remaining in its universality. The *I* that expresses itself is *heard;* it is a contagion in which it has immediately passed over into a unity with those for whom it is there, and in which it is universal self-consciousness.[99]—In being *heard* its *determinate being* itself has immediately *died away;* its otherness has been taken back into itself; and its determinate being, as the self-conscious *now,* is just this: it is there, to be not there, and by means of this disappearing to be there. Thus this disappearing is itself immediately its remaining; it is its own knowing of itself, and its knowing of itself as one that has passed over into another self, one that has been heard and is universal.

Spirit acquires this actuality here because the extremes, whose *unity* it is, have just as immediately the determination of being proper actualities for-themselves. Their unity is broken up into rigid sides, each of which is for the other an actual object excluded from it. In this way the unity steps forward as a *middle* [term] that is excluded and distinguished from the departed actuality of its sides; hence it has an actual objectivity itself, distinguished from its sides, and is *for them,* that is, it is extant. As such, *spiritual substance* enters into existence only because it has won self-consciousnesses for its sides, which know this pure self as an *immediately* [277] *valid* actuality, and yet, just as immediately, they know that this is the case only through the estranging *mediation.* Through the first knowledge the moments are purified to the category of knowing themselves and thus to the point where they are moments of spirit; by means of the second knowledge, spirit enters into determinate being as spirituality. 72–509

---

that he had prohibited, permitting them only if they could be made in writing and only after the decree was already obeyed. This testament [i.e., the document of protest] was read in a low voice, rapidly, and only for form's sake," p. 326.

99. The Spirit of Law has become the spirit of the monarch. When the monarch says, "I am the state," there is only one identification possible for actual self-consciousness—namely, I am a divine being. The divinity, however, belongs to what the English call the "corporate sole"—the legal institution of the monarchy. The death of an individual king means nothing to the institution because it does not die with him. As such the claim to divinity is unlike that of the Roman emperor, because with the emperor and "Legal Right" it was the person who was divine. Here, instead, it is the *name* that is divine. That "name" is heard through the land in decrees, edicts, taxes, and criminal proceedings. It is the king's proclamations that make something legal; it is his words that grant privilege or disgrace. All who hear the words partake of his Spirit and are to be honored simply because they hear him. In this case there is no longer a genuine *person* on the throne. The determinate being of the individual is lost: he is just a name. For Hegel this is the state of complete facticity.

—Thus spirit is the middle [term], which presupposes those extremes, and is generated by their determinate being—but equally it is the spiritual whole, breaking forth in their midst, that divides itself among them and only through this contact incorporates each one into the whole in [the person of] its prince.[100] —That both extremes are already *implicitly* sublated and broken up brings forth their unity; this is the movement that links the two together, exchanges their determinations and [then] even links them together *into each extreme*. Hence this mediation posits the *concept* of each of the two extremes in its actuality or makes what each is *in itself* into its *spirit*.[101]

73–510   The two extremes, the state power and the noble consciousness, are broken up by this mediation: the first into the abstract universal that is obeyed and into a will that exists for itself, but which may not yet itself come up to the universal; the second into the obedience of sublated determinate being (or into the *being-in-itself* of self-respect and honor) and into the not yet sublated, pure being-for-self, that is, into the will that still remains in reserve. The two moments, into which both sides are purified and which are thus moments of speech, constitute the *abstract universal,* which is called the common good, and the *pure self,* which renounced in service the consciousness that is submerged in the manifold diversity of being. In concept both are the same, for the pure self is just what is abstractly universal; in this way their unity is posited as their middle [term]. But the *self* first becomes actual only in the extreme of consciousness, and the *in-itself* becomes actual only in the extreme of state power. What is lacking to consciousness is that the state power should have

---

100. *in seinem Principe.* The modern German editions (Hoffmeister, Moldenhauer) have "in seinem Prinzip," which would read "in its principle." We, who are following the original spelling, take Hegel to mean the person who is the prince of the estates. Hegel is borrowing *Princeps* from the Latin, not using the ordinary early nineteenth-century German, *das Princip.*

101. The paragraph is actually about what constitutes the *être suprême.* The supreme being of this World consists in the name and words of the monarch, but the spiritual essence of this being is not in the king's name but in the knowledge that the monarch is God's anointed and, as such, he is the state power itself. The king knows this through the Church triumphant. The first estate sanctifies the connection between this one man and the law of God. In the act of anointment the *être suprême* lives in the monarch, and it will continue to live there as long as a monarchy exists. This is why when, near the end of this chapter, Hegel discusses the Reign of Terror—the guillotine not only kills the king, it kills the *être suprême,* because not only did Louis XVI die but the entire institution of monarchy (with its connection to the Church) died as well. The spiritual unity and identity of the estates dies with him, but this means that the bourgeoisie lose their place and role as well. They are cut off from their self-defining substance.

passed over into it, not only as *honor* but [as something] actual; what is lacking to state power is that it should be obeyed not simply as the so-called *common good*, but as a will, or as the decisive self. The unity of the concept, within which the state power still stands, and to which consciousness has been purified, is actual in this *mediating movement*, whose simple determinate being, as the *middle* [term], is speech. —Nevertheless, the middle [term] does not yet have as its sides two selves that are present as *selves;* for the state power only comes to be self when it is animated. Hence this speech is not yet spirit the way it completely knows and expresses itself.[102]

Because it is the extreme of the self, the noble-minded consciousness appears as the one from which the *speech* proceeds, which transforms the sides of the relation into animated wholes. —The heroism of mute service [278] becomes the *heroism of flattery.* This reflection of service in speech constitutes the spiritual middle that breaks itself apart, and reflects not only its own extreme into itself but also the extreme of universal authority back into itself; it makes the authority, which at first is *in itself,* into the *being for itself* and the singularity of self-consciousness. In this way the spirit of this power comes into being—an *unlimited monarch;* one, *unlimited:* the language of flattery raises the power into its purified *universality* (the moment as product of speech or of determinate being purified into spirit is a refined self-identity); two, *monarch:* it equally raises *singularity* to its peak, (that by which the noble-minded consciousness externalizes itself on this side of simple spiritual unity is the pure *in-itself of his thinking,* [that is,] his *I* self). More precisely, speech elevates singularity (which otherwise is only something *intended*) into its purity of being, thereby giving the monarch his own *name;* for it is only with the name that the *distinction* between this single [being] from the others is not simply *intended* but is actually made by everyone. In the name, the single [being] *counts* as

---

102. With the identification of the supreme being as one with the crown, the estates are united into a spiritual bond. But the actual consciousness of the king is not a deified lord; he is only a power that speaks its thoughts and exerts its will. Thus we return to the realm of actuality and see that what has been achieved in this spiritual connection is that the sovereign, when he speaks for himself, must speak for everyone. His individual will must be the universal will that also knows itself. In the course of events it does not matter what he actually says, because whatever he says expresses the common will—the universal good. Again, Voltaire gives an account of this in the case of Louis XIV: "Louis XIV prepared the most important decisions for the entire nation. He quickly set to work to make laws uniform and fixed the manner of procedures in all the judicial courts, both civil and criminal. He set the preferences of the judges: what cases they were permitted to attend and which they had to give up," p. 322.

something purely singular, no longer simply in his own consciousness but in the consciousness of everyone. By virtue of his name, therefore, the monarch is separated from everyone else absolutely: [he is] isolated and alone. In his name, he is the atom that can share nothing of its essence and has no peer. —This name is thus reflection-into-self, or the *actuality* that universal power has in *its own self;* through the name this power is the *monarch.* Conversely, he, *this single* [being], knows *himself:* [he knows] *this single* [being] to be the universal power, because the nobles place themselves around the throne, not only as ready for service to the state power but as *ornaments;* and he knows himself because they *are* always *telling* the one who sits on the throne what he *is.*[103]

75–512   In this way the speech of their praise[104] is the spirit that links the two extremes together in the *state power itself;* it reflects the abstract power back into itself and gives it both the moment of the other extreme—the willing and decisive *being-for-self*—and henceforth self-conscious existence. In other words, this *singular actual* self-consciousness thus comes to the point of *knowing with certainty* that he is the power. The power is the point of the self, into which the many points have flowed together by means of the externalization of *inner certainty.* —But since this peculiar spirit of state power consists in having its actuality and nourishment in the sacrifice of the noble consciousness's deed and thought, the state power is *self-estranged independence.* The noble-minded consciousness, or the extreme of *being-for-self,* receives the extreme of *actual universality* in return for the universality of thinking, which it externalized from itself; the power [279] of the state has *passed over* to it.[105] In the noble-minded

---

103. Here Hegel shows the poverty of this actuality. The king does not actually know who he is; it is the courtiers who know and constantly assert that he is an absolute monarch. The contradiction is self-evident, the absolute monarch as the shape of a knowing will is within himself absolutely vacuous. All ethical connections have been lost; the "divination" of the crown has been raised to such a universality that there is no longer any foundation for it. This Self who has been anointed has lost his Self to the state—he is nothing but the expression of the state-corporation. It is *this* being who is the absolute monarch, and he is completely impotent in himself. Hegel now seems to be referring to the time of the regency of Louis XV and perhaps to Louis XV's own reign.

104. *Die Sprache ihres Preises;* that is, they name their price of service.

105. The noble-minded consciousness becomes the first minister and chief executive of the state; the power of the state rests in his and not the absolute monarch's hands. Here "noble-minded" can refer to either a member of the first or the second estate. Cardinals Richelieu and Mazarin are obvious examples of this consciousness. That the first minister is a member of the first estate is no accident; to have the head of government as a Prince of the Church only confirms the bond

consciousness, the state authority is for the first time genuinely activated; in its *being-for-self* the state authority ceases to be the *inert essence* that it appeared to be as the extreme of abstract being-in-itself. —Considered *in itself,* the *state power reflected into itself* (or the fact that it becomes spirit) means nothing other than that it has become *the moment of self-consciousness*—that is, that it is only as *sublated.* As a result, it is now the essence as something whose spirit is to be sacrificed and surrendered; that is, it exists as *wealth.* —Over against the wealth, which always comes to be according to the concept, state power still persists, to be sure, as an actuality as well, but as one whose concept is just this movement of going over into its opposite, or into the externalization of power, through the very service and reverence by which it comes to be. Through the abandoning of the noble-minded consciousness, therefore, its own *self,* which constitutes its will, comes to be for itself a self-alienating universality, a complete singularity and contingency, which is surrendered to every more powerful will; what remains to it of a *universally* acknowledged and incommunicable independence is the empty name.[106]

Thus, although the noble consciousness defined himself as one who 76–513 might approach the universal power as an *equal,* the truth of the situation is rather that in his service he retained his own being-for-self, and in the very abdication of his personality there was still the actual sublating and rending asunder of the universal substance. His spirit is the relation of complete inequality; for on the one hand he retains his own will in rendering honor, and on the other hand, in giving up his will, he estranges his inner self and achieves the greatest inequality with himself for one thing; and for another, he subjects himself thereby to the universal substance, and makes this completely unlike himself. —It is clear that in this way the contrast that noble consciousness had in *judgment,* in respect to what was called contemptuous consciousness, has disappeared, and consequently contemptuous consciousness has disappeared too. The latter has achieved its aim: to bring universal power under being-for-self.[107]

---

between the institution of the monarchy and the Church triumphant. After Louis XIV's reign, the first estate has to play the roles of minister, courtier, and surrogate monarch.

106. The reign of Louis XV is when the state power loses its honor and respect. The monarch is admired only in name. The real state power lies in the ministers of government.

107. Earlier, the contemptuous consciousness was the haughty vassal and the privileged nobility. But here Hegel has in mind both the wealthy aristocrats and the bourgeoisie. They have made the monarch like themselves, one who enjoys wealth and entertainments. Once this occurs, then the rebelliousness within privilege vanishes.

77–514   Enriched in this way by the universal power, self-consciousness exists
as *universal beneficence,* or it is *wealth,* which is once again itself the object
of consciousness. After all, for consciousness, wealth is the universal,
which has indeed been subordinated, but not yet returned absolutely into
the self through this initial sublating. —The *self* does not yet have itself
qua self for its object but only the *sublated universal essence.* Since this
object has just now come to be, the *immediate* connection of consciousness
with it is posited; hence consciousness has not yet exhibited its inequality
with it. It is the noble consciousness, which retains its being-for-self with
respect to a universal, that has now become inessential, and that therefore
recognizes its object and is thankful to the benefactor.[108] [280]

78–515   Wealth already has the moment of being-for-self within it. It is neither the selfless universal of state power, nor [yet] is it the unaffected
inorganic nature of spirit; instead, wealth is state power that, through the
will, holds fast to itself against anyone who would seize possession of it
for his own enjoyment. But since wealth has only the form of essence,
this one-sided being-for-self (which is not *in itself* but is rather the sublated in-itself) is the individual's return into himself which, being enjoyment, lacks essence.[109] Thus, even wealth needs to receive life, and the
movement of its reflection consists of this: in being only for-itself, it
becomes *in-* and *for-itself,* and as being sublated essence, it becomes
essence. In this way, wealth preserves its own spirit within itself. —Since
the form of this movement was spelled out above, it is sufficient here to
specify its content.

---

108. The second estate, which has lost its identity in service by becoming
desirous of power and wealth, must now turn to the third estate, who labor and
grow wealthy. Even the first estate looks to the third for its strength. For instance,
the emergence of the "clerks regular," who were bourgeois religious, e.g., the
Jesuits, become the source of new wealth. The Jesuits controlled both great plantations in America, e.g., Louisiana's sugar plantations, and the silk trade in the
Orient. The dependency on honor and sacred trust has been reversed: it is now
the king and the nobles who need both the recognition and money of the bourgeoisie. The context of this paragraph points to the time when the first two estates
are in decline and the third has the real power. Most likely Hegel is referring to
the policies of Louis XV's court. Here the Paris *parlement* has virtually equal
power to the monarchy. Cf. Voltaire's account of this period and how the Paris *parlement* rose in prominence, pp. 333–43.

109. The bourgeois class obtains what the upper classes do not have, namely,
an *individual Self.* But the lower class has no spiritual unification: it only has its
money. Thus it seeks to find an essence that will preserve its freedom and give it
satisfaction. As we will soon see, it does this politically by becoming the government; it will do this spiritually by becoming the benefactor, especially for the arts
and salons.

The noble-minded consciousness does not here connect itself with the   79–516
object as essence in general; instead, it is precisely *being-for-self* that is
strange to it. The noble-minded consciousness *finds* itself *already*
estranged as such—that is, as a fixed, objective actuality, which it has to
receive from another fixed being-for-self. Its object is being-for-self and
thus what is *its own*. But by virtue of being an object, consciousness is, at
the same time, immediately a foreign actuality, which has a being-for-self
of its own and a will of its own; that is, it sees itself dominated by a foreign
will, upon which it depends, since the foreign will either allows consciousness its own being-for-self [or does not].[110]

Self-consciousness can abstract from every singular side; it retains its   80–517
recognized status, therefore, and its *inherent worth* as an essence existing
for itself in any obligation affecting a singular side. But here, from the side
of its pure, most proper *actuality,* of its *I,* it sees itself outside itself and
belonging to another; self-consciousness sees its *personality* dependent, as
such, on the contingent personality of another: on the chance of a glance,
of a whim, or else of the most trivial circumstance. —In the condition of
Right, what is under the dominion of the objective essence appears as a
contingent content from which one can abstract, and the dominion does not
affect the *self* as *such;* on the contrary, the self is recognized. Here, however, self-consciousness sees the certainty of itself as such to be most inessential. It sees the pure personality to be absolute nonpersonality. The
spirit of its gratitude is, thereby, as much the feeling of deepest rejection
as of deepest insurrection. Because the pure *I* intuits itself outside itself
and as torn apart, everything together that has continuity and universality—everything called law, good, and right—has come apart and perished
in this tearing. Every identity is dissolved; for the *purest inequality* is
present there; the absolute inessentiality of what is absolutely essential;
the being outside itself of being-for-self: that is, the pure *I* itself is absolutely decomposed.[111]

---

110. The bourgeois type has been raised to the privileged estates by *la noblesse
de robe* but finds that in-itself it has lost itself. It is not autonomous and free but a
Knecht, a servant, to the higher powers of Church and State. Its autonomy
remains alien to it, while it recognizes that the higher powers prevent it from
obtaining its *real* Self—that is, the power to govern the whole. The bourgeoisie
will attempt to wrest power from the higher estates in the law courts; it will form
the "social life" of manners and present its values in the "beautiful arts," especially in the opera houses.

111. The problem with *la noblesse de robe* is clearly seen. The law declares the
equality and nobility of the bourgeoisie, but the reality of power defeats the declaration. The power of the old guard will not yield real equality, even when they
grant it formally.

81–518   If, therefore, this consciousness does indeed get back from wealth the objectivity of being-for-self and sublates it, then consciousness is not only incomplete according to its concept [281] (as in the previous reflection), but is not satisfied with itself. Since the self receives itself as something objective, this reflection is the immediate contradiction posited in the pure *I* itself. But, at the same time, consciousness qua self stands immediately above this contradiction: it is the absolute elasticity that this sublatedness of the self again sublates, that rejects this rejection (in which its being-for-self becomes foreign), that revolts against this receiving of itself, and is *for itself* in this *receiving*.

82–519   Since, then, the relationship of this consciousness is tied to this absolute tearing, there falls away in its spirit its distinction of being defined as noble-minded as against *contemptuous:* both are the same. Furthermore, the spirit of beneficent wealth can be distinguished further from that of the consciousness that receives the benefit, and has to be considered separately. —This spirit of wealth was the inessential being-for-self; it was the prostituted essence. But through sharing, it comes to be *in–itself.* Since spirit has fulfilled its determination by sacrificing itself, it now sublates the singularity of only getting enjoyment for itself, and as sublated singularity, it is *universality* or *essence.* —What this spirit of wealth shares, what it gives to others, is *being-for-self.* But it does not give itself up as a selfless nature or as the naively self-surrendering[112] condition of life, but rather as self- conscious essence that keeps to itself. This spirit of wealth is not the inorganic power of the elements, known by the receptive consciousness to be inherently transitory. Instead, it is the power over the self that knows itself to be *independent* and *arbitrary,* and that knows, at the same time, what it disburses is the self of another.[113] —Thus wealth shares rejection with the clients, but in the place of insurrection there enters arrogance. For on the one side, like the client, wealth knows *being-for-self* to be a contingent *thing;* but it is itself this contingency under whose dominion personality stands. In this arrogance, which believes that with a supper it has acquired a foreign "I-self" and has, thereby, secured the submission of that self's innermost essence, wealth overlooks the inner rebellion of the other; it overlooks the complete casting off of all fetters, this pure tearing for which (because the *self-identity* of being-for-self has become thoroughly unequal to it) everything equal and subsistent is torn apart, and

---

112. *Sich preißgegeben,* which can also mean "to prostitute oneself."

113. This is the first indication that we are approaching *Rameau's Nephew.* The reference here to the arrogance of the bourgeoisie and the reference two sentences later to ". . . with a supper it has acquired a foreign 'I-self' . . ." looks to be a gloss on Rameau's account of his servitude to the family of M. Bertin.

which, therefore, tears apart most of all the belief and opinion of the benefactor.[114] Wealth stands at the brink of this innermost abyss, of this bottomless depth in which all stability and substance have disappeared. It sees in this depth nothing but an everyday thing, a play of fancy, an accident of whim. Its spirit has become a belief quite without essence, a surface forsaken by spirit. [282]

Just as self-consciousness has its way of speaking vis-à-vis state power   83–520 (that is, spirit emerged between these extremes as an actual middle term), so it has, as well, a way of speaking vis-à-vis wealth. But the insurrection of self-consciousness has its way of speaking to a greater extent. The speech that gives wealth the consciousness of its essentiality and, thereby, seizes possession of it, is once more the speech of flattery, but of ignoble flattery; for what it asserts to be essence, it knows to be the surrendered essence, the essence without being-*in-itself*. But the speech of flattery, as we remarked before, is still a one-sided spirit. For its moments, of course, constitute the *self*—purified through the culture of service to the point of pure existence—and the *being-in-itself* of power. But the pure concept (in which the simple self and the *in-itself*, the pure I and this pure essence of thinking, are the same)—this unity of both sides (between which reciprocity occurs) is not in the consciousness of this speech. For consciousness, the object is still the *in-itself* in contrast to the self; in other words, for consciousness the *object* is not at the same time its own *self* as such. —But the speech of tearing is the way of speaking, and the true, existing spirit of this whole world of culture. This self-consciousness, to which the insurrection of its rejected rejection may come, is immediately absolute self-identity in absolute tearing, the pure mediation of pure self-consciousness with itself. It is the identity of the identical judgment in which one and the same personality is just as much subject as predicate. But this identical judgment is, at the same time, an infinite judgment; for this personality is absolutely divided, and the subject and predicate are strictly *indifferent entities*. They have nothing to do with each other and have no necessary unity, to the point that each is the power of a personality of its own.[115] The *being-for-self* had *its being-for-self*

---

114. Rameau first appears in the dialog as one whose clothing is torn, but soon it is made clear that his mind is torn because of his service to Bertin's family.

115. Rameau assumes several personalities in the dialog. His personality identity is torn apart, even though he continues to make "sense" regarding his own life, the state of French music, and general condition of the arts. His mania is due to his social identity and not any biological condition. His persona demonstrates the point that both Diderot and Rousseau were making that Culture debases the "natural" being of man.

for its object as something quite *other,* and, also, at the same time, immediately as *itself.* It has itself as an other, not in the sense that this other has another content; rather, the content is the same self in the form of absolute opposition and with an indifferent determinate being all of its own. —Thus what is present here is the spirit of this real world of culture, spirit *conscious* of itself in its truth and in its *concept.*[116]

84–521   This spirit is the absolute and universal inversion and estrangement of actuality and of thought: *pure culture.* What is experienced in this world is that neither the *actual essence* of power and of wealth, nor their determinate *concepts,* good and bad (that is, the consciousness of what is good and bad), nor the noble-minded and contemptuous consciousnesses have truth; rather, all of these moments are inverted instead into one another, and each is the contrary of itself. —Since it has come to its own spirituality through the principle of individuality, the universal power that is *substance* receives a self of its own only as the name attached to it; and since it is *actual* [283] power, it is rather the powerless essence that sacrifices itself. —But this surrendered, selfless essence, that is, the self that has become a thing, is instead the return of essence to itself; it is the *being-for-self* that is *for itself,* the existence of the spirit. —Equally, the *thoughts* of this essence, of *good* and of *bad,* invert themselves in this movement: what is determined to be good is bad, and what is determined to be bad is good. When the consciousness of either of these moments is judged to be the noble or contemptuous consciousness, in truth they are instead much more the inversion of what, according to these determinations, they ought to be. The noble-minded consciousness is contemptuous and rejected, in the same way as the rejection turns over into the nobility of the most cultivated freedom of self-consciousness.[117] —From a formal$_2$ point of view as well, everything is *outwardly* the inverse of what is for *itself;* and again,

---

116. We have transversed the progression of the actuality of this *bonne société,* and we now enter into the Concept of that experience. This Concept articulates the manners of the salon culture, where wit effectively grants entrance to high society. Such mores are actually perverted, and we begin to see that people who live with them are unbalanced.

117. We see here an inversion of the previous movement of actuality; the reference has changed too. While the first movement concerned privileged members in *bonne société,* the second concerns the "noble-minded" *philosophe* and artist: those whose formal standing are in the third estate but whose actuality, as contemptuous of social manners, has ejected them from the material sustenance of that privileged place. The *mise en scène* is now Diderot's world of literature, where satire replaces flattery as the mode of "true" thought and speech. It is also the World where, if you offend your patrons, you will find yourself without income and estranged from your "friends."

what is for itself is not true, but is something other than what it wants to be: instead, being-for-self is the loss of itself; estrangement from itself is rather self-preservation. —So what is present here is this: all moments execute on one another a universal justice; each estranges itself in itself just as much as it depicts itself in its contrary and is in this way inverted. —The true spirit, however, is just this unity of what is absolutely separated, and it does come to existence through the *free actuality* of these *self-less* extremes precisely as their middle term. Its determinate being is the universal *speaking* and torn *judging* into which all of those moments that ought to count as essences and actual members of the whole dissolve and that is equally this self-dissolving play with itself. Hence, for as long as it overwhelms everything, this judging and speaking are what is true and invincible; it is the *only truthful* thing with which one has to deal in this world. In this judging, each part of this world comes to the point where its spirit is expressed, or where it is spoken of spiritedly, and what is said of it is what it is. —Honorable consciousness takes every moment as an abiding essentiality and is the uncultured thoughtlessness of not knowing that it is equally doing the inverse. But the torn consciousness is the consciousness of this inversion and, indeed, of the absolute inversion. The concept is what is dominant in it, and it brings together the thoughts that lay far apart for honor, so that its speech is full of spirit.

    The content of spirit's talk on and about itself, therefore, is the inversion of all concepts and realities, the universal deception of itself and others;[118] and just for this reason, the shamelessness of expressing this deception is the greatest truth. This talk is the lunacy of the musician "who assembled and scrambled thirty arias of every sort and character: Italian, French, tragic, comic; [284] at one moment with a deep bass he descended into hell; at the next he contracted his throat and in falsetto rent the heights of the heavens, by turns raging, soothing, imperious, and mocking."[119] —For the placid consciousness that honorably posits the melody of the good and true in equality of tone,[120] that is, in one note, this talk appears as "a hotch potch of wisdom and foolishness, as a mix of

85–522

---

  118. The "universal deception" is nothing other than the facticity of the individual's consciousness that now speaks of itself through self-mockery, wit, and satirical buffoonery against members of "good society." Michel Foucault is quite right to think that we are seeing here a "social schizophrenia" produced from the "logic" of this society. Cf. *Madness and Civilization*, trans. Richard Howard (NY: Vintage, 1965), p. 199ff.

  119. The line is from Diderot's *Rameau's Nephew* (Goethe's translation), p. 1000.

  120. The "placid consciousness" would refer to the "philosopher" in *Rameau's Nephew*—that is, to Diderot's doppelgänger, "*Moi*."

equal parts of taste and vulgarity, of right ideas and wrong ones, of a complete perversion of sensibility, hence perfect shamefulness and total openness and truth."[121] The placid consciousness cannot prevent the musician
from shifting into all these tones and from running up and down the
whole scale of feelings, from the deepest contempt and dejection to the
highest admiration and sympathy; "with these latter feelings a touch of
the ridiculous is fused, which divests them of their nature."[122] In their
openness the former feelings have a reconciling touch; in their quaking
depths is the touch of omnipotence that restores spirit to itself.

86–523   If we consider the discourse of this self-transparent confusion in contrast with the talk of that *simple consciousness* of the true and good, then it
can only be monosyllabic in contrast with the open and self-conscious elo-
quence of the spirit of culture; for consciousness can say nothing to the
latter that the latter does not itself know and say.[123] If it goes beyond its
monosyllables, what it then says is the same as what the spirit of culture
utters, but in so doing it commits the additional folly of thinking that it is
saying something new and different. Its very syllables—"shameful,"
"contemptuous"—are already this folly; for the spirit of culture says them
about itself.[124] If in its speech this spirit inverts everything monotonous
(since this self-identity is only an abstraction, but within its actuality is
implicitly the inversion), and if, on the other hand, the upright consciousness stands up for the good and noble, that is, for what maintains itself in
its utterance, in the only way possible—namely, that the good and noble
does not lose its value just because it is *tied* to or *mixed* with what is bad
(since this is its *condition* and *necessity* and that is what the *wisdom* of
nature consists in)[125]—then, although it meant to contradict the talk of
spirit, this consciousness has thus only summarized its content in a trivial
way by speaking. In making the *opposite* of the noble and good the *condition* and *necessity* of the noble and good, this summing up thoughtlessly

---

121. A paraphrase from *Rameau's Nephew,* cf. pp. 984, 1000.

122. The line is from *Rameau's Nephew,* p. 1001.

123. The "simple consciousness" in the dialog seems to refer to the minor
nobility and the *petite bourgeoisie,* in particular, Rameau's employer, M. Bertin. Cf.
Rameau's Nephew, p. 988. However, Hegel probably has in mind the "typical"
consciousness that identifies itself as both worldly and pious. We will see in a few
paragraphs that this "simple consciousness" is the Jansenist, who becomes the
real opponent to the *philosophe.* Again, Hegel is alluding to controversies of the
time, when the Jansenists are victorious against the Jesuits (having them expelled
from France in 1762) and now plot battle against the "freethinkers."

124. See, for instance, *Rameau's Nephew,* p. 984.

125. The reference is to J. Robinet's *De la nature* (1783), T. 1, p. 67f.

intends to say something other than this; what is called noble and good is in its essence the inverse of itself, just as the bad is, inversely, the excellent.

If the simple consciousness compensates for these spiritless *thoughts* 87–524 with the *actuality* of the excellent by specifying the latter in the *example* of a [285] fictitious case, or even of a true anecdote, and shows in this way that it is no empty name but *is here present,* then the *universal* actuality of the inverted conduct stands opposed to the whole of the real world, in which the example thus constitutes only something quite isolated, an *espèce.* And to display the determinate being of the good and noble as a singular anecdote, whether fictitious or true, is the most biting comment that can be made about it. —And when the simple consciousness finally demands the dissolution of this whole world of inversion, it cannot ask the *individual* to distance himself from it; for Diogenes in his tub is conditioned by it, and the demand made of the singular is precisely what counts as the bad, namely, to care *for itself* as *singular.* And when the demand for this distancing is directed toward the universal *individuality,* the demand for this distance cannot mean that reason should, once more, give up the spiritually formed consciousness that it has reached, that it should submerge the extensive wealth of its moments in the simplicity of the natural heart and fall back into the wildness and proximity to the animal consciousness that is called "nature" or "innocence." No! The demand for this dissolution can only be addressed to the *spirit* of culture itself as a requirement that it should return out of this confusion to itself as *spirit* and earn a yet higher consciousness.[126]

But in fact spirit has already in an implicit way accomplished this. The 88–525 self-conscious and self-declared tearing of consciousness is its scornful laughter at determinate being and hence at the confusion of the whole and at itself. At the same time, it is the silent self-audible echoing of all this confusion. —This "self-audible" vanity of all actuality and of every determinate concept is the twofold reflection of the real world within itself: first, in *this self* of consciousness as *this,* and secondly, in the pure

---

126. "Simple consciousness" is now specified to be a moralist who opposes the words and "folly" of inversion. In the Diderot dialog the Countess de la Mark and her salon are described as the "espèce," meaning that they are the "type" who make these moral judgments. The Countess and her salon were supporters of Diderot's nemesis, the Jansenist playwright, Palissot. In his play, *Le Philosophe,* he ridiculed Diderot as a rake. Diderot and Rameau speak both of this play and of the Jansenist party in the dialog. Cf. *Rameau's Nephew,* p. 998. The reference to Diogenes, the Cynic, and the return to nature is a reference to *Rameau's Nephew,* p. 1021ff. (The critical editors believe that Hegel is referring to Rousseau here, but the clear allusions to Diogenes and Rameau, being the cynic who returns to nature, suggest that Hegel is continuing with his allusions to Diderot's dialog.)

universality of consciousness or in thinking. In the first case the spirit that has come to itself directs its glance into the world of actuality and still has this world as its purpose and immediate content. But in the second case its glance in part is only into itself, and is negative in contrast with the world; and in part it is turned away from the world of heaven, and its object is the beyond of that world.[127]

89–526   On the former side, the return to self, the *vanity* of all *things* is *its own vanity*, that is, the self *is* vain. It is the self-subsisting self that knows not only how to criticize and chatter about everything, but also how to express with spirited wit the fixed essences of actuality, as well as the fixed determinations that the judgment posits in their *contradiction;* this contradiction is their truth. —Formally considered, this self knows everything to be self-estranged: *being-for-self* separated from *being-in-self,* meaning and purpose separated from truth, and from both again *being-for-other* (the ostensible separated both from the genuine meaning and from the true matter and intention). —Thus the self knows each [286] moment in contrast with the other, and in general it knows the inversion of everything. More exactly, it knows better what each thing is than [the way] it is, determined in whatever way it may be. Since the self is familiar with the substantial from the side of the *disunity* and the *conflict* that it unites within it, but not from the side of this uniting, it understands very well how to *pass judgment* on the substantial, but has lost the capacity to grasp it. —Hence, this vanity needs the vanity of all things in order to get from them the consciousness of the self; it thereby produces this vanity and is the soul that bears it.[128] Power and wealth are the highest purposes of its exertion; it knows that through renunciation and sacrifice it forms itself into the

---

127. Hegel seems to accept Diderot's comment that the "simple consciousness" of the cynic is that of the Carmelite and the Capuchin; in other words, Rameau's "state of nature" is parallel to the religious self's denial of the world. Cf. *Rameau's Nephew,* p. 1022. From here on, the viewpoint of piety becomes more pronounced, especially the piety espoused in Jansenism. Hegel's "equation" between simple piety and Rameau's simplicity is a case of Hegel reconciling opposites. He believes that from the vantage point of "sane reason," that is, from Diderot's viewpoint, the two are in fact equivalent.

128. As Pascal says in his *Pensées,* "Les vrays Chrestiens obéiessent aux folies néantmoins, non pas qu'ils respectent les folies, mais l'ordre de Dieu, qui pour la punition des hommes, les a affervis à ces folies. *Omnis creatura subjecta est vanitati. Liberatur,*" *Les Pensées de Blaise Pascal,* ed. by H. F. Stewart (NY: Pantheon Books, 1950), § 589, p. 329. Hegel is presenting Jansenism as the true form of religious consciousness within the world of Culture. The French and Latin mean, "True Christians are nonetheless obedient to folly, not that they respect folly but the order of God, who to punish men made them subject to folly. *All creatures are subject to vanity. They shall be liberated.*"

universal, achieves the possession of it, and has universal validity in this possession: power and wealth are the actual, recognized powers. But this value is itself vain, and precisely by having possession of them the vain self knows them to be not selves; instead, it knows their power and knows them to be vain. The fact that in the very possession of them it is thus outside them is exhibited in the witty speech that, therefore, is its greatest interest and the truth of the whole. In that speech *this* self, as the pure self that belongs neither to the determinations of actuality nor to those of thought, comes to be spiritual and has universal validity in a genuine way. It *is* the self-tearing nature of all relations and the conscious tearing of them. But only as a rebelling self-consciousness does it know its own tearing, and in this knowledge it has immediately raised itself above its torn state. In that vanity all content becomes something negative, something that can no longer be grasped positively. The positive object is only the *pure I itself,* and the torn consciousness is *in itself* this pure self-identity of the self-consciousness that has returned to itself.

b. Faith and Pure Insight

The spirit of self-estrangement has its determinate being in the world of culture, but since this whole has been estranged from itself, there stands beyond it the nonactual world *of pure consciousness* or of *thinking.* The content of this world is purely thought, and thinking is its absolute element. But since thinking is in the first instance the *element* of this world, consciousness only *has* these thoughts; it does not yet *think* them, that is, it does not know that they are thoughts. Instead, they exist for it in the form of *representation.* For although consciousness steps from actuality into pure consciousness, in principle it is itself still in the sphere and the determinacy of actuality. To begin with, the torn consciousness is *in-itself* [287] the *self-identity* of pure consciousness—it is so for us, not for itself. So it is only the *immediate* elevation that is not yet inwardly completed; it still has within it its own opposite principle, by which it is conditioned, and has not become the master of it through the mediated movement. Hence, the essence of its thought counts for it not as *essence* only, in the form of the abstract in-itself, but in the form of something *actual in common sense*—an actuality that has merely been elevated into another element without losing in the latter the determinacy of an actuality that is not thought. —This in-itself is essentially to be distinguished from the *in-itself* that is the essence of *Stoical* consciousness; for Stoicism only the *form of thought* counted as such, and so it has some content foreign to it, taken from actuality. But for this present consciousness, it is not the *form of thought* that counts. (Equally, it must be distinguished from the *in-itself* of the virtuous consciousness, for which

90–527

the essence does indeed stand in connection with actuality—it is the very essence of actuality, but only an essence that is initially not actual.) For this present consciousness, the essence still counts as something actual, even though it is admittedly beyond actuality. In the same way, what is right and good in itself for reason as the lawgiver, as well as the universal of the consciousness that tests laws, does not have actuality as its vocation. —Hence, although pure thinking fell within the world of culture itself, namely, on the side of estrangement (specifically in judgment as the standard of abstract good and bad), it has been enriched by the moment of actuality and hence of content, because it has gone through the movement of the whole. But, at the same time, this actuality of the essence is only an actuality of *pure*, not of *actual*, consciousness—although it is elevated into the element of thinking for this consciousness but is beyond the proper actuality of consciousness; for the first actuality is the flight from the second.[129]

91–528   As *religion* makes its entrance here as the faith of the world of culture—for it is evident that we are talking about religion—it does not yet enter as religion *in- and for-itself.* —It has already appeared to us in other determinacies—specifically as *unhappy consciousness*—or as the shape of the substanceless movement of consciousness itself. It appeared again in the ethical substance as faith in the underworld, but the consciousness of the departed spirit is properly speaking not *faith*, not the essence posited in the element of pure consciousness beyond the actual one; instead it has itself an immediate presence: its element is the family.[130] —But religion has emerged from *substance* and is, in part, the pure consciousness of it, and, in part, this pure consciousness is estranged from its actual consciousness, but it has still the determinacies of being antithetical to actuality as "this" in general, and antithetical to [288]

---

129. What makes the Jansenist different from the Stoic is that the Jansenist acknowledges the world of actuality, that is, the society of manners, as its World. Pascal can go to his gambling tables with ease. But the truth of consciousness does not lie in the actual World but in its faith; or at least its faith conceived through pure thinking. What this consciousness actually disdains is profane thinking, that is, Jesuitical thinking, that attempts to appease the World of Actuality and the World of Religion. But the Jesuits, under this view, have no true sense of virtue either, since virtue (as in the section of Chapter 5, called "Virtue and the Way of the World") stands against the actuality of the political order. The Jansenist opposes the worldliness of the Jesuit, but its "simple consciousness" belongs also to the political order that it disdains.

130. The references are back to Unhappy Consciousness in Chapter 4 of *Phenomenology*, to the movement of consciousness that occurs in the first three chapters of the book, and finally to "True Spirit," sections a–b, in Chapter 6.

the actuality of self-consciousness in particular; hence it is essentially just a *faith*.[131]

This *pure consciousness* of the absolute essence is something *estranged*. 92–529 Now, we have to see closer how its other determines itself, and it is only to be considered in conjunction with this other. Initially, then, this pure consciousness seems to have the *world* of actuality simply opposed to it, but since it is the flight from this world (and for that reason it has the *determinacy* of *antithesis* to this world), it has the world in itself. Hence, pure consciousness is estranged from itself essentially, and faith constitutes only one of its sides. But this means that the other side has already arisen for us. In other words, pure consciousness is the reflection out of the world of culture in such a way that the substance of that world and the masses into which it is articulated might show themselves for what they are in themselves, namely, *spiritual* essentialities, [that is,] absolutely restless motions or determinations that are sublated immediately in their contraries. Thus their essence (the simple consciousness) is the simplicity of the *absolute difference* that is immediately no difference. It is pure *being-for-self*, therefore, not as *this singular* [being] but the universal inward self as restless motion, which attacks and penetrates the *restful essence* of the *facticity*. Hence, there is present in it the certainty that knows itself immediately as truth: pure thinking as the *absolute concept* in the power of its *negativity*, which wipes out every objective essence that is supposed to be contrary to consciousness and makes the essence into a being of consciousness. —At the same time, this pure consciousness is *simple* as well, because *its* difference is no difference. But as this form of simple reflection in itself, pure consciousness is the element of faith in which the spirit has the determinacy *of positive universality* or of *being-in-itself,* as opposed to the being-for-self of self-consciousness.[132]

---

131. The pure thoughts of the Jansenists appear here as the form of religious consciousness. Their thoughts belong to Unhappy Consciousness, but Unhappy Consciousness that has achieved rational insight. Even the freethinkers point to the Jansenist as a "true religious" Self inasmuch as he renounces the values of Culture.

132. In this retreat from the actual world into religious thought, the absolute substance of the *ancien régime* itself is known through the first estate, that is, the Church. It is in this "element" that the Concept has its identity, since in it the sanctify and worth of the whole "good society" is secured. However, in this moment the truth of the whole is challenged by the religious reformers. They disclose the facticity of self-consciousness and show its worthlessness. Since this facticity constitutes the self-identification of the bourgeoisie, with their thoughts of status and wealth, to show the worthlessness of it challenges the very essence of the "good" society.

Driven back into itself out of the world that lacks essence and is only self-dissolving, the spirit is truly one and indivisible; [that is, it is] both the *absolute movement* and *negativity* of its own appearing, and the inwardly *satisfied* essence and positive *rest* of that appearance. But these two moments go asunder to become a doubled consciousness, because they lie in general under the determinacy of *estrangement*. The negative movement is *pure insight*, as the spiritual *process* of gathering itself within *self-consciousness*. It is confronted by, and directed against, the consciousness of the positive—the form of objectivity or of representing—but its own object is just the *pure I*. —Alternatively, the simple consciousness of the positive, or of the resting self-identity, has the inner *essence* qua essence for its object. This means that pure insight has, to begin with, no content within it, because it is the negative being-for-self; [289] on the contrary, the content belongs to faith, but without insight. While pure insight never steps outside of self-consciousness, faith does have indeed its content in the element of pure self-consciousness, but the content is in *thinking* and not in *concepts—in pure consciousness, not in pure self-consciousness*. So, of course, faith is pure consciousness of the *essence,* which means it is pure consciousness of the *simple inner,* and it *is,* therefore, thinking. This is the cardinal aspect of the nature of faith that is usually overlooked: the *immediacy,* which the essence has in it, lies in the very fact that faith's object is *essence,* and that means it is *pure thought.*[133] But this *immediacy* obtains the significance of an objective *being* that lies beyond the consciousness of self, inasmuch as *thinking* enters into *consciousness,* or pure consciousness enters into self-consciousness. Because of this significance, which obtains the immediacy and simplicity of *pure thinking* within *consciousness,* the *essence* of faith falls from thinking down to *representation* and becomes a supersensible world, which is essentially an *other* for self-consciousness. —In pure insight, on the contrary, the transition of pure thinking into consciousness has the opposite determination: objectivity has the significance of a merely negative content that sublates itself and

---

133. The thoughts that constitute faith are here divided into the negative and the positive, or between science and faith per se. The negative movement is thinking itself, that is, the domain of logic and science, not the thoughts of pious or moral sentiments. In terms of the religious position depicted here, we should think of simple pious belief, even if it embraces "science." Perhaps Hegel has in mind the famous Port Royale, which fostered both Jansenistic piety and logical rigor. "Science" is portrayed as the "way of the concept" in its retreat from the false values of the world, especially away from the pretensions of the royal court, but the substance of this position is still simple faith: a form of renewal for the Catholic World.

turns back into the self; that is, only the self is properly the object of itself, or the object has truth only to the extent that it has the form of the self.[134]

Just as faith and pure insight belong in common to the element of pure consciousness, so too they belong in common to the return [to consciousness] out of the actual world of culture. Therefore, they present themselves under three aspects. First, there is each of them *in* and *for itself,* outside all relations; next, each of them is connected with the *actual* world opposed to pure consciousness; and in the third place, each is connected with the other within pure consciousness. 93–530

In *believing* consciousness, the aspect of *being in* and *for itself* is its absolute object, whose content and determinacy is already given. For, according to the concept of faith, its object is nothing but the real world elevated into the universality of pure consciousness. Hence, the articulation of the real world constitutes the organization of the world of faith as well, except that, in becoming spiritual, the parts of the latter are not estranged from themselves but are essences that exist in and for themselves.[135] They have turned into themselves and are spirits that abide by themselves. —Only for us, therefore, is the movement of their transition an estrangement of the determinacy in which they are in their difference, and only for us is it a *necessary* sequence; but for faith their difference is a resting diversity, and their movement *has happened.* 94–531

Let us name them [that is, the essences] briefly according to the outward determinacy of their form. Just as the state power, or the good, was the first [determinacy] in the world of culture, so here too the first is [290] *the absolute essence,* the spirit that exists in and for itself because it is simple, eternal *substance.* But its concept is to be spirit, and in realizing it, the substance passes over into *being for another.* Its self-identity becomes an *actual,* self-*sacrificing* absolute essence, which becomes a *self,* but a perishing self. Hence, the third [determinacy] is the return of this estranged self and of the humiliated substance into their initial 95–532

---

134. The thoughts of the *philosophes* are based in mechanical representations. Here the Self is an object and nature has the form of the Self. The allusion is probably to Diderot or D'Holbach and the *image* of nature as the great living organization of Reason.

135. As the actual World is divided into classes, so too is the religious community, but unlike the secular World the religious fraternities are motivated by love and the denial of worldly values (that is, wealth and power). The Jesuits, for instance, divided their religious community into three classes: the professed priests, who take special vows; the "ordinary" priests; and the brothers. The distinctions, however, are based on "spiritual vocation" and not on either wealth or privilege.

simplicity. That is how it comes to be represented as spirit.[136]

96–533   When, through thinking, these differentiated essences have been taken back into themselves out of the alterations of the actual world, they are changeless, eternal spirits whose being is to think the unity that they constitute. Although withdrawn from self-consciousness in this way, these essences encroach upon it nonetheless. Were the essence left undisturbed in the form of the original, simple substance, it would remain foreign to self-consciousness, but the externalization of this substance and its resulting spirit has a moment of actuality in self-consciousness, and for that reason it gives itself a share in the believing self-consciousness, or the believing consciousness belongs to the real world.

97–534   In this second relation, the believing consciousness, on the one hand, has its very actuality in the real world of culture; it constitutes the spirit and the determinate being of that world (which we have already considered). But, on the other hand, it confronts this actuality of its own as vanity; it is the movement of sublating it. This movement does not consist in its having a spirited and witty consciousness of its own inversions; after all, it is the simple consciousness that takes a witty spirit to be vanity, because wit still has the real world as its purpose. Rather, actuality, as spirited determinate being, stands against the restful realm of its thinking; hence, this determinate being has to be overcome in an external way. Through the sublation of sensuous knowing and doing, this obedience in service and praise produces the consciousness of unity with the essence existing in and for itself, though not as an intuited actual unity; rather, this service is only a perpetual producing, which does not completely achieve its goal in the present. The community is indeed coming to be here, since it is the universal self-consciousness; but, for the singular self-consciousness, the realm of pure thinking remains necessarily something beyond its own actuality. Or, inasmuch as this beyond has stepped into actuality (through the externalization of the eternal essence), it is a sensuous actuality that is not comprehended.[137] One sensuous actuality

---

136. Hegel is referring to the Trinity and its "progression" as what the religious community imitates. God the Father is the eternal substance; the Son is the "self-sacrificing essence," who as the "perishing self" is Jesus, the God-Man; and the Holy Spirit comes into the world as the "humbled" God and becomes one with the World in the form of the Church triumphant. The religious community imitates this progression: the Church itself is the "eternal substance" with the Pope as its father; the clergy and religious houses with their vows of poverty and chastity represent the self-sacrificing essence; and the worldly but "sacramental" life of all baptized Christians represents the humble stance of the Holy Spirit.

137. Hegel seems to be referring to organized religion—that is, the specific confessional attitudes in the Christian religion. What is not comprehended by

remains, however, indifferent to the rest, and in addition to that, the beyond has only acquired the determination of being distanced in time and space. —But in the believing consciousness, the concept, as the actuality of the spirit present to itself, remains the *inner,* which is and effects everything but does not itself step forth.

In *pure insight,* however, the concept is solely what is actual; and this third aspect of faith, namely, that it is the object for pure insight, is the genuine [291] relationship in which faith now makes its entrance.[138] —Pure insight itself has to be considered in the same way: first, in and for itself; secondly, in relationship with the actual world so far as it is still positively present, namely, present as vain consciousness; and finally, in the relationship to faith that was just mentioned. 98–535

We have already seen what pure insight is in and for itself. Just as faith is the resting pure *consciousness* of the spirit as *essence,* so pure insight is the *self-*consciousness of spirit; hence it knows the essence not as *essence,* but as absolute *self.* Consequently, it aims to sublate for self-consciousness every *other* independence, whether actual or existing *in-itself,* and to make it into a *concept.* Pure insight is not just the certainty of self-conscious reason that it is all truth; it also *knows* that this is what it is. 99–536

As the concept of pure insight makes its entrance, however, it is not yet *actualized.* Accordingly, its consciousness appears still as something *accidental, singular,* and that which is for it the essence as *purpose* that it has to actualize. Initially it has the *intention* of making *pure insight universal;* that is, of making everything that is actual into the concept, and of making it into a concept in every self-consciousness. The intention is "pure" because it has pure insight for its content; and this is not restricted in itself. Two sides are immediately involved in the unrestricted concept: that everything objective have only the significance of *being-for-self,* that is, of self-consciousness; and that this self-consciousness have the significance of a *universal,* that is, that pure insight becomes a property of every self-consciousness. This second side of intention is the result of culture, inasmuch as therein the differences of objective spirit (the parts and determinations of the judgment of its world), and so also the differences that appear as the original determinate natures, have gone to ground. Genius, talent, the particular capacities in general, belong to the world of 100–537

---

them is the universal self-consciousness that lies within. In the next chapter, "Religion," Hegel will identify this universal self-consciousness as the living God, or absolute spirit.

138. Hegel may be referring to the fact that the *philosophes* were especially interested in the alleged miraculous character of the religious life, e.g., the idea that bread could be turned into flesh.

actuality inasmuch as they still have in the world the aspect of being a spiritual animal kingdom that, amid mutual violence and confusion, struggles and deceives itself concerning the essences of the real world. —Indeed, the differences have no place in the world of noble *espèces:* neither is individuality satisfied by the nonactual *facticity itself,* nor has it a *particular* content or goals of its own. Instead, it counts [itself] only as something universally valid, namely, as cultured; and the difference is reduced to one of lesser or greater energy—or to a difference of *magnitude,* that is, to the unessential.[139] This last differentiation has therein gone to ground, because in the complete tearing of consciousness the difference converts into the absolutely qualitative one. Therein, what is other for the I is just the I itself. In this [292] infinite judgment all the one-sidedness and selfishness of the original being-for-self is eradicated. The self knows itself to be its object as pure self; and this absolute equality of the two sides is the element of pure insight. —Hence, pure insight is the simple inward undifferentiated *essence.* In the same way, it is the universal *work* and universal possession. In this *simple* spiritual substance self-consciousness both gives itself and maintains in every object the consciousness of *this* its *singularity* or of its *doing;* while conversely the individuality of self-consciousness is there *self-equivalent* and universal. —So this pure insight is the spirit that cries aloud to *every* consciousness: *Be for yourselves* what you are *in yourselves—be rational.*

II. The Enlightenment

101–538   The specific object against which pure insight directs the force of its concept is faith, as the form of pure consciousness that confronts it in the same element. It has, however, a connection with the actual world as well,

---

139. The "unrestricted concept" is reason qua "pure intention," which now begins its development to identify itself with nature. The *differentiae* of nature are simple magnitudes of energy; what matters is reason's return to the "Spiritual Kingdom of the Animals" (section c in Chapter 5, "Reason"), that is, to enjoy the talents and capacities of invention *isolated* from the estranged world of actuality. Hegel is alluding to Rousseau's essay, "The Origin of Inequality," since talents and capacities come from nature, and if we return to nature we would somehow return to "purity." A "pure culture" is possible on this basis, as Rousseau discusses in *Emile* (1762). But this view is deceptive, however. A "pure" Self does not exist in and of itself. Any Self must have an identity to its World and reflect that World. With Rousseau and the other *philosophes* nature has a formative energy, but Hegel is denying this. Nature supplies us only with quantity of energy; it does not supply us with any formative principle. Despite these deceptions the philosophical concept progresses through this "rational insight" that the "pure" Self is the object of knowledge.

since, like faith, it is the return from that world into pure consciousness. We must first of all see what constitutes its activity in respect to the impure intentions and perverted insights of the actual world.

We have already referred to the tranquil consciousness that stands 102–539 opposed to the self-dissolving and self-reproducing turmoil; it constitutes the side of pure insight and intention. As we saw, however, this tranquil consciousness contains no *particular insight* about the world of culture; rather, the world of culture itself has the most painful feeling and truest insight concerning itself: it is the feeling of having everything fixed dissolve, of being on the rack at every moment of its existence, and shattered in every bone; it is equally the speech of this feeling and the witty talk that appraises every aspect of its condition. Pure insight, then, can have here no activity and content of its own and so can only behave as the formal, true *apprehending* both of the world's own witty insight and of its speech. Since this speech is disjointed—its appraisal is a fad of the moment that is straightaway forgotten—and exists as a whole only for a third consciousness, this latter can only be distinguished as *pure* insight when it gathers these disjointed features into a general picture and then makes them into an insight of everything.[140] [293]

By virtue of this simple medium, pure insight will dissolve the confu- 103–540 sion of this world. For we have demonstrated that it is not the masses, the determinate concepts, and individualities that are the essence of this actuality, but that it has its substance and support solely in the spirit that exists in judging and discussing, and that the interest of having a content for this babble and argumentation alone preserves the whole as well as the masses into which it is articulated. In this speech of insight, its self-consciousness is still something *existing-for-itself, this singular;* but the vanity of the content is at the same time the vanity of the self that knows it to be vain. When, therefore, the placidly apprehending consciousness compiles the most telling conceptions, penetrating to the core of all this witty babbling of vanity, then the soul, which still retains the whole, goes over to the remaining vanity of determinate being, and the vanity of witty judgments perishes.[141] The compilation shows to most people a better wit than their own, and to everyone at least a more varied one, and shows that knowing better and judging are in general something universal and now

---

140. The third consciousness is the encyclopedist who has insight into everything.

141. Hegel seems to be referring to the conclusion of *Rameau's Nephew*, when Rameau leaves aside his arias and jokes, and both he and Diderot discuss the importance of their families, the existence of a "paternal molecule," and how society is bound together by power, money, and material connections. Cf. p. 1006ff.

universally known. With this the sole interest, which was still present, extinguishes itself, and the singular inspection dissolves itself into the universal insight.

104[142]   Knowledge of the essence, however, still stands firm over vain knowledge; pure insight initially appears in its own proper activity when it makes its entrance against faith.

a. The Struggle of the Enlightenment with Superstition

105–541 The various modes of the negative attitude of consciousness—on the one hand, that of skepticism and, on the other hand, that of theoretical and practical idealism—are subordinate shapes with respect to that of *pure insight* and of its expansion—the *Enlightenment;* for it is born from the substance, knows the pure *self* of consciousness to be absolute, and is a match for the pure consciousness of the absolute essence of all actuality. —Faith and insight are the same pure consciousness but are opposed formally: the essence is for faith mere *thought,* not *concept,* and therefore something quite opposed to *self*-consciousness, whereas for pure insight the essence is the *self;* thus they are reciprocally each absolutely negative for the other.[143] —In their emergence as mutually opposed, all the *content* belongs to faith, for in its tranquil element of thinking each moment wins subsistence—[294] but, initially, pure insight is without content and is its pure vanishing instead. Yet through the negative moment against its own negative, it will realize itself and give itself a content.

106–542   Pure insight knows that faith is opposed to it, to reason and truth. Just as faith is for it universally a web of superstitions, prejudices, and errors, so in addition the consciousness of this content is organized for it into a kingdom of error wherein false insight is in the first instance the *universal mass* of consciousness:[144] immediate, naive, and without reflection into self. But faith also has within it the moment of reflection into self; or of self-consciousness, separated from its naiveté, under the aspect of an insight that remains on its own in the background; or of an evil intention by which that mass is deluded. This mass is sacrificed by the deceit of a *priesthood* that promotes both its jealous vanity of remaining in sole possession of insight

---

142. In the Miller translation this paragraph is attached to the preceding one.

143. The "Concept" referred to here is religion's essence. Religion has not reached the truth of its concept. It is here only a profession (a form of representational thinking). It has its certainty through the content of its confessions, doctrines, and acts of faith. We should think of Rousseau's "Profession of Faith of the Vicar of Savoyard," in *Emile,* as an example of such piety.

144. *die allgemeine Masse.* The "universal mass" is here the people, identified as believing in superstitions, miracles, and other "errors" of judgment.

and its self-conceit as well.[145] At the same time priesthood makes common cause with *despotism* that, as the synthetic, nonconceptual unity of the real and this ideal kingdom—an oddly inconsequential essence—stands above the bad insight of the multitude and the bad intentions of the priests, yet unites both within itself. From the stupidity and confusion of the people and through the means of a deceitful priesthood, despotism, despising both, at once draws the benefit of tranquil domination, the fulfillment of its desires and whims, and is itself the same mustiness of insight, the equal [in] superstition and error.[146]

The Enlightenment does not concern itself with these three aspects of the enemy indiscriminately.[147] After all, since its essence is pure insight, that is, that which is *universal* on its own account, its true connection with the other extreme is the one in which it concerns itself with what the two have *in common* and how they *are equivalent*. The side of *singularity*, which isolates itself from the universal naive consciousness, is its opposite, which it cannot immediately influence. The will of the deceitful priesthood and of the oppressive despot is, therefore, not the immediate object of its doing; [its object is] rather the insight, lacking will, which does not individuate itself to the point of being-for-self, [that is,] the *concept* of rational self-consciousness that has its determinate being in the mass but is not yet present there as concept.[148] Since, however, pure insight wrenches the honorable insight, with its naive essence, free from

145. The reference is to Baron D'Holbach's *System of Nature* (1773): "Are not those priests, so careful of the soul's health, who insolently break into the sanctuary of the thoughts, to the end that they may find in the opinions of man motives for injuring him, odious knaves and disturbers of the mind's repose, whom religion honors and whom reason detests? What villains are more odious in the eyes of humanity than those infamous *inquisitors*, who, by the blindness of princes, enjoy the advantage of judging their own enemies, and of committing them to the flames? Nevertheless the superstition of the people makes them respected, and the favor of kings overwhelms them with kindness!" trans. by H. D. Robinson, vols. I–II (1868; rpt. NY: Burt Franklin Press, 1970), p. 319.

146. The sentiment of materialism is against despotism, as D'Holbach says, "[S]overeigns are dispensed from the trouble of instructing themselves; they neglect the laws, they enervate themselves in ease and sloth . . . [T]hey confide the instruction of the people to priests, who are commissioned to render them good, submissive, and devout. . . . It is thus that politics, jurisprudence, education, and morality are everywhere infected with superstitions," p. 322ff.

147. Namely, the universal mass, priesthood, and despotism.

148. The mode of insight that "lacks will" and does not have the Concept qua rational concept in it is most likely deism: D'Alembert seems to be the target of *pure* rational insight, since while rejecting Catholicism he espoused a god beyond nature. Diderot attacks this view in *D'Alembert's Dream* (c. 1769).

its prejudices and errors, it wrests from the hands of the bad intention the reality and power of its deceit. The kingdom of this bad intention has its *basis* and *material* in the nonconceptual consciousness of the universal mass, and the *being-for-self* has its *substance* in the *simple* consciousness in general.[149]

108–544   The connection of pure insight with the naive consciousness of absolute essence has now a double side: on the first side, pure insight is *in itself* the [295] same as that consciousness; on the second side, this naive consciousness, in the simple element of its thought, endorses the absolute essence as well as its parts, gives itself subsistence, and lets pure insight count only as its *in-itself,* and for that reason [lets it count] in an objective way, while yet disavowing its *being-for-self* in this in-itself. —Insofar as, according to the first side, this faith is for pure insight *implicitly* pure *self*-consciousness and needs only to become so *explicitly,* pure insight possesses in this concept of self-consciousness the element wherein it realizes itself instead of false insight.[150]

109–545   Since from this [first] side both are essentially the same and the connection of pure insight takes place through and in this same element, their communication is an *immediate* one and their give and take [is] an undisturbed flow of the one into the other.[151] Whatever more may be stuck into consciousness to pin it down, then, it is *in itself* this simplicity in which everything is dissolved, forgotten, and remains naive, and which is, therefore, absolutely receptive to the concept. For this reason the communication of pure insight is comparable to a tranquil expansion, to the *diffusion,* for example, of a fragrance in an undisturbed atmosphere. It is a

---

149. This is accomplished by an appeal to Reason inherent in thought, which "popular notions" have obscured. D'Holbach states the following proposition, "Thus every rational thinker, in renouncing his prejudices, may feel the lack of utility and the falsity of so many abstract systems . . . in consulting reason, man will discover that of which he needs a knowledge and undeceive himself of those chimerical causes which enthusiasm, ignorance, and falsehood, have everywhere substituted for true causes and to real motive-powers," p. 329.

150. The first side is the unity between the freethinkers, deists and the atheists alike. D'Alembert and Rousseau accept a justified and reformed faith, Diderot and D'Holbach, among others, accept only pure insight. The first side has a positive connection to unsophisticated belief, the other has only a negative attitude, and its very negativity realizes the concept of the materiality of rational self-consciousness.

151. The deism of the freethinker is closely tied to "enlightened" faith, since the latter sees the former as a colleague against superstitions and Jesuitical thought. We should remember that Diderot had governmental support until the *Encyclopédie* was brought out (1751ff.). That all changed in a dramatic way when

penetrating infection that gives no prior indication that it is something opposed to the indifferent element into which it insinuates itself; hence it cannot be warded off. Only when the infection breaks out is it *for the consciousness* that unheedingly yielded to it. For it was indeed the essence that was simply itself and equally equivalent to consciousness, which took it into itself; but what consciousness received was also the simplicity of a *negativity* reflected into itself, which in due course also develops, in accordance with its nature, into something opposed to it, and so reminds consciousness of its former state. This simplicity is the concept that is the simple knowing that knows itself and its opposite as well, but knows the opposite as sublated within it.[152] Hence by the time consciousness is aware of pure insight, that insight is already diffused; the struggle against it betrays that the infection has already occurred. The struggle is too late, and every remedy only aggravates the disease, for it has attacked the very marrow of spiritual life: namely, consciousness in its concept or its own pure essence. For this reason consciousness has no strength to overcome the disease. Because it lies in the essence itself, it allows its still isolated expressions to be repressed and the superficial symptoms to be suppressed.[153] This is very much to the advantage of the disease, for it does not now dissipate its strength or show itself to be unworthy of its essence, as it does when it breaks out in symptoms and singular eruptions antagonistic to the content of faith and to the cohesion of its external actuality. Rather, since it is now an invisible and unnoticed spirit, it creeps into the

---

people actually read the *Encyclopédie*'s articles on faith and religion, and from that point on the proponents of religion indicted him and his work. The Paris prosecutor began proceedings against Diderot. He lost his funding and right to control the publication of the *Encyclopédie*. The other *philosophes* either left Paris or kept to their salons without engaging in public debate. An account of this controversy and Hegel's views on it can be found in Shannon, "Hegel: Philosophy versus Faith," *Philosophy and Theology*, 9, No. 3–4 (1996), 351–88.

152. The infection is the "free thought" of materialism, but what is more important to Hegel is that the concept of thinking—pure thinking—is a contamination that spreads throughout the body politic. Even the University of Paris is not immune to this infection. The Abbé d'Prades, a member of the Sorbonne, defended D'Alembert's deism, which produced a scandal. The charge that "free thinking" was an infection must have been a common complaint, since D'Holbach responds to the charge, when he says, ". . . the discipline of reason is not an irrational being, which seeks to poison you, or to infect you with a dangerous delirium," p. 332.

153. Even with the temporary suppression of the *Encyclopédie*, true insight has become victorious because philosophy has taken hold of consciousness. Specifically, faith must become rational, and the naive scholastic idea of truth being derived from sense or from Church authority is now dead.

noble parts thoroughly and has soon completely mastered all the vitals and members of the unconscious idol: then [296] "*one fine morning* it gives its comrade a shove with the elbow and bash! crash! the idol lies on the floor."[154] —"One fine morning," that is, whose noon is bloodless if the infection has penetrated every organ of spiritual life. Memory alone still preserves the dead ways of the spirit's previous shape as a history, vanished one knows not how, and in this way the new serpent of wisdom held up for adoration has painlessly shed a shriveled skin.[155]

110–546   But this mute and ceaseless weaving in the simple inwardness of its substance by the spirit that hides its deed from itself is only one side of the realization of pure insight.[156] Its diffusion consists neither in the simple fact that like goes with like nor is its actualization only an expansion without antithesis. Rather, the deed of the negative essence is just as essentially a developed, intrinsically self-differentiating movement, which, as a conscious deed, must set up its moments in a specific and revealed determinate being and must be present as a frightful din and violent struggle with an opposite as such.

111–547   We have to see, therefore, how "pure insight and intention" is related *negatively* to the other where it found its opposite. —Pure insight and intention, which is related negatively, can only be the negative of itself, since its concept is all essentiality and nothing is outside it. As insight, therefore, the other comes to be the negative of pure insight; it becomes untruth and unreason; and, as intention, the other comes to be the negative of pure intention—to the lying and impurity of purpose.

112–548   In this contradiction pure insight entangles itself because it gets itself into strife and means to do battle with something *other*. —This is only "meant," because its essence, as absolute negativity, is to have otherness within itself. The absolute concept is the category; it is this, that knowledge and the *object* of knowledge are the same. Thus what pure insight

---

154. Line from Diderot's *Rameau's Nephew*, p. 999. The line refers to the Jesuit missionaries who placed an alien god on the altar of China, and also to the iconoclasm of the Jansenist who would replace the sounds and images of the Mass with a "bloodless" God. Rameau, who is speaking, says that these alien gods of the Christian faith are also idols. In their place he would have the god of nature and its "Trinity": that is, the True, the Good, and the Beautiful.

155. "[A]nd the Lord said to Moses, Make thee a fiery serpent, and set it upon a pole: and it shall come to pass, that everyone that is bitten, when he looketh upon it, shall live," Numbers 21: 8.

156. This is the first instance where the "truth of Enlightenment" is likened to the motion of a venomous thing. Hegel uses the image of the serpent here, a seraph, which is to remind us that we are considering an "idol" created in the image of reason that is becoming the god of the Enlightenment.

pronounces to be its other, what it pronounces to be an error or lie, can be nothing other than itself; it can condemn only what it is.[157] What is not rational has no *truth*, or, what is not conceived *is* not. Thus when reason speaks about something *other* than itself, it is in fact speaking only of itself; it does not therein go beyond itself. —Hence this struggle with the opposite unifies within itself the significance as reason's *actualization*. For this consists precisely in the movement of developing the moments and taking them back into itself. One part of this movement is the distinguishing by which conceptual insight confronts itself as *object;* as long as it remains in this moment, it is estranged from itself. As pure [297] insight it lacks all *content;* the movement of its actualization consists in this: that *it itself* comes to be as content for itself; another cannot become so for it, because it is the self-consciousness of the category. But since, at first, insight knows the content in the opposite merely as *content* and not yet as itself, it fails to recognize itself therein. Its fulfillment has thus the sense of coming to know as its own the content that was at first objective to it. The result, however, will thus be neither the reinstating of the errors against which it struggles, nor merely its initial concept, but an insight that recognizes the absolute negation of itself as its own actuality, as its own self. In other words, it will be insight's own self-recognizing concept. —The nature of Enlightenment's struggle with errors, that is, struggling with itself in the errors, and condemning in them what it itself asserts, is *for us;* or it is what Enlightenment and its struggle is *in itself.* But the first side of this struggle, which is its defilement through the adoption of a negative relation in its self-identical *purity*, is the way that it is *an object for faith*.[158] Faith thus experiences Enlightenment as lying, unreason, and bad intention, just as faith is error and prejudice for Enlightenment. —With regard to its content, it is first of all an empty insight whose content appears to be other than itself; consequently, it *already finds* its content in this shape where the content is not yet its own; in faith [it finds it] as a determinate being completely independent of pure insight.

Enlightenment, then, grasps its object initially and generally so that it 113–549 takes it to be *pure insight* and, failing to recognize itself therein, explains it to be an error. In *insight*, as such, consciousness so grasps an object that

---

157. The "other" is religion, but deistic religion, which has the same essential concept as materialistic reason. They are the "same" in terms of their object. Thus when pure insight, as materialism, turns against deism, it is only attacking itself, since they have the same object and they share the same form.

158. That is, pure insight only appears as the defilement of the "purity" of self-consciousness. Pure insight has betrayed the accomplishment of reform, since it turns against the spiritual world: this is how religion sees materialism.

the object comes to be the essence of consciousness for it or comes to be an object that consciousness penetrates, in which it maintains itself, stays at home with itself, presents to itself, and, since it is the movement thereby of the object, brings it forth. This is just what Enlightenment correctly pronounces faith to be, when it says that what is for faith the absolute essence is a being of faith's own consciousness, its own thought, [that is,] something produced by consciousness. Enlightenment explains faith as an error and a fiction concerning the very thing that Enlightenment itself is. —Enlightenment, which wants to teach faith the new wisdom, does not thereby tell it anything new. After all, for faith too its object is just this: a pure essence of its own consciousness, such that this consciousness does not take itself to be lost or negated in it, but rather puts its confidence in it; to be precise, it finds itself *therein as this* consciousness, that is, as *self*-consciousness. Whomsoever I trust, the *certitude* of *his* own self is for me the *certitude* of *my* self; in him I am aware of my being for myself in that he recognizes it, and that it is purpose and essence for him. Trust, however, is faith, because the consciousness of the believer is *immediately connected* with its object and [298] thus also intuits that the consciousness is *one* with it and in it. —Furthermore, since what is object for me is that in which I recognize myself, I am for myself, at the same time, in the object as *another* self-consciousness in general that means, one that has become estranged therein from its particular singularity, from its natural and contingent state, but that in the object remains partly self-consciousness and partly, indeed, *essential* consciousness as its pure insight. —Implied in the concept of pure insight is not merely that consciousness is aware of itself in the object of its insight and (without first leaving this thought and returning then into itself) possesses itself *immediately* therein, but, even more, that consciousness is conscious of itself as the *mediating* movement as well, or of itself as *doing* and producing. The unity of consciousness, as unity of *self* and object, is thereby *for consciousness* in its thought. —Even this consciousness is faith as well; "obedience and the deed" form a necessary moment, through which the certainty of its being in the absolute essence is given status. This deed of faith, of course, does not operate in such a way that the absolute essence itself is thereby brought forth. But the absolute essence of faith is essentially not the *abstract* essence that could exist beyond the believing consciousness; on the contrary, it is the spirit of the community, the unity of abstract essence and self-consciousness. In order for the essence to be this common spirit, the communal deed must be an essential moment. This spirit is the essence *only through the productive act* of consciousness; or, instead, it is essence *not without* having been produced by consciousness; or, even though the production is essential, it is just as essentially not the sole ground of the essence but rather only a moment.[159] The essence is at the same time on its own.

From the other side the concept of pure insight is itself something 114–550 *other* than its object; for just this negative determination constitutes the object.[160] Hence from its other side as well, pure insight expresses the essence of faith as something *foreign* to self-consciousness, which is not *its* essence but is foisted upon it like a changeling. Except that Enlightenment is here quite stupid; faith experiences it as a way of speaking that does not know what it says and that does not understand the issue when it talks of priestly deceit and popular delusion. It speaks about it as if, through the hocus pocus and sleight of hand of priests, something absolutely *foreign* and *alien* was foisted on consciousness in place of the essence, and says at the same time that it is something essential in consciousness that it believes in it, trusts it, and seeks to make it enjoyable; this means that it intuits therein *its pure* essence just as much as *its* singular and universal *individuality*, and through its own deed produces this unity of itself with its essence. Enlightenment immediately expresses that what it declares to be *foreign* to consciousness is what is *most its own*.[161] —Therefore, how [299] can it speak of deceit and delusion? since that Enlightenment *at once* asserts the opposite of what it affirms about faith, instead it shows *itself* to faith as the conscious *lie*. How may delusion and deceit occur where consciousness has immediately in its truth the *certainty of itself*, where it possesses *itself* in its object[?], since it finds itself therein as much as it produces itself. The distinction is no longer present even in words. —If the general question has been posed: "Whether it is permissible to deceive a people[?]"[162] the answer in fact must be that the

---

159. The reference is back to the identification of the universal mass and the Self. Free thought must accept what religion already knows: the absolute essence is the unity between the people and religion. What has to be overcome is the superstition and despotism, *not faith*.

160. The "other side" refers not to the object of the Concept but to the form of the concept itself. Here we are looking at "pure insight" from the vantage point of the purity and simplicity of self-consciousness, and from that viewpoint "pure insight" is just being stupid in its criticisms of religion. (The references to pure insights' objections to religion are in ¶107–543).

161. That is, the pure insight of Enlightenment claims that it is "pure" and "simple"; that it is a "religious" being. So, either Enlightenment is not opposed to religion, since it embraces the form of the religious concept, or it is opposed to it, but then it could not claim to have the "truth" of self-consciousness.

162. This question was suggested by D'Alembert for an essay competition to be given by the Berlin Academy of Science. The competition was won by D'Alembert's friend, the astronomer Frédéric de Castillon, in 1779. To be even more

question is senseless, because it is impossible to deceive a people on this question. —Bronze instead of gold, a counterfeit bill instead of a genuine one may well be sold to some, a lost battle may be palmed off as a victory to many, and other lies about sensory things and singular events may be made believable for a period; but in the knowledge of the essence where consciousness has the immediate *certainty of itself* the thought of deception falls away entirely.[163]

115–551   Let us see further how faith experiences Enlightenment in the *differentiated* moments of its consciousness, to which the indicated intention initially only went into the universal. These moments are: pure thinking or (as object) *absolute essence* in and for itself; second, its *connection* with the essence as a *knowing,* or the *ground of its faith;* and finally, its connection with it in its act, in other words *its service.* Just as pure insight has misjudged and belied itself generally in faith, so it will behave in an equally perverted way in these moments.

116–552   Pure insight behaves negatively to *the absolute essence* of believing consciousness. This essence is pure *thinking;* pure thinking posited within its own self as object or as *essence.* In the believing consciousness, this *in-itself* of thinking acquires at the same time, for consciousness, the form that is for itself—but still only the empty form—of objectivity; it is determinate as something *represented.* Since pure insight is pure consciousness from the side of the *self that exists for itself,* however, the *other* appears to it as something *negative in self-consciousness.* This could still be taken either as the pure *in itself* of thinking, or else as the *being* of sense-certainty. However, since it is, at the same time, actual consciousness for the *self* and for

---

precise, D'Alembert raised two questions in his correspondence with Frederick II of Prussia. The first question was whether religion (that is, superstition) was useful for the control and maintenance of the populace. Frederick argued that it was, considering that the populace was stupid and that it needed to be educated, thus religious instruction was useful for that purpose. It was useful for the government as well, since religion is a vehicle to control people. D'Alembert replied that "The people is undoubtedly a stupid animal, but give it the truth it will grasp it;" further, that it is a disease and the only way to cure a disease is to remove the cause of infection (see his letter 18 December 1769). The second question concerned whether the people should be deceived if it was in their interest. D'Alembert urged that error and superstition should be combated with "finesse and patience" and not to draw attention to the views of philosophy, otherwise the philosophers themselves will be indicted for stirring up trouble. (See his letter 7 May 1770.)

163. In part Hegel is agreeing with the *philosophes,* who held that there are "natural truths" that we all know by our own rational faculties, but he is also saying that this entire question is moot, since the people have never been deceived by fraudulent religion; they always have known that the "true religion" is in the form of pure and simple self-consciousness that lies in a communal spirit.

it as a *self* that has an object, its proper object as such is a *common existing thing of sense certainty.*[164] Its object appears to it under the *representation* of faith. Pure insight condemns the representation, and in it its own object. [300] Against faith, however, it already commits the injustice of considering the object of faith as if it were its own. Hence it says about faith that its absolute essence is a piece of stone, a block of wood that has eyes but does not see, or else a bit of dough, grown in a field, transformed by men, to be returned there;[165]—or [it speaks of] whatever other way faith anthropomorphises the essence, [that is,] makes itself objective and representational.

At this point the Enlightenment, which purports to be what is pure,   117–553 makes what for spirit is eternal life and the Holy Spirit into an actual *perishable thing,* and defiles it with the inherently null perspective of sense-certainty. This perspective is in no way present in faith's act of worship, so that Enlightenment is simply lying when it attributes it to faith. What faith reveres is not stone for it at all, or wood, or bread, or any other temporal, sensible thing. If it occurs to the Enlightenment to say that faith's object is *also* this, or indeed it is this implicitly and in truth, then faith on the one hand is equally aware of *that* "also," but it lies outside of its worship; on the other hand, no stone or anything of that kind is something "in itself" for faith; rather what is in itself for faith is the essence of pure thinking alone.

The *second moment* is the connection of faith as *knowing* conscious-   118–554 ness with this essence. For faith as a thinking pure consciousness, this essence is immediate, but the pure consciousness is just as much a *mediated* connection of certainty with truth; it is this connection that constitutes the *ground* of *faith.* This ground becomes for the Enlightenment a contingent *knowing of contingent* events as well. The ground of knowing, however, is the *knowing* universal, and in its truth the absolute spirit that in the abstract pure consciousness or thinking as such is only the absolute *essence,* yet as self-consciousness is the *knowing* of itself. Pure insight posits this knowing universal, the *simple self-knowing spirit,* as the negative of self-consciousness too. Indeed, it is itself the *pure, mediated* thinking, that is, self-mediating thinking; it is pure knowing. But since it is *pure insight, pure knowing* that does not yet know itself—that is to say, it

---

164. The accusation is that faith has as its object the worship of some material thing; so for pure insight faith is *material* and in religion it is idolatry. Materialism pretends that faith is just like itself in terms of content.

165. "Their idols are silver and gold, the handiwork of men. They have mouths but do not speak; they have eyes but do not see. . . . Their makers shall be like them, everyone who believes in them," Psalm 115: 4ff. Cf. also Psalm 135: 15–18.

is not yet aware that it is this pure, mediating movement, which, like everything that pure insight itself is, appears to pure insight to be something else. Grasped thus in its actualization, it develops its essential moment; however this appears to pure insight as belonging to faith, and in its determinacy to be external to insight, [that is,] as a contingent knowing of just such ordinary everyday stories. It thus attributes to religious belief at this point that its [301] certainty is based on some *singular, historical testimonies* that, considered as historical testimonies, clearly do not evidence the degree of certainty concerning its content that newspaper stories offer us about any event whatever; that, in addition, its certainty rests on the chance of the *preservation* of these testimonies—on the one hand, preservation on paper and, on the other hand, preservation by the skill and trustworthiness of the transmission from one paper to another—and finally rests on the correct interpretation of the meaning of dead words and letters.[166] In fact, however, it does not occur to faith to tie its certainty to such testimonies and contingencies. In its certainty faith is an ingenuous relation to its absolute object, a pure knowing of it, which does not mix letters, paper, and scribes with its consciousness of the absolute essence, and which therefore is not mediated through things of that sort.[167] Rather, this consciousness is the self-mediating ground of its knowing; it is the spirit itself that is the witness to itself, as much in the *inwardness* of the *singular* consciousness as through the *universal presence* of everyone's faith in it. If, by appealing to history, faith also wants to offer that kind of support, or at least of confirmation, of its content about which the Enlightenment speaks, and seriously supposes and acts as if it depended on it, then it has already let

---

166. Hegel seems to be referring to the argument of Pastor Johann Melchoir Goeze, author of *Something Provisional, Lessing's Weakness* (1777)—in which he attempted to show that Lessing was an atheist and that Christianity is proven true through historical documents—and to Lessing's reply to this tract, called *Anti-Goeze* (1778). The debate arose from Lessing's work *Concerning the Proof of Spirit and Might* (1777). In the latter he argues that the testimony of the Gospels are not proofs, and that the worth of the Gospels is only moral insofar as morals agree with reason. Goeze uses traditional religious arguments against Lessing: the divine inspiration of scriptures; the rightness of authority; and, if one accepted Lessing's propositions, the undermining of moral authority.

167. In part three of *Something Provisional* Goeze argues that religion is something "subjective," and its truth consists in *die Gemütsfassung der Menschen*—"the human beings' constitutive character of mind"—which can be seen in all religions and in all peoples. This character of mind gives the individual certainty and knowledge of God. Hegel appears to side with Pastor Goeze in this debate, at least to the extent that faith is a character of mind that is not concerned with the contingencies surrounding the historical texts on which faith is based.

itself be seduced by the Enlightenment;[168] and efforts of this sort to support or defend itself are only testimonies that it offers of its infection.

Still the third side remains: the *connection of consciousness with the abso-* 119–555
lute essence as an *act.* This act is the sublating of the particularity of the individual, or of the natural mode of its being-for-self, from which his certainty proceeds of being pure self-consciousness or of being one with the essence by his act, that is, as singular consciousness *which is for itself.*
—Since purposiveness and purpose are distinct in the act, and since pure insight also *relates negatively* in connection with this act and, as in the other moments, disavows itself, it must display itself with respect to the *purposiveness* as ignorant, since the insight that is bound up with the intention to make purpose and means agree appears to pure insight as something other, indeed as its opposite. With respect to *purpose,* however, it takes evil, enjoyment, and possession to be its purpose, and demonstrates itself thereby to be the most impure intention; for in this way the pure intention, as other, is impure intention.[169]

---

168. Hegel plays on the definition of faith given by St. Paul, "Faith is the substance of things hoped for, the evidence of things not seen," Hebrews 11:1. Faith that has given itself over to a material justification of belief is just not "faith."

169. The purpose of faith is salvation of the individual, which is of material interest to each person. But the purposiveness of faith is to worship God for no other reason than this is what the purity of faith demands. These two components of faith are used against it by the materialist.

With this third moment faith sees pure insight as the evil enemy, and it begins to develop its case against the materialist. In its first moment, faith's pure thinking recognizes that the accusations against it are factitious because the object of faith is not the relic, the statute, or the dough that makes the Eucharistic; its object is its own pure and simple thinking. Faith does not know its essence as of yet, because it does not recognize that its thinking is its essence. In the second moment the necessary connection is made between thinking and knowledge of its essence. The religious understanding is not contingent upon the accidents of history but only upon its own character of mind. Thus the accusation that faith relies on historical truth, which is subject to doubt, is a misleading claim. The *true* witness of faith is the religious experience itself, which is known in simple feeling and pure thought. The third moment is the act of religious consciousness as what makes the connection between consciousness and its absolute object. This act is purely moral. The true purpose of faith is *virtue,* specifically to attain the qualities of poverty, chastity, and obedience (that is, the Evangelical Counsels). These virtuous deeds are *purposive,* since we have no material interest in them—they serve our spiritual life only, not our material benefit. With the evangelical virtues the individual attains self-satisfaction defined beyond the limits of pleasure, wealth, and material interest. The secular thought of the Enlightenment *misidentifies* the genuine purpose of life. Its attacks reveal that it supposes that the purpose of life is pleasure, and thus they show its ignorance. The religious consciousness, on the

120–556   Henceforth with respect to *purposiveness* we see that the Enlightenment finds it foolish whenever the believing individual presents himself as
the higher consciousness, [302] not bound to natural pleasure and satisfaction, by *actually* denying himself natural pleasure and satisfaction and
demonstrating *by his action* that the disdain of them is no *lie*, but that it is
true. —It finds it equally foolish that by divesting himself of his property
the individual absolves himself of his determinacy of being absolutely singular, of excluding everyone else and possessing property; by this he does
in truth show that he is not in earnest about his isolation but is, on the
contrary, exalted above the natural necessity of making himself singular,
and in this absolute singularity of being-for-self he disavows the other as
being the same *as himself*. —Pure insight finds both as pointless as they
are unjust. It is *pointless* to deny oneself enjoyment and give one's possessions away in order to show oneself free from enjoyment and possessions;
conversely, it will therefore take for a *fool* the one who, in order to eat,
avails himself of the means of really eating. —Pure insight finds it unjust,
as well, to deny oneself a meal, and give butter and eggs away, not for
money, and money not for butter and eggs, but directly without getting
anything back.[170] It declares a meal or the possession of such things to be
a selfish goal, and itself thereby to be in fact a very impure intention, for
which it is quite essential to be involved with such pleasure and possessions. Or again it asserts that pure intention necessitates elevation above
natural existence and above coveting the means for that; only it finds it to
be foolish and unjust that this elevation should be demonstrated *in action;*
in other words, this pure intention is in truth the deception of pretending
to, and requiring, an *inner* elevation, but of declaring that doing so in earnest—*actually* putting it *into practice* and *demonstrating its truth*—is
superfluous, foolish, and even unjust. —In this way it belies *itself* both as
pure insight (for it belies the immediately purposive action) and as pure
intention (for it belies the intention of proving itself to be freed from the
ends of singularity).

121–557   This is how the Enlightenment offers itself for faith to experience. It
makes its entrance in this evil garb because, precisely through the relation
to an other, it gives itself a *negative reality,* in other words, displays itself
as the contrary of itself; pure insight and intention must take this relation

---

contrary, knows itself in its acts, and with this knowledge it shows the wickedness
of pure insight. Genuine virtue is only the *service* of worship. To pure insight, the
separation of pleasure from the "good life" is absurd, and the religious concept
remains alien to it.

170. The attack is directed against the Evangelical Counsels and, in general,
the thought that virtue is the selfless activity of the self.

upon themselves, however, for it is their actualization. —At first this appears as negative reality. But perhaps its *positive reality* is better constituted; let us see how it behaves. —When all prejudice and superstition have been banned, the question arises: "But now what? What is the truth that the Enlightenment has promulgated instead of this?" —It has already expressed this positive content in its rooting out [303] of error, for that self-estrangement is equally its positive reality. —In what, for faith, is absolute spirit, pure insight takes whatever *determinate aspect* it discovers—wood, stone, and so on—to be singular actual things; since in this way it conceives *any determinacy* whatever, that is, all content and its fulfillment, to be *finitude*, as *human essence and representation*, the *absolute essence* becomes for it a *vacuum* with which no determination, no predicate, can be coupled. A coupling of this kind would be criminal, and it is just from this coupling that the monstrosities of superstition have been begotten. Of course reason, or *pure insight*, is not itself empty, since its negative is *for it* and is its content; on the contrary it is rich, though only in singularity and limits; neither allowing such things to come near the absolute essence nor coupling them with it—that is reason's enlightened way of life, which knows how to put itself and the riches of finitude in their place, and how to treat the absolute with due dignity.

Over against this empty essence and as *the second moment* of the positive truth of the Enlightenment, the *singularity* of consciousness and of all being in general, which has been excluded from absolute essence, stands *as absolute being in and of itself.* Consciousness, which in its primordial actuality is *sense-certainty* and *meaning,* here turns back from the whole path of its experience and is once again a knowing of the *pure negative of itself,* that is, of *sensible or subsisting things,* which stand indifferently over against its *being-for-self.* At this point, however, it is not *immediate* natural consciousness, but it has *become* so. Abandoned at first to all the complications where it is brought to ruin through its development and now brought back to its first shape by pure insight, consciousness has *experienced* this shape as *result. Grounded* on the insight of the nullity of all other shapes of consciousness, and hence of all "beyonds" of sense-certainty, this sense-certainty is no longer meaning but is rather the absolute truth. This nullity of everything that goes beyond sense-certainty is, to be sure, only a negative proof of this truth. But it is amenable to no other; for the positive truth of sense-certainty with respect to itself is just the *unmediated* being-for-self of the concept as object—of the concept, indeed, in the form of otherness. In other words, it is for every consciousness *absolutely certain* that it *is* and *other actual things* are outside it, and that consciousness as well as these things are *in and for themselves,* or *absolute,* in their *natural* being. [304]

122–558

123–559   Finally, *the third moment of the truth of the Enlightenment* is the relation of the singular essences to the absolute essence, the connection of the first two moments. As pure insight into the *equal* or *unrestricted,* insight *goes beyond* the *unequal* (namely finite actuality) as well or beyond itself as mere otherness. As the beyond of this otherness, it has *the void,* with which it thus connects sensible actuality. The two sides do not both enter in the determination of this *relation* as *content,* for one is the void, and so a content is present only in virtue of the other, namely, of sensible actuality. The *form* of the connection, however, to whose determination the side of the *in-itself* contributes, can be fashioned as one pleases; for the form is what is *in itself negative,* and hence what is self-opposed: being as well as nothing; *in-itself* as well as *contrary;* or what is the same thing, the connection *of actuality* with the *in-itself* as the *beyond* is just as much a *negating* as it is a *positing* of it. Finite actuality, then, can in fact be taken just as one requires. So the sensible is now connected *positively* with the absolute as with the *in-itself,* and sensible actuality itself is *in itself.* The absolute makes, cherishes, and protects it. Again, it is connected with it as with its contrary, or with its *nonbeing;* according to this relation it is not in itself, but only *for an other.* If in the preceding shape of consciousness the *concepts* of the antithesis were determined as *good* and *bad,* here for pure insight they turn instead into the purer abstractions of being *in itself* and being *for an other.*

124–560   Both types of consideration—the positive as much as the negative connection of the finite with the in-itself—are nevertheless in fact equally necessary, and everything is therefore just as much *for another* as it is *in itself;* in other words, everything is *useful.*[171] —Everything gives itself up to others, now allows itself to be used by others, and is *for them;* and now again digs in its heels, so to speak, acts stubborn to the other, is for itself, and uses the other in its turn. —For man, as the thing that is *conscious* of this connection, his essence and station result therefrom. As natural consciousness *in itself,* he is *good* the way he immediately is, as singular he is *absolute,* and the other is *for him;* and indeed, since for him as the animal conscious of itself the moments have the significance of universality, *everything* is for his pleasure and delight; as one comes from the hand of God, he goes about in the world as in a garden planted on his account.[172] —He must have plucked from the tree of the knowledge of good and evil,

---

171. Hegel is referring to the idea of utility. In particular he has Helvétius in mind, who says "The idea of utility; and, taking this idea as it is generally understood, I understand by this word every idea proper to our instruction or our amusement," *De l'esprit* (2nd ed., 1795), II, p. 9.

172. "Then the Lord God planted a Garden in Eden, in the east, and he placed there the man whom he had formed," Genesis 2: 8.

too.[173] [305] He thereby possesses a usefulness that distinguishes him from all others; for as it happens, his nature, good in itself, is *also* so created that an excess of delight does it harm, or rather, his singularity has *also its beyond* in it, and can go beyond itself and destroy itself. To counter this reason is for him a useful means to set a convenient limit to this transgression or rather to maintain himself even while going beyond the determinate, for this is the force of consciousness. The enjoyment of the conscious essence, which is implicitly *universal,* must throughout all multiplicity and duration not be something determinate, but universal. Its measure therefore has the determination of preventing the pleasure from being interrupted in its multiplicity and duration; in other words, the determination of the measure is the measureless. —Just as everything is useful for man, so he is useful too, and his determination is just as much to make himself generally useful and a universally serviceable member of the troop. So far as he looks after himself, to just that extent does he have to put himself out for the others, and so far as he puts himself out, to that extent does he look after himself; one hand washes the other. Wherever he finds himself, it is right for him, he uses others and is used.

It is quite another thing to be useful to each other in different ways; but all things have this reciprocity of use through their essence, namely, of being connected with the absolute in a double way: positive—thereby to be *on its own account;* negative—thereby to be *for another.*[174] The *connection* with the absolute being, or religion, is thus, in all utility, the most useful; for it is *pure usefulness itself:* it is this persistence of all things, or their being *on their own account,* and the fall of all things, or their *being for another.*[175]

125–561

---

173. "Out of the ground the Lord God made various trees grow . . . with the tree of life in the middle of the garden and the tree of the knowledge of good and bad," Genesis 2: 9. Hegel is showing how the Enlightenment imitates religious consciousness but also perverts the sense of what is good.

174. The absolute for the materialist is nature, which has been deified. See D'Holbach's invocation to the Goddess of Nature, in *System of Nature:* "'O Nature, sovereign of all beings! And ye, her daughters, Virtue, Reason, and Truth! Remain forever our only Divinities," p. 338. However, this invocation is empty, unless he means that nature is spirit, in which case we return to an attitude of faith.

175. The critical editors cite Frédéric de Castillon, who contested this question in his *Dissertation sur la question: Est-il utile au Peuple d'être trompé, soit qu'on l'induise dans de nouvelles erreurs, ou qu'on l'entretienne dans celles où il est?* (Berlin, 1780)—*The Dissertation on the Question: Is it Useful for the People to be Deceived. . . .* But the point that religion is actually useful for the people is also contested by D'Holbach, p. 312ff.

126–562   For faith, of course, this positive result is as much an abomination as
Enlightenment's negative attitude. This *insight* into the absolute essence,
which sees nothing in it except the *absolute* essence, the *être suprême* or *the
void*—this *intention* that everything in its immediate mode of being is *in
itself* or good, that finally the *connection* of the singular conscious being
with the absolute essence or *religion* is completely expressed in the concept of utility, is simply *abhorrent* to faith. This *wisdom* peculiar to the
Enlightenment necessarily appears to faith both as mere *platitude* and, at
once, as the *confession* of platitudes, because it consists of knowing nothing
of the absolute essence, or, which is the same thing, of knowing this quite
banal truth, that it is simply just the *absolute essence*. On the contrary, it
consists of knowing only about finitude, indeed knowing it to be the true,
and of knowing the knowledge of it as the true to be what is highest.

127–563   As against the Enlightenment, faith has the divine right—the right of
absolute *self-identity* or of pure thinking, and experiences [306] nothing
but injustice at its hands; for the Enlightenment distorts it in all its
moments and makes them into something other than they are in faith. As
against faith and for its truth, however, the Enlightenment has only human
right; for the injustice that it perpetrates is the right of *inequality*, and it
consists of inverting and transforming—a right that belongs to the nature
of *self-consciousness* in contrast to the simple essence, or *thinking*. But since
its right is the right of self-consciousness, the Enlightenment will not only
also maintain its right (so that two equal rights of spirit remain confronting each other and neither can satisfy the other) but it will assert the absolute right; for self-consciousness is the negativity of the concept which is
not just *for itself* but also overreaches its opposite, and because faith itself
is consciousness, it cannot deny to Enlightenment its right.

128–564   For the Enlightenment relates to the believing consciousness not in
terms of its own peculiar principles but in terms of those that the believing consciousness has in it. The Enlightenment brings together for it only
its own thoughts, which unconsciously fall apart for it. It reminds believing
consciousness in *one* of its modes about the *other*, which it has *as well*, but
which it always forgets when it is in the other mode. Enlightenment
proves itself to believing consciousness to be pure insight, just because in
one *determinate* moment it sees the whole, hence it brings into play the
opposite that is connected with each moment and, by transmuting the one
into the other, highlights the negative essence of both thoughts, [which is]
the *concept*. To faith, Enlightenment thus appears to be a distortion and a
lie, because it points out the *otherness* of its moments; it thus appears to it
to be immediately making something other out of them than they are in
their singularity. But this *other* is equally essential; and it is in truth
present in the believing consciousness itself, except that the latter does

not think about it, but has it somewhere else. Hence this other is neither alien to it, nor can it be disavowed by it.

The very Enlightenment that reminds faith of the opposite of its sepa- 129–565 rated moments is, however, no more enlightened about itself. It relates quite *negatively* to faith to the extent that it excludes its own content from its purity, and takes it to be the *negative* of itself. Hence it neither acknowledges itself in this negative—in the content of faith—nor, for this reason, does it bring the two thoughts together: the one that it advances, and the one against which this latter is advanced. Since it does not acknowledge that the very thing it damns in faith is immediately its own thought, it is itself [involved] in the opposition of the two moments, of which it only recognizes one, in every case the one opposed to faith; [307] but it separates the other from this one just as faith did. It therefore does not produce the unity of both as their unity, that is, as the concept; but the concept *originates* for it on its own; in other words, Enlightenment discovers the concept only as *present*. For implicitly this is just the realization of pure insight: that it, the essence of which is the concept, first comes to be something absolutely *other* to itself and disavows itself, since the antithesis of the concept is the absolute antithesis; then out of this otherness it comes to itself, or to its concept. —The Enlightenment *is*, however, just this movement; it is the still unconscious activity of the pure concept, which does indeed come to itself as object, but takes this to be an *other;* the nature of the concept is not within its ken either: namely, that it is the not-differentiated that divides itself absolutely. —Against faith, therefore, pure insight is the *might* of the concept to the extent that it is the movement and the connecting of the moments that lie apart from each other in the believing consciousness—a connecting in which their contradiction comes to light. Herein lies the absolute *right* of the dominion it exercises over faith. The *actuality* to which it brings this dominion, however, is just this: that the believing consciousness is itself the concept and hence itself recognizes the opposite that insight brings to it. Enlightenment thereby maintains its right against faith, because it makes effective for faith what is indeed necessary for it and what it has in itself.

At first the Enlightenment asserts the moment of the concept to be an 130–566 *act* of *consciousness;* it asserts this *against* faith: that its absolute essence is the essence of *its own* consciousness as a self, in other words, that the essence is *produced* by consciousness.[176] For the believing consciousness its

---

176. Hegel might well be thinking of Spinoza and his followers. The *Theological-Political Treatise* (1670) is a good case in point to show that the "truths" of religion are to be rationalized, and that the rational virtues (demonstrated in Part IV of the *Ethics*) are compatible with Christian teaching. During the

absolute essence, just because it is *in-itself* for it, is at the same time not like an alien thing that *has arisen,* one knows not whence or why. On the contrary, its confidence consists precisely in finding itself as *this* personal consciousness in this essence, and its obedience and service consist in bringing it forth as *its own* absolute essence through its own *act.* Enlightenment in fact reminds faith of this only when faith simply expresses the *in-itself* of the absolute essence to be *beyond* the *act* of consciousness. —However, since Enlightenment does highlight, in the one-sidedness of faith, the opposite moment of its *act* over against the *being,* which is all that faith thinks of here, while for itself it does not bring its own thoughts together either, it isolates the pure moment of the *act,* and says of faith's *in-itself* that it is *only* something *produced* by consciousness. For the isolated act, opposed to the *in-itself,* is a contingent act and as something represented it is a spawning of fictions—representations that have no being *in themselves;* that is how Enlightenment views the content of faith. [308] —But, on the other hand, pure insight says the contrary as well. To the extent that it affirms the moment of *otherness,* which the concept contains, it says that the essence of faith is the kind of thing that *does not concern* consciousness but is *beyond* it, alien and unknown. For faith, just as on the one hand it trusts in the essence and finds the *certainty of itself* therein, so on the other hand the essence is unsearchable in its ways and unattainable in its being.[177]

131–567   In addition, the Enlightenment asserts against the believing consciousness a claim that faith itself concedes when it considers the object of its devotion to be wood or stone, or to be any other finite, anthropomorphic determinacy. For, since it is this split consciousness—in having a *beyond* of *actuality* and a pure *this-side* of that beyond—there is in fact present in faith this view of sensible things *as well,* in which the sensible thing *is valid in* and *of itself;* but it does not bring these two thoughts of *what is in and of itself* together, the one which is the *pure essence* for it, the other a common *sensible thing.* —Even its pure consciousness is affected by the latter view, after all; because it lacks the concept, the distinctions of its supersensible realm are a series of independent *shapes,* and their movement a *happening;* that is to say, they are only in *representation* and have the characteristics of sensible being about them. —In a similar way, the Enlightenment on its part isolates *actuality* as an essence forsaken by spirit, determinacy as an undisturbed finitude, which would not be itself a

---

Enlightenment Moses Mendelssohn in Germany espouses this form of reconciliation, as did Kant, at the end of the Enlightenment, in *Religion within the Bounds of Reason Alone* (1793).

177. "How deep are the riches and wisdom and the knowledge of God! How inscrutable his judgments, how unsearchable his ways!" Romans 11: 33.

moment in the spiritual movement of the essence, neither nothing nor a something *that was* in and for itself, but rather something disappearing.

It is clear that the same thing happens with the *ground* of *knowing.*   132–568
Believing consciousness itself acknowledges a contingent *knowing,* for it has a relation to contingencies, and the absolute essence itself is for faith in the form of a represented common actuality. As a result, the believing consciousness is *also* a certainty that does not possess the truth, and it confesses itself to be an unessential consciousness of this kind, on this side of the self-confirming and self-authenticating spirit. —This moment is forgotten, however, in its spiritual, immediate knowing of the absolute essence. —But the Enlightenment, which reminds it thereof, again thinks *only* about the contingent knowing and forgets the other; it thinks only about the mediation that occurs by means of a *foreign* third, not about the mediation in which the immediate itself is the third by which it is mediated with the other, namely, with *its own self.*

Finally, the Enlightenment discovers in its intention of the *act* of faith   133–569
that throwing off [309] enjoyment and possessions is unjust and pointless. —With respect to this injustice, Enlightenment obtains the agreement of the believing consciousness because the latter itself acknowledges this actuality of possessing, maintaining, and enjoying property. In its assertion of property it behaves in so much the more stiff-necked and isolated a way, (just as it throws itself all the more crudely into its enjoyment) since its religious act—of *giving* possession and enjoyment *up*—lies beyond this actuality, and purchases for it freedom for this side. Because of this antithesis in the deed, this service of sacrificing natural drives and pleasures has no truth; the retention coexists *with* the sacrifice.[178] It is only a *sign,* which accomplished the genuine sacrifice only in a small part, and only *represents* it in the deed.

From the perspective of *purposiveness,* the Enlightenment finds it inapt   134–570
to renounce *one* possession, to deny *one* pleasure in order to know and prove oneself free of *all* possessions and of *all* pleasure. The believing consciousness itself takes the absolute act as a *universal* act; not only is the action of its absolute essence as its object something universal for it, but the singular consciousness should also show itself completely and universally free from its sensuous essence.[179] The renunciation of a *singular*

---

178. The religious houses espouse poverty as a virtue (one of the Evangelical Counsels), but they in fact grow rich. Voltaire satirizes the Jesuits in *Candide* (1759) for their great wealth.

179. This is typical of the Jansenist's doctrine in eighteenth-century France and Belgium. Stendhal's character of Julien Sorel in *The Scarlet and Black* (1830) has this type of Jansenistic outlook.

possession or the repudiation of a *singular* pleasure, however, is not this *universal* activity; and since in the activity the *purpose,* which is universal, and the *execution,* which is singular, must stand before consciousness in their incompatibility, the activity shows itself to be the kind of action in which the consciousness plays no part, and thereby this action is in fact too naive to be an activity. It is too naive to fast in order to free itself from the pleasure of meal time, too naive to remove other pleasures *from the body* as Origen did, to show itself rid of them.[180] The activity in fact shows itself to be an *external* and *singular* act; but desire is rooted *internally* and is something *universal;* its pleasure disappears neither with the instrument nor through singular abstinence.[181]

135–571   But the Enlightenment for its part isolates what is *internal* and *inactual* from actuality, in just the same way that it maintains the externality of thinghood against the inwardness of faith in its intuition and devotion. It makes the *intention* or the *thought* what is essential and spares itself thereby the actual accomplishment of liberation from natural goals. On the contrary, this inwardness is itself the formal kind that has its satisfaction in natural drives, and that is justified by the very fact that it is internal, that it belongs to *universal* being, namely, to nature. [310]

136–572   The Enlightenment thus has an irresistible dominion over faith by virtue of the fact that the moments to which it ascribes value are found in faith's own consciousness. When we look more closely at the effect of this power, the behavior of the Enlightenment to faith seems to rend the *beautiful* unity of *trust* and of immediate *certainty,* to defile its *spiritual* consciousness with lowly thoughts of *sensuous* actuality, and to destroy its *peacefully* submissive and *secure* demeanor with the *vanity* of understanding and of selfish will and accomplishment. But, on the contrary, it does in fact start the sublating of the *thoughtless* or rather the *unconceiving separation* that is present in faith. The believing consciousness lives by a double measure and a double weight; it has two kinds of eyes, two kinds of ears, two kinds of tongue and speech; it has doubled all its representations without ever comparing these two senses. In other words, faith lives within two realms of perception: one, the perception of the *sleeping* consciousness, living simply with unconceiving thoughts, the other the perception of waking consciousness, living simply in sensible actuality; in each realm faith maintains its own domestic economy. —The Enlightenment

---

180. . . . *wie Origines.* Origen, a father of the Church, castrated himself in order to avoid sexual temptation.

181. The comment is directed against the virtue of chastity. This is another one of the Evangelical Counsels, and one that the religious houses had difficulty keeping.

illuminates that heavenly world with the representations of the sensible one and shows the former the finitude of the latter; faith cannot deny this because it is self-consciousness and, hence, the unity to which both ways of representing belong and in which they do not fall asunder. After all, they belong to the same indivisible *simple* self into which faith has passed.

Faith has thereby lost the content that was its element and collapses 137–573 into a dank weave of the spirit within itself.[182] It has been expelled from its kingdom, or rather, this kingdom is plundered, since the waking consciousness has snatched to itself every discrimination and elaboration of the kingdom and laid claim to all its parts, for the earth as its property restored them to it.[183] But faith is not satisfied by this, for with this illumination nothing but singular essence has arisen everywhere, so that only actuality without essence and finitude divested of spirit has a claim on spirit. —Since faith lacks content and cannot remain in this void—in other words, since in going beyond the finite that is its only content it finds nothing but the void—it is a *pure yearning;* its truth is an empty *beyond* for which no appropriate content remains to be found, since everything has ties elsewhere. —In fact, faith has become the same as the Enlightenment, namely, the consciousness of the connection of the finite that is in itself with the predicateless, unknown, and unknowable absolute, only *that the Enlightenment* is the *satisfied, faith,* the *unsatisfied* Enlightenment. It has yet to be seen whether the Enlightenment can rest in its satisfaction; that yearning of the troubled spirit, which grieves for the loss of its spiritual world, stands in reserve. The Enlightenment, too, has this defect of unsatisfied yearning within itself: as *pure* [311] *object,* in its *empty* absolute essence; as *act* and *movement,* in *going out* of the bounds of its singular essence to an unfulfilled beyond; as *fulfilled object* in the *selflessness* that pertains to what is useful. It will sublate this defect. From a closer consideration of the positive results that are its truth, it will emerge there that the defect has already been implicitly sublated.

b. The Truth of Enlightenment

Thus the dank weave of spirit that no longer differentiates itself has 138–574 entered into itself beyond consciousness, which in contrast has become transparent to itself. The first moment of this clarity is determined in its necessity and condition by the very fact that pure insight, or that which is

---

182. The reference is probably to the weaving of the serpent of wisdom, cf. Genesis 3: 14: "Then the Lord said to the serpent: . . . On your belly you shall crawl, and dirt you shall eat all the days of your life."

183. Cf. "The Lord God therefore banished him from the garden of Eden to till the ground from which he had been taken." Genesis 3: 23.

in-itself the concept, actualizes itself. It does so by positing otherness or determinacy within itself. In this way it is negative pure insight, that is, the negation of the concept; this is equally pure, and therefore it has come to be a *pure thing,* or an absolute essence, which has no further determination in any other way. More exactly defined, insight qua absolute concept is the distinguishing of distinctions that are such no longer; of abstractions, or pure concepts, which no longer maintain themselves; rather, they gain support and differentiation only through the *whole of the movement.* This distinguishing of what is not distinct consists just in the fact that the absolute concept makes itself into its own object and posits over and against itself the *movement* as *essence.* This therefore dispenses with the aspect in which the abstractions or distinctions come to be *held apart,* and thus there comes to be *pure thinking* as *pure thing.* —This, then, is just the dank nonconscious weaving of spirit within itself that faith sank into when it lost its distinct content. At the same time, the weaving is that *movement* of pure self-consciousness for which it ought to be the absolutely foreign beyond. Because this pure self-consciousness is the movement within pure concepts, that is, within distinctions that are no more, it in fact collapses into nonconscious weaving, that is, into pure *feeling* or into pure *thinghood.* —The concept that is self-estranged (for here it still stands at the stage of estrangement) is not aware of the *equal* essence of both aspects: of the movement of self-consciousness and of its absolute essence; it is not aware of their *equal essence* that in point of fact is their substance and subsistence. Since it is not aware of this unity, essence is valid for it only in the form of an objective [312] beyond, but the differentiated consciousness that has the in-itself outside it in this way is valid as a finite consciousness.

139–575   With regard to this absolute essence, the Enlightenment gets into the conflict that previously it had with faith but now has with itself; so it divides into two parties.[184] The one party proves itself *victorious* just by disintegrating into two parties; for by so doing it shows that it possesses intrinsically the principle that it has fought against, and thus it has sublated

---

184. The one party that becomes two seems to refer to the *philosophes:* some, such as D'Alembert, were deists who opposed institutional religion but nonetheless claimed that there was a god beyond nature, but there were others, such as Diderot and D'Holbach, who were atheists and claimed that only nature could be called a "god." So the *philosophes* split into two, but it is the atheists who say that they have the principle of Reason that the deists also lay claim to; thus they are the true party of humanity. Even this division is for them proof that the Enlightenment supports liberty and equality, since the division and conflict among the *philosophes* is only the "natural"outcome of a democratic and rational principle at work.

the one-sidedness with which it had previously come on the scene. The interest that divides itself between that party and the other one now enters entirely into the first and forgets the other, because interest finds in it the very antithesis with which it is preoccupied. But at the same time, this antithesis has been raised into that higher victorious element where it presents itself purified, so that the dissension arising in the one party, which seems a misfortune, proves its good fortune instead.

The pure essence itself has no distinction within it; hence distinction 140–576 comes to it in that [there are] two such pure essences for consciousness; in other words, a two-sided consciousness of essence comes to the forefront. —The pure absolute essence is only in pure thinking, or rather it is pure thinking itself; therefore it is quite *beyond* the finite, or *self*-consciousness, and is only the negative essence. But in this way, it is just being—the negative of self-consciousness. As the *negative* of self-consciousness, being is *also* connected with it: it is *external being* that, connected with the self-consciousness in which distinctions and determinacies fall, preserves therein the distinctions of coming to be tasted, seen, and so on; the relation is *sense*-certainty and perception.[185]

If we start from this *sensible* being, into which that negative beyond 141–577 necessarily passes, but abstract from these determinate modes of conscious connection, then pure *matter* is left over as dank weaving and moving within itself. Consequently, it is essential to see that *pure matter* is only that that is left *over* when we *abstract* from seeing, feeling, tasting, and so forth, that is, matter is not what is seen, tasted or felt, and so on; it is not *matter* that is seen, tasted, or felt, but color, a stone or a grain of salt, and so on. Matter is rather a *pure abstraction*, and thereby it is the *pure essence* of *thinking*, or pure thinking itself, which is present as the absolute, not distinguished internally, not determinate, and lacking predicates.

The first Enlightenment calls absolute essence the unpredicated abso- 142–578 lute, which exists beyond actual consciousness in thinking, and from which we started; the second one calls absolute essence *matter*.[186] If these two views were distinguished as *nature* and spirit, or *God*, then the wealth of developed life needed for nature would be wanting in the unconscious

---

185. Hegel is referring to Chapters 1 and 2 of the *Phenomenology:* perception is the truth of sense-certainty; it unifies and universalizes the things of sense but still maintains the sensuous content of representation.

186. The first part of the Enlightenment is the initial form of pure insight: either the deist who adheres to the *être suprême,* e.g., D'Alembert or Rousseau, or the reforming religious who has a subjective religion, e.g., the Jansenist. The second is the materialist who is either an atheist, e.g., D'Holbach or Diderot, or a pantheist, e.g., Lessing.

weaving within itself, and the self-differentiating consciousness would be wanting in spirit or God. The two of them, as we have already [313] seen, are strictly the same concept. The difference does not lie in the subject matter, but simply and solely in the divergent starting points of the two formations and the fact that each stands fast in its own point of view within the movement of thought. If they would set aside their divergent viewpoints, they might come together and realize that what one alleges to be a monster and the other a folly are the same thing. After all, for the first Enlightenment the absolute essence in its pure thinking (or immediately for pure consciousness) is outside finite consciousness; it is its *negative* beyond. Would it but reflect on the fact that, on the one hand, the simple immediacy of thought is nothing but *pure being* and that, on the other hand, what is *negative* for consciousness is at the same time connected with it—that in the negative judgment the copula "is" both separates and also conjoins—then there would result the connection with consciousness of this beyond in the character of an *external entity*, and, hence, the same thing as what is called *pure matter*, [then] the missing moment of the *present* would be achieved.

The second Enlightenment starts from sensible being and then *abstracts* from the sensory connection of tasting, seeing, and so on, and makes being into the pure *in-itself*, into *absolute matter*, which is neither felt nor tasted. This being has become in this way the unpredicated simple, the essence of *pure consciousness:* it is the pure concept as existing *intrinsically* or *pure thinking within itself.* In its consciousness this insight does not take the opposite step from the *entity*, which is *purely* existent, into thought, which is the same as the *purely* existent; nor the step from the purely positive into the purely negative, since the positive is *pure* simply and solely through the negative, while the *pure* negative qua pure is internally self-equivalent and, just for that reason, positive.

In other words neither side has reached the concept of Cartesian metaphysics according to which *being* and *thinking* are *intrinsically* the same;[187] they have not reached the thought that *being, pure being,* is not something *concrete* and *actual*, but rather a pure *abstraction;* and conversely, that pure thinking, self-identity, or essence, in part is the *negative* of self-consciousness, and hence *being;* and in part, as immediate simplicity, is again nothing else than *being: thinking* is *thinghood* or *thinghood* is *thinking.*

---

187. The allusion is to Descartes's *Discourse on Method* (1637), "Ego cogito, ergo sive existo" ("I think, therefore I am or I exist"), better known as *cogito ergo sum.* However, the notion that thinghood is thinking or vice versa is not Cartesian. Hegel is probably referring to how the second party of the Enlightenment, the atheists, treated Descartes's principles. See next note.

Here the essence has *division* in it in such a way that initially two sorts   143–579
of consideration are involved: on the one hand, essence must have the distinction in itself; on the other hand, by this very fact, both types of consideration come together into one—for the abstract moments of pure
being and of the negative, by which they are differentiated, are then
united in the object of these considerations. —The universal they share is
the abstraction of a pure vibration within itself, or of a pure self-thinking.
The simple oscillating movement must sift itself, for it [314] is only movement insofar as it differentiates its moments.[188] This differentiation of
moments leaves behind the unmoved as the empty husk of pure *being*,
which has no actual thinking, no life, within it any longer; for this differentiation as difference is the whole content. However the differentiation
that posits itself *outside of* that *unity* is thus the exchange of moments—of
being *in itself* and *for another* and of being-*for-self*—an exchange that *does
not return into itself;* in other words, it is actuality in the way it is the object
for the actual consciousness of pure insight: it is *usefulness.*

As bad as usefulness may appear to faith, or to sensibility, or also to the   144–580
abstraction that calls itself speculation (which congeals the *in-itself*), nevertheless usefulness is where pure insight completes its realization and
becomes its own *object* (the object that insight no longer rejects and that,
moreover, does not have the value of the pure beyond or the void for it).
For pure insight, as we have already seen, is itself the existent concept, or
the purely self-equivalent personality, which differentiates itself internally
in such a way that each of the differentiated [moments] is itself a pure
concept, that is, is immediately nondifferentiated; pure insight is simple,
pure self-consciousness, which is as much *for itself* as *in itself* within an
immediate unity. Its *being-in-itself* is, therefore, not an abiding *being;*
rather it immediately ceases to be something in its difference. But such a

---

188. A fairly clear reference to Julien de la Mettrie's "principle of the vibration of organic bodies," which he develops in his tract, *L'homme Machine* (1748).
The tract is directed primarily against Descartes and his followers. The thesis is
that the body is a machine comprised of springs and levers. Mettrie says at one
point, "This oscillation [of the material and sensible part of the brain], which is
natural or suited to our machine, and with which each fibre and even each fibrous
element, so to speak, seems to be endowed, like that of a pendulum, can not keep
up forever. It must be renewed. . . . The body is a watch, whose watchmaker is the
new cycle." The soul by this account is just a force within the brain—what
Mettrie calls, following Hippocrates, the *enormôn* or the principle of impetus,
"This principle exists and has its seat in the brain at the origin of the nerves, by
which it exercises its control over all the rest of the body. By this fact is explained
all that can be explained." Cf. *Man a Machine,* ed. Gertrude Carman Bussey (La
Salle, IL: Open Court, 1912), p. 135, 132.

being, which has no hold immediately, is not an *inherent* being but is essentially for *another*, which is the power that absorbs it. But this second moment, opposite to the first—to the *being-in-itself*—vanishes just as immediately as does the first; or, as *being* that is *only for another*, it is rather the *vanishing* itself: *being returned* into itself, or *being for itself*, is posited. But this simple being for itself is as self-equivalent rather *one being*, and thereby it is *for another*. —The nature of pure insight in this *unfolding of its moments*, in other words nature as object, expresses the useful. The latter is something *inherently* subsisting, or is a thing. At the same time, this inherent being is only a pure moment. Consequently, it is absolutely *for another*, but it is just as much only for another as it is in itself. These opposite moments have returned into the indivisible unity of being-for-self. But even though the useful expresses the concept of pure insight, it is nevertheless not pure insight as such but as *representation* or as its *object;* it is only the restless exchange of each moment, in which, indeed, one is itself being that has returned into itself but only as being *for-self*, namely, as an abstract moment that issues forth on one side against the other. The useful itself does not consist in its having intrinsically the negative essence, that is, these moments at once in their opposition are *unseparated* in *one* and the *same respect*, or as a *thinking*—the way they were [315] in pure insight: the moment of *being-for-self* is indeed in the useful but not in such a way that it *overreaches* the other moments, [namely] the *in-itself* and *being for another*, in which case it would be the *self*. In the useful, therefore, pure insight has for its *object* its own concept in its *pure* moments: pure insight is the consciousness of this *metaphysics* but not yet the conception of it: consciousness has not yet come to the *unity* of *being* and *concept* itself. Because the useful still has the form of an object for insight, pure insight has a world that, although no longer subsisting in and for itself, is still a *world* that insight distinguishes from itself. Only when the antitheses have emerged at the pinnacle of the concept shall this be the next stage: that they collapse and the Enlightenment tastes the fruit of its deeds.

145–581   When we consider the attained object in connection with this entire sphere, the actual world of culture is summed up in the *vanity* of self-consciousness—in the *being-for-self* that still has for its content the confusion of culture and that is still the *singular* concept, not yet the explicitly *universal* one. But returned into itself, the concept is *pure insight;* it is pure consciousness as pure *self*, as negativity, just as faith is the very same as *pure thinking*, or positivity. In that self, faith has the moment that completes it, but because faith founders by means of this conception, it is now in pure insight that we see both moments: as absolute essence that is purely *thought*, or the negative, and as *matter* that is positive *being*. This completeness still lacks that *actuality* of self-consciousness that belongs to the *vain* consciousness—the world out of which thinking rises to itself. In usefulness what was lacking has now been attained insofar as pure insight acquires there positive objectivity: insight thereby is actual self-satisfied consciousness. This objectivity now constitutes the *world* of insight: it has become the truth of the preceding whole, of the ideal world as well as the real one. The first world of spirit is the widespread realm of its self-dispersing being,[189] and of the singularized *certainty* of itself, similar to the nature that disperses its life into an infinite manifold of shapes without the *species* of these being present. The second world contains the *species* and it the realm of *inherent being* or *truth* that is opposed to that certainty. But the third world, or the useful, is the *truth* that is the *certainty* of itself as well. The realm of the truth of *faith* lacks the principle of *actuality* or certainty of itself as this *singular*. But the actuality or self-certainty as this singular lacks the *in-itself*. In the object of pure insight both worlds are united. The useful is the object insofar as self-consciousness sees through it, and the [316] *singular certainty* of itself has its pleasure (its *being-for-self*) therein; self-consciousness *intuits* the object in this way, and this *insight* contains the *true* essence of the object (to be something transparent *for another*). Therefore it is itself *true knowledge,* and self-consciousness has just as immediately the universal certainty of itself; it has its *pure consciousness* in this relationship, in which, therefore, presence and *actuality* as well as *truth* are united. Both worlds are reconciled, and heaven is transplanted onto the earth below.

III. Absolute Freedom and Terror

In usefulness consciousness has found its concept. But this concept is 146–582 partly still an *object* and, precisely for this reason, partly still *purpose,* of which consciousness does not immediately find itself in possession. Usefulness is still the predicate of the object, not the subject itself, or [it is] the object's immediate and unique *actuality*. It is the same thing that appeared before: that is, *being-for-self* [has] not yet shown itself to be the substance of the rest of the moments, as a result of which the useful would immediately be nothing other than the self of consciousness, and thereby the latter would be in its possession. —However, this resumption of the form of objectivity on the part of usefulness has already happened *in itself;* and out of this inner convolution, the actual convoluting of actuality—the new shape of consciousness or the *absolute freedom*—issues forth.

In actual fact what is at hand is nothing more than an empty show of 147–583 objectivity, separating self-consciousness from possession. For, on the

---

189. <Daseyn>

one hand, all the subsistence and validity of the determinate members of
the organization in the actual world and the world of faith have, in general, retreated into this simple determination as into their ground and
spirit. But, on the other hand, this determination has for itself nothing
more of its own; it is rather pure metaphysics, pure concept or the knowing of self-consciousness. That is to say, from the being *in-* and *for-itself*
of the useful as object, consciousness is aware that *its being-in-itself* is
essentially *being for another;* the *being-in-itself* as *selfless* is in truth what is
passive, or what is for another self. But the object is for consciousness in
this [317] abstract form of *pure being-in-itself,* because consciousness is a
pure *inspecting,* whose distinctions are in the pure form of the concept.
—The *being-for-self,* however, into which the being for other retreats—
the self—is not one that belongs to what is called "object," a self separate
from the *I*. For consciousness as pure insight is not a *singular* self, over
against which the object would also stand as its *own* self, but is the pure
concept, the showing of the self in the self: the absolute twofold seeing of
its self. Its certainty is the universal subject, and its knowing concept the
essence of all actuality. If, therefore, the useful was only the exchange of
moments that does not return to its own *unity,* and hence was still object
for knowledge, so it [now] ceases to be this, for knowledge is itself the
movement of those abstract moments; it is the universal self, the self
equally of itself as object, and, as universal, the unity that returns to itself
of this movement.

148–584   Henceforth spirit is present as *absolute freedom.* It is self-consciousness
grasping itself—that its self-certainty is the essence of all the spiritual
masses of the real world as well as the supersensible one; or conversely,
that the knowledge that consciousness has *of itself* is essence and actuality.
—It is conscious of its pure personality and, in it, of all spiritual reality.
And all reality is only spiritual. For it the world is simply its will, and this
will is the universal will. It is not, indeed, the empty thought of the will
posited in consent, whether tacit or through being represented, but real$_2$
universal will: the will of all singulars as such.[190] For in itself the will is
the consciousness of personality, or of each someone. And it should be as
this truly actual will, that is, as *self-*conscious essence of each and every
personality, so that each always does everything undividedly, and what
emerges as the deed of the whole is the immediate and conscious deed of
each someone.

---

190. Hegel is following, and later criticizing, Abbé de Sieyès, the political
advocate for the National Convention. He, unlike Rousseau, identified the General Will with the decision of the majority. Sieyès's position is found in his *What
Is the Third Estate?* (1789).

This undivided substance of absolute freedom ascends the throne of 149–585
the world, without any power able to offer resistance. For, since consciousness alone is truly the element in which the spiritual essences, or powers, have their substance, their whole system that was organized and preserved through the partition into masses falls apart when the singular consciousness grasps the object in such a way that it does not have any other essence than self-consciousness itself; in other words, it is the concept absolutely. What made the concept into a subsisting *object* was its being distinguished into divided, *persisting* masses. But since the object [now] comes to be concept, nothing is left persisting in it; negativity has permeated all its moments. It steps forth into existence in such a way that each single consciousness is raised above the sphere to which it had been apportioned, and in such a way that it no longer finds its essence and its work in this particularized mass, but grasps its self as the *concept* of the will, all the masses [318] as the essence of this will, and hence can only be made actual in a labor that is total labor. In this absolute freedom all the estates that are the spiritual essences, into which the whole is articulated, are abolished. The singular consciousness that belonged to any of these members, and willed and accomplished its will in each, has sublated its boundary: its purpose is the universal purpose, its speech the universal law, and its work the universal work.

Here the object and the *distinction* have lost the meaning of *usefulness* 150–586
that was the predicate of all real being. Consciousness does not begin its movement in the object as in *something foreign,* out of which it first turned back into itself; rather, the object for consciousness is consciousness itself. So the antithesis consists solely in the distinction of *singular* and *universal* consciousness. The singular consciousness is, however, in its own eyes immediately what had only *the show* of antithesis; it is universal consciousness and will. The *beyond* of this actuality it has hovers over the corpse of the departed independence of the real, or believed, being only as the stench of a stale gas—of the empty *être suprême.*

Thus, after the sublation of the distinct spiritual masses and the 151–587
restricted life of individuals, as well as after the sublating of the two worlds of this life, only the movement into itself of universal self-consciousness is present as a reciprocal action of this self-consciousness in the form of *universality* and of *personal* consciousness. The universal will goes *into itself,* and it is a *singular* will to which the universal law and work stands opposed. But this *singular* consciousness is just as immediately conscious of itself as universal will; it is conscious that its object is a law that it gives and a work that it carries out. So as it passes over into activity and creates objectivity it does not produce anything singular, but only laws and acts of state.

152–588   This movement is thereby the reciprocal action of consciousness with itself, in the course of which it releases nothing in the shape of a *free object* confronting it. From this it follows that it can yield no positive work: the universal work neither of speech nor of actuality, neither the laws and universal institutions of *conscious* freedom, nor the deeds and works *of willed* freedom. —The work that freedom could achieve in making itself *conscious* would consist in this: that as *universal* substance, it makes itself into an *object* and *abiding being*. This otherness would be the distinction in freedom, according to which it would divide itself into persisting spiritual masses and into the elements of several powers[191]—in such a way that these masses would be, on the one hand, the *ens rationes* of a separated legislative [319], judicial, and executive *power;* on the other hand, however, they would be the *real essences* that emerged within the real world of culture and, since the content of the universal deed would be more closely attended to, they would be the particular masses of labor, further distinguished as more specific *estates.*[192] —The universal freedom that in this way would have divided itself into its members, and just because of this would have made itself into an *existing* substance, would thereby be free of singular individuality and would apportion the *multitude* of the *individuals* among its various members. But the deed and being of personality would thereby find itself restricted to one branch of the whole, to one kind of deed and being. Posited in the element of *being*, it would acquire the meaning of a *determinate* personality; it would cease truly to be universal self-consciousness. This self-consciousness does not let itself be defrauded out of its *actuality* in this way, either through the *presentation*[193] of obedience under *self-imposed* laws that allotted it a portion or through its *representation*[194] in the imposing of law and universal action. [It does not let itself be defrauded] out of the actuality of imposing the law *in person*[195] and brings to completion *in person* not a singular work but universal work; for wherever the self is only *represented* and *presented* it is not *actual;* wherever it is *delegated*, it does not exist.[196]

---

191. <Gewalten>

192. Hegel is referring to the tri-part division of power in the old regime. More specifically he has in mind Montesquieu's treatment of the constitution of France's government in his *Spirit of the Laws* (1748), Bk. XXXI, ch. xxi–xxxiv. Cf. *The Spirit of the Laws*, ed. by Anne Cohler, et. al. (Cambridge: Cambrige Univ. Press, 1989), 701–22. Montesquieu in these chapters explains how the bonds of the three estates became dissolved.

193. <*Vorstellung*>

194. <*Representation*>

195. <*selbst*>

196. A gloss on Rousseau's *Social Contract*: "the moment a people gives itself representatives, it is no longer free; it no longer exists," III, xv.

Just as the singular self-consciousness does not find itself as existent 153–589
substance in this *universal work* of absolute freedom, neither does it find
itself in its will's own *deeds* and *individual* actions. For the universal to
arrive at a deed, it must collect itself into the *one* of individuality, and
ensconce a singular self-consciousness at the pinnacle, for the universal
will is *actual* will only in a self that is *one*. As a result, however, *all other
singulars* are excluded from the *whole* of this deed, and only have a limited
share of it, so that the deed would not be deed of the *actual universal* self-
consciousness. —Hence, the universal freedom cannot bring forth any
positive work or deed; it is left only with the *negative act;* it is only the
fury of vanishing.[197]

But the highest actuality, which is also most opposed to the universal 154–590
freedom—indeed the one and only object that still comes to be for it—is
the freedom and singularity of the actual self-consciousness itself. For
that universality, which does not allow itself to come to the reality of
organic articulation and whose aim is to preserve itself in undivided continuity, is internally distinguished all the same because it is movement or
consciousness in general. And indeed, for the sake of its own abstraction it
sunders itself into extremes just as abstract, that is, into simple, inflexible,
cold universality and into the discrete, absolutely rigid brittleness and
stiff-necked punctilio of actual [320] self-consciousness.[198] Now that the
universal has finished with the obliteration of the real organization and
stands on its own, this is its only object—one that has no other content,
possession, determinate being, or external extension left, but in only this
knowledge of itself as absolutely pure and free singular self.[199] There is
only its *abstract* determinate being in general by which it can be grasped.
—Since, then, they are undividedly and absolutely on their own and

---

197. Cf. Hegel's Jena lecture on the *Philosophy of Spirit* (1805–6), "The *free
universal* is the point of individuality. This individuality, free of the knowledge
shared by all, is not constituted through them. . . . The spiritual tie is public opinion; this is the genuine legislature, the national assembly . . . The declaration of
the universal will, which lives in the execution of all commands, [is the improve-
ment of law] . . . ,"*GW,* viii, p. 262. Hegel is describing the development of government through the third estate, which by 1789 formed the legislature and
government under the authority of Louis XVI.

198. These types are represented in the persons of St. Just and Robespierre.

199. The "fury" of the revolution leads to the abolishment of the Estates General, which was the old government of the universal. The new government that
claims universality breaks into extremes. In the French National Assembly the
extremes were presented by the "plain"—or moderate faction that looked to Necker
and Lafayette as its leaders—and the "mountain"—or radical faction that looked to
Robespierre, Danton, and St. Just as their leaders. It is the third estate that has
moved and annulled the entirety of the universal; it becomes the universal class.

hence cannot yield any part to the middle by means of which they would
be connected, the relation of the two is totally *unmediated* pure negation—
indeed, the negation of the singular as *subsistent* in the universal. The
unique work and deed of universal freedom is therefore *death*—more precisely a *death* that has no inner reach or fulfillment, for what is negated is
the unfulfilled point of the absolutely free self. It is therefore the coldest,
dullest death, with no more significance than the chopping off of a cabbage head or a gulp of water.[200]

155–591   In the dullness of this syllable ["death"] constitutes the wisdom of the
government and the universal will's understanding of how to fulfill itself.
The government is itself nothing else than the point that fixes itself, or the
individuality of the universal will. A willing and fulfilling that emanates
from one point, the government wills and, at the same time, fulfills a definite order and policy. It thereby excludes, on the one hand, the rest of the
individuals from its action; on the other, by excluding them, it constitutes
itself as the kind of government that is a determinate will, and hence it is
opposed to the universal will.[201] It cannot possibly present itself, therefore, in any other way than as a *faction*. Only the *victorious* faction is called
government; and just in its being a faction there lies immediately the
necessity of its demise; in its being government—this is conversely what
makes it a faction and guilty.[202] Whereas the universal will takes the actual

---

200. The reference is to the guillotine, which when dropped on the victim's
neck was said to produce a "tickling" at the back of the neck but no pain. Dr.
Guillotine demonstrated his device by cleaving a head of cabbage.

201. Cf. Hegel's Jena lecture on the *Philosophy of Spirit* (1805–6): "Thus the
universal is against individuals as such, who want to know their immediate positive
will asserted as absolute—as lord, tyrant, pure force—for the universal is something foreign to them; and the state power that knows what is must have the courage, in every case of need where the existence of the totality is compromised, to
take completely tyrannous action. Through tyranny we have the immediate externalization of the individual's actual will—transcended, immediate—this is education toward obedience," *GW,* viii, p. 259. The new government of the individual
claims for itself universality, which is ironically directed against the individuals of
society; the government of the individual becomes the force directed to destroy the
individual. Hegel in his lectures explicitly refers to the republican form of government that Robespierre and Danton established when Louis XVI was arrested,
tried, and convicted before the National Assembly; cf. *GW,* viii, p. 260.

202. The two leading factions were the Girondists, lead by Danton, and the
Jacobins, led by Robespierre. They will take on the universal work of government,
but simply because they are factions they oppose both the universal and each
other. The "necessary result" of such opposition is strife, which will eventually
lead to the deaths of the Girondists' leaders, and finally to the trial and death of
the Jacobin leaders.

operation of this governing faction to be a crime committed against it, the faction, on the contrary, has nothing determinate and external to it by which it portrays to itself the guilt of the will that stands opposite; for opposed to the faction as *actual* universal will there is only the nonactual pure will or *intention. Falling under suspicion,* therefore, takes the place of, or has the meaning and effect of, *being guilty.* And the external reaction against this actuality that lies in the simple inwardness of intention consists in the arid extermination of this subsisting self, from which there is nothing else to be taken away but only its being.

In this *work* that is peculiar to it, absolute freedom comes to its own object; and self-consciousness experiences what freedom *is. In itself* freedom is precisely this *abstract self-consciousness* that exterminates within itself all distinction and any persistence of distinction. As such an abstract self-consciousness, it is [321] its own object; the *terror* of death is the intuition of this, its negative essence. But the absolutely free self-consciousness thus finds its reality to be quite other than the concept that freedom had of itself, that is, that the universal will is only the *positive* essence of personality, and the latter knows itself in that will only positively or as received. But here it is the absolute *transition* from the one to the other that in its actuality is present to self-consciousness, which, as pure insight, simply divides its positive and negative essence—an absolute without predicates as pure *thinking* and as pure *matter.* —The universal will, as absolutely *positive* actual self-consciousness, converts into the *negative* essence; because it is self-consciousness, this self-conscious actuality is *raised* to *pure* thought or to *abstract* matter, and so proves itself to be the *sublation* of the *thinking of itself* or of self-consciousness. 156–592

As *pure* self-identity of the universal will, therefore, absolute freedom has *negation* within it—and hence *the distinction* in general, which it develops again as *actual* distinction. For in the self-equivalent universal will, the pure *negativity* has the *element* of *subsistence,* or the *substance,* in which its moments are realized; it has the matter that it can make use of in its determinacy. And inasmuch as this substance has shown itself to be the negative for the singular consciousness, the organization of spiritual masses builds itself up again, and the multitude of individual consciousnesses is apportioned to them. These consciousnesses that have felt the fear of their absolute Lord, death, submit again to negation and distinction; they subordinate themselves to the masses, and return to a partitioned and restricted work; through this, however, they return to their substantial actuality. 157–593

Out of this tumult, spirit would be hurled back to its starting point, to the ethical and real world of culture that has merely been restored and rejuvenated by the fear of the Lord that has returned to men's minds. If 158–594 the result were only the complete interpenetration of self-consciousness and substance, spirit would have to run through this cycle of necessity once more, and repeat it over and over again. For in that interpenetration self-consciousness, having experienced the negative counterforce of its universal essence, would want to know and find itself, not as this particular, but only as a universal, and hence it could also endure the objective actuality of universal spirit that excludes self-consciousness as particular. —In absolute freedom, however, it was not the consciousness that was submerged in manifold determinate being (that is, has fixed self-determined purposes and thoughts) and an *external,* valid world (be it of actuality or thought) that were [322] in reciprocal action with each other, but rather the world was simply in the form of consciousness as universal will, and, just so, self-consciousness was simply contracted into the simple self out of all extended determinate being, that is, out of manifold purposes and judgments. So the culture that self-consciousness attains in reciprocal action with that essence consists in seeing what is most sublime and final; its simple and pure actuality immediately disappears and passes over into empty nothingness. In the world of culture itself, self-consciousness does not come to the point of intuiting its negation or estrangement in this form of pure abstraction. For, on the contrary, its negation is full [of content]: it is either the honor or the wealth that it gains to replace the self from which it has become estranged; or it is the speech of spirit and insight, which the torn consciousness has attained; or it is the heaven of faith or the usefulness of the Enlightenment. All these determinations are forfeit in the total loss that the self experiences in absolute freedom. Its negation is meaningless death, the pure terror of negation that has nothing positive, nothing fulfilling, within itself. —But, at the same time, this negation in its actuality is of something *foreign.* It is neither the universal *necessity,* lying beyond, into which the ethical world passes away, nor the singular accident of private property, nor the whim of its owner, on which the torn consciousness sees itself dependent. It is rather the *universal will* that has nothing positive in this, its last abstraction, and hence it can render nothing back in sacrifice but is immediately one with self-consciousness for this very reason. That is, it is the pure positive because it is the pure negative; and in the inner concept meaningless death, or the unfulfilled negativity of the self, converts into absolute positivity. For consciousness, its immediate unity with the universal will and its requirement that it know itself as this determinate point in the universal will is transformed into the exactly opposite experience. What here disappears for consciousness is abstract *being,* or the immediacy of a point without substance. And this immediacy that has disappeared is the universal will itself that consciousness now knows itself to be, inasmuch as it is *sublated immediacy,* inasmuch as it is pure knowing and pure will. Through this it knows the will as its self, and itself as essence, but not as an essence *existing immediately.* Neither does it know the will as revolutionary government or as anarchy striving to constitutionalize anarchy, nor itself as middle point of this faction or its opposite.[203] The *universal will* is rather its *pure knowing* and *willing,* and *it* is universal will, [323] as this pure knowing and willing. It does not lose *itself* therein, for the pure knowing and willing are rather itself as the atom point of consciousness. It is therefore the reciprocal action of pure knowing with itself; the pure *knowing* as *essence* is the universal will; but this *essence* is simply and solely pure knowing.[204] Thus self-consciousness is the pure knowing of the essence as pure knowing. Moreover, as *singular self,* it is only the form of the subject or of actual doing that is known by self-consciousness to be *form.* Similarly, for self-consciousness, the *objective* actuality, the *being,* is strictly a selfless form since the objective actuality would be what is not known, whereas this knowing knows the knowing as essence.

Absolute freedom has therefore brought the antithesis of universal and   159–595
individual will into balance. The self-estranged spirit, driven to the extreme of its antithesis, in which the pure willing and the pure willed are still differentiated, reduces the antithesis to transparent form, and finds itself therein. —Just as the kingdom of the actual world passed over into the kingdom of faith and insight, so absolute freedom passes from its self-destroying actuality over into another land of self-conscious spirit, where it counts as what is true in this inefficacy; with the thoughts of this truth spirit is comforted, inasmuch as *it is,* and remains, *thought* and knows this

---

203. Most likely the references are to the failed governments of France preceding Napoleon's coup d'état.

204. In *Philosophy of Spirit* Hegel explains this moment as becoming of the citizen-ruler or the republican spirit: "the universal will has been taken into this oneness. It has *itself initially* come forth from the *will of the singular being to be constituted* as something universal . . . the universal is absolutely there for the singular being; they are not *immediately* the same. The constitution of the universal one may introduce as *all burghers coming together* . . . and thus the *plurality* of the *universal will is constituted,*" *GW,* viii, p. 256f.

From here on there are some strong parallels between *Phenomenology of Spirit* and *Philosophy of Spirit* (1806). This is not surprising, since the *Phenomenology* is to introduce us to the other parts of the system, and the *Philosophies of Nature and Spirit* are the only other extant parts. It is important to note the connection, and there are times when we should interpret the *Phenomenology* from the viewpoint of *Philosophy of Spirit,* especially on how the universal will and its articulation into the masses (i.e., the estates) continues throughout the rest of the chapter. Only *Philosophy of Spirit* shows us how Spirit Certain of Itself, or Morality, continues this pattern of identity.

being, contained within self-consciousness, as the perfect and complete essence.[205] The new shape of *moral spirit* has emerged.

C. SPIRIT CERTAIN OF ITSELF. MORALITY

160–596   The ethical world showed the spirit that in it was departed, the *single self,* as its destiny and truth. But this *legal person* has its substance and fulfillment outside of the ethical world. The movement of the world of culture and of faith sublates this abstraction of the person, and through the completed estrangement, through the highest abstraction, substance becomes, for the self of spirit, first the *universal will,* and finally its property. Thus knowing seems here to have become at last perfectly equivalent to its truth, since its truth is this knowing itself, and every antithesis of the two sides has vanished: not merely *for us* or *in itself,* but for self-consciousness itself. That is, self-consciousness has become master over the antithesis of consciousness [324] itself. The latter rests on the antithesis between the certainty of itself and the object. But now the object for consciousness is its self-certainty—that is, knowing; just as self-certainty as such no longer has purposes of its own, so too it no longer consists in determinacy but is pure knowing.

161–597   The knowing of self-consciousness is thus for self-consciousness *substance* itself. The substance is for it both *immediate* and absolutely *mediated* in one undivided unity. *Immediate:* like ethical consciousness, it knows and does its duty and belongs to it as to its nature; but it is not *character* in the way ethical consciousness is, which, because of its immediacy, is a determinate spirit belonging only to *one* of the ethical essentialities and having the aspect *of not knowing.* —It is *absolute mediation,* like the consciousness that cultivates itself and has faith: for it is essentially the movement of the self to sublate the abstraction of the *immediate determinate being,* and to become universal, but neither through pure estrangement and tearing of itself and actuality nor through flight. On the contrary, it is itself *immediately present*[206] in its substance, for the substance is its knowing. It is the intuited pure certainty of its self; precisely *this immediacy,* which is its own actuality, is all actuality, for the immediate is *being* itself;

---

205. The "other land of self-conscious spirit" is a nordic kingdom, e.g., the German states. As Hegel says in his *Philosophy of Spirit,* "spirit is purified of the immediate existence; it has entered into its pure element of *knowing* and is indifferent to existing individuality. Here spirit begins *to be* knowledge; i.e., its formal existence is that of self-knowing. Spirit is this nordic essence that is within itself, although it has its determinate being in the self of all," *GW,* viii, p. 264.

206. <gegenwärtig>

and as pure immediacy purged through absolute negativity it is pure, it is *being* in general or *all* being.

Absolute essence is therefore not exhausted in the determination of 162–598 being the simple *essence* of *thinking* but is all *actuality,* and this actuality consists only in knowing. Whatever consciousness did not know would have no sense and can be no power for it. All objectivity and the world have withdrawn into its knowing will. It is absolutely free in that it knows its freedom, and just this knowing of its freedom is its substance and purpose and sole content.

a. The Moral World-View

Self-consciousness knows duty to be the absolute essence; it is bound 163–599 only by duty, and this substance is its own pure consciousness. For self-consciousness duty cannot acquire the form of something foreign. But as closed up within itself [325], moral self-consciousness is not yet posited and viewed as *consciousness.* The object is immediate knowing, and as thus permeated purely by the self it is not an object. But being essentially mediation and negativity, moral self-consciousness has in its concept the connection with an *otherness* and is consciousness. Because duty constitutes its unique and essential purpose and object, this otherness is, on the one hand, completely *meaningless* actuality for consciousness. But because this consciousness is thus perfectly closed up within itself, it then relates in a perfectly free and indifferent way to this otherness, and therefore determinate being is, on the other hand, one that is completely freed from self-consciousness, a determinate being that in the same way is just self-related. As self-consciousness becomes freer, so much the more free does the negative object of its consciousness become in turn. Thereby the object is a world complete within itself with its own individuality, an independent whole of laws peculiar to it, as well as an independent operation and free actualization of these laws; it is one *nature* in general whose laws, like its deeds, belong to it as an essence that is untroubled by moral self-consciousness, just as self-consciousness is untroubled by nature.[207]

---

207. Hegel is describing what he calls in *Philosophy of Spirit* the "nordic essence," which forms its own world as a community of the Estates General. This northern essence will have three objective moments culminating in a moral constitution: "first is trust; second is the division within it that is abstract right; the third is absolute mistrust . . . thus the object [of self-consciousness] enters as implicitly the universal: the state is [its] purpose—knowledge of duty; morality, but this universal is in particular branches; [namely,] the business estate . . . the learned [estate]; and finally the military estate . . . " *GW,* viii, p. 266; cf. p. 264.

164–160   Starting from this determination, a *moral world-view* is formed that
subsists in the *connection* between *moral* being in and for itself and the *natural* being in and for itself. Underlying this connection as its ground are
both the complete *indifference* and proper *independence* of *nature*, which
stand against *moral* purpose and activity, and also, on the other side, consciousness of the unique essentiality of duty and the complete noninde-
pendence and nonessentiality of nature. The moral world-view contains
the development of the moments that are contained in this connection of
such completely conflicting presuppositions.

165–601   At first, then, moral consciousness is in general presupposed: duty
counts as the essence for this consciousness that is *actual* and *active*, and
which in its actuality and act fulfills duty. But for this moral consciousness there is, at the same time, the presupposed freedom of nature; in
other words, the *experience* of consciousness is that nature is unconcerned
about giving it a consciousness of the unity of its actuality with that of
nature, and therefore consciousness will *perhaps* be *fortunate*, or, as well,
perhaps not. The immoral consciousness in contrast finds its actualization,
perhaps by accident, at the point where the moral one finds only the *occasion* for action; but because of this it does not see the good fortune in performing or in enjoying the accomplishment for its own sake. Hence, it
rather finds a basis for complaint about such a condition of discord
between itself and existence,[208] and about the injustice that limits it to
having only *pure duty* for its object and denies it the sight of either the
object or *itself* actualized. [326]

166–602   Moral consciousness cannot renounce happiness and leave out this
moment from its absolute purpose. The purpose, which is expressed as
pure duty, is essentially characterized in that it contains this *singular* self-
consciousness; the *individual conviction* and the knowing of it constituted
an absolute moment of morality. This moment in the *purpose* that has
objectively come about in the *fulfilled* duty is the *singular* consciousness
that sees itself realized; in other words, it is the *enjoyment* that, thereby, is
viewed not immediately in the concept of morality as *disposition*,[209] but
solely in the concept of morality's *actualization*. But on that account it
also lies within morality as *disposition;* for this does not remain disposition in antithesis to action, but rather it comes to the point of *acting*, or to
actualizing itself. Hence, to express purpose as a whole with the consciousness of its moments involves, therefore, the fulfilled duty being

---

208. <Daseyn>

209. *Gesinnung*. It can also mean sentiment. In *Philosophy of Spirit* this is a
category that characterizes the "lower estate" or the business community, cf. *GW,*
viii, p. 267ff.

equally [both] pure moral action, as realized *individuality*, and *nature*, as the side of *singularity* vis-à-vis abstract purpose, being *one* with that purpose. —As necessary as the experience of disharmony is to both sides because nature is free, so too duty alone is essential, and nature, in contrast to duty, is without self. That whole *purpose*, which harmony constitutes, contains within it actuality itself. It is, at the same time, the *thought* of *actuality*. The harmony of morality and nature—or, since nature only comes into view insofar as consciousness experiences its unity with it, the harmony of morality and happiness—is *thought* to be necessarily *existing;* that is, it is *postulated.*[210] For "requirement" expresses that something comes to be thought *as existing* that is not yet actual; a necessity not of the *concept* as concept but of *being.*[211] But necessity, at the same time, is essentially connection by way of the concept. Therefore, the required *being* does not belong to the presentations of a contingent consciousness; rather it lies within the concept of morality itself, the true content of which is the *unity* of *pure* and *singular* consciousness. What belongs to singular consciousness is the fact that this unity should be *for it* as an actuality; what is happiness in the *content* of the purpose is yet determinate being in general in its *form.* —This required determinate being, or the unity of both sides, is consequently neither a wish nor, when viewed as a purpose, something whose accomplishment is still uncertain; rather, it is a requirement of reason, its immediate certainty and presupposition.

That first experience and its postulate are not unique, but rather they open up a complete circle of postulates. That is to say, nature is not only this completely free and *external* mode in which consciousness [327] might have realized its purpose as a pure object. *Of itself* this consciousness is essentially something *for which* this free and actual other exists, that is, it is itself something accidental and natural. This nature, which for consciousness is its own, is *sensuality*, which, within the *shape* of the willing as *drives* and *inclinations*, has for itself its own *determinate* essentiality or *specific purposes*, and thus is opposed to pure will and its pure   167–603

---

210. In *Critique of Practical Reason* (1788) this is Kant's definition of the highest good (*summum bonum*): "Now insofar as virtue and happiness together constitute the possession of the highest good in a person, and, thereby, the distribution of happiness as well, in exact proportion to morality, . . . is the *highest* good of a possible world," *Akad.*, v, 110. This is the first postulate of morality.

211. There are two requirements as stated in Kant's *Critique of Judgment* (1790): the formal rational condition of employing our freedom to strive for the highest good attainable by freedom, that being morality; the subjective condition that is human happiness set as "the highest possible physical good in the world, and the one to be furthered so far as in us lies the end purpose . . . " *Akad.*, v, 450.

purpose.[212] But in contrast to this opposition, the essence for pure consciousness is rather the connection of sensuality with consciousness, their
absolute unity. Both of them, pure thinking and the sensuality of consciousness, are *in themselves one consciousness,* and pure thinking is just
that for which and in which this pure unity exists; but for thinking as consciousness there is the antithesis between its own self and the drives. In
this conflict of reason and sensuality the essence for reason is that the
conflict be resolved, and that as a *result* there emerges the unity of both—
not the *original* unity where both reason and sensuality are in one individual, but rather one that emerges out of the *known* antithesis of both.[213]
Only such a unity constitutes *actual* morality; for in it the antithesis is
contained, whereby the self is consciousness or is for the first time actual
and, in fact, is universal; in other words, it expresses this same *mediation*
in it, which, as we have seen, is essential to morality.[214] —Since under
both moments of antithesis sensuality is simply *otherness,* or the negative,
whereas the pure thinking of duty is the essence from which nothing can
be surrendered, it seems that the unity that has emerged could only come
about by virtue of the sublation of sensuality. But sensuality is itself a
moment of this becoming, the moment of *actuality;* hence for this unity
one must be content, at first, with the expression that sensuality be *appropriate* to morality. —Likewise, this unity is a *postulated being;* it *is* not
there.[215] For what *is there* is consciousness, that is, the antithesis between

---

212. Hegel is stating that there is a dilemma within the concept. He is initially
presenting it in terms of Kant's "Antinomy of Practical Reason," (cf. *Akad.,* v,
111ff.). The "Antinomy of Practical Reason" occurs in the identification of virtue
and happiness, either, as the Stoics claimed, by pursuing virtue, happiness follows,
or, as the Epicureans claimed, by pursuing happiness, virtue follows. But Hegel
does not believe that Kant has resolved the dilemma; in fact, Kant's solution,
which makes a further postulate—namely, that there is a noumenal Self whose sole
purpose is complete virtue—is only an abstract way of stating the Stoical position
(a position that Hegel has already analyzed in Chapter 4, "Self-Certainty," and
that constitutes "Legal Right" in the "True Spirit" section of this chapter).

213. Hegel is referring to a distinction made by Kant between human nature,
which is prone to the weakness of self-love and is itself "evil," and a pure rational
nature, which exists only as a rational idea but that is "true" to humanity's moral
capacities.

214. The reference is to Kant's solution to the Antinomies of Practical Reason, namely, the positing of the noumenal self—"to think my determinate being
as noumenal in a world of understanding," *Akad.,* v, 114. This noumenal world
"exists" only as a kind of necessary fiction: what is "as if" but is not actual.

215. The first postulation is that the highest good consists in the possession of
happiness under morality in some possible world; the second postulate is to think
of my determinate being as noumenon in the world of understanding. For Kant

sensuality and pure consciousness. But, at the same time, it is not an in-itself like the first postulate in which free nature constituted one aspect, so that the harmony of nature with moral consciousness falls outside it; rather, nature is here something in consciousness itself, and we are here dealing with morality, that is, with a harmony that is proper to the acting self. Hence consciousness itself has to bring about this harmony, and always has to make progress in morality. But the *completing* of the progress lies in its *infinite deferral;*[216] for if it were actually to occur, then moral consciousness would be sublated. For *morality* is only moral *consciousness* as negative essence; and for this pure duty, sensuality has only a *negative* significance, and is simply *not appropriate*. But in the harmony *morality* as consciousness, or the *actuality* of it, disappears, just as [328] in the moral *consciousness* or the actuality of it, *harmony* disappears. Hence the completion is not actually to be achieved but is only to be thought of as an *absolute task*, that is, as one that simply remains a task. Yet, at the same time, its content is to be thought of in such a way that it must simply *be* and not remain a task; whether one now represents that consciousness be sublated entirely in this goal or that it is not, how it ought properly to be regarded is left in the dark distance of infinity, where, just for this rea-son, the achievement of the goal is deferred, and is no longer clearly dif-ferentiated.[217] It must really be admitted that the determinate representa-tion should not interest us and should not be sought, because it leads to contradictions: to a task that remains a task and yet may be fulfilled; to a morality that should not be consciousness, should not be actual any longer. Through the consideration that perfect morality might involve a contradiction, however, the holiness of moral essentiality would suffer and absolute duty appear as something nonactual.

The first postulate was the harmony of morality and objective nature— 168–604
the final purpose of the *world;*[218] the second was the harmony of morality

---

the second postulate relates to the religious belief in the immortality of the soul. Notice that Hegel has changed the claim: the postulation is not the immortal soul but an actual union between sensual and pure consciousness. This is how Schiller interprets Kant, and Hegel is following Schiller's interpretations.

216. Hence this is why Kant believes that happiness has to be put off until after death, since we cannot hope to attain the harmony between our sensible and noumenal natures in life. Hegel rejects this conclusion.

217. Cf. "This infinite progress exists [*ist*], however, only under the presup-position of an *existence* and personality of some rational being continuing into *infinity*," *Critique of Practical Reason, Akad.*, v, 122.

218. Kant goes through great pains to define the concept of *World:* "[world] signifies the mathematical sum-total of all appearances and the totality of their synthesis, alike in the great and in the small, that is, in the advance alike through

and sensual will—the final purpose of *self-consciousness* as such. The first, then, was the harmony in the form of the *in-itself,* the second in the form of *being-for-self.*[219] But what serves as a means to bind together these two final purposes as extremes, which are thought, is the movement of *actual* conduct itself.[220] They are harmonies whose moment in their abstract differentiation has not yet come to be the object; this occurs in the actuality whereby each of the aspects within genuine consciousness comes forth to be the *other* of the other. The postulates arising from this now contain the harmony *in and for itself,* just as previously they contained only the separated harmonies, one *being in itself* and the other *being for itself.*

169–605   As the *simple knowing* and *willing* of pure duty, moral consciousness is connected in action to the object opposed to its simplicity—to the actuality of a *case with many aspects*—and as a result it has a moral *relation* with many aspects. On the side of the content, there here originate the *many* laws in general, and on the side of the form, there originate the contradictory powers of knowing consciousness and the nonconscious.[221] —In the former, where the *many duties* are concerned, what counts for moral consciousness in general is just the *pure duty* in them: the *many duties* qua many are *determinate,* and as such they are thus not at all holy for moral consciousness. But *necessarily* at the same time, by virtue of the concept of *action,* which includes within it the one actuality with many aspects and thus the one moral connection with many aspects, [329] they must be viewed as existing in and for themselves. Furthermore, since they can only be in some moral *consciousness,* they are, at the same time, in an other one than the one for which only the pure duty exists, [namely] what is pure in and for itself and is holy.[222]

----

composition and through division," *Critique of Pure Reason,* A418 = B446. The idea of the World, then, is the idea of a mathematical progression considered *in toto.* All appearances are ordered under this totalizing conception.

219. Hegel follows Fichte's analysis of the highest good in the latter's *Critique of all Revelation* (1792): "But the determination of the above desiring faculties to will the good is rational *in itself,* for they act [*geschieht*] immediately through a law of reason . . ." §2, "Deduction of Religion," p. 9.

220. Cf. Fichte, p. 19ff. What binds these two together is the fear of God and the hope of things to come, namely, pleasure in paradise; Hegel bypasses this step and goes right to the action deemed right by practical reason.

221. A fairly clear reference to Kant's *Anthropology* (1798), "*To have representations* and *still not be conscious of them,* therein seems to lie a contradiction . . ." §5, *Akad.,* vii, 135. The nonconscious powers are described as that which produces "*dark* representations," such as the fantasy produces; these are often connected with our sexuality, or our animal nature.

222. The pure moral laws are divine laws; thus the holy is known in and through abstract morality.

It is postulated, therefore, that there is an *other* consciousness that 170–606
makes them holy, or which knows and wills them as duties.[223] The first
consciousness maintains pure duty *indifferently* against all *determinate
content,* and duty is only this indifference vis-à-vis content. The other
consciousness, however, contains the equally essential connection with
action and the *necessity* of the *determinate* content; since for it duties are
valued as *determinate* duties, it follows that the content as such is just as
equally essential for it as the form by which it is duty. Consequently, this
consciousness is one wherein the universal and the particular are simply
one, and its concept is thus the same as the concept of the harmony
between morality and happiness. For this antithesis also expressed the
separation of the *self-equivalent* moral consciousness from the actuality
that, as *manifold being,* conflicted with the simple essence of duty. However, if the first postulate expresses only the existent harmony of morality
and nature, because in it nature is this negative of self-consciousness or
the moment of being, now, in contrast, this *in-itself* is posited essentially
as consciousness. For what exists has only the form of the *content* of *duty;*
in other words, it is the *determinacy* in the *determinate duty.* So the in-itself
is a unity of [moments] which as *simple essentialities* are essentialities of
thinking and hence are only in one consciousness. This consciousness,
then, is from now on a Lord and ruler of the world who brings forth the
harmony of morality and happiness, and at the same time sanctifies duties
as *many.*[224] What the latter means is just that for the consciousness of *pure
duty* the determinate cannot immediately be holy; because it is for the sake
of the actual doing, which is something determinate and likewise *necessary;* however, its necessity then falls outside that consciousness into an
other one which, consequently, mediates the determinate duty and the
pure duty and is the ground whereby the former duty is also valid.

But in the actual doing, consciousness behaves as this self, as a com- 171–607
pletely singular consciousness. It is directed toward actuality as such, and

---

223. For Kant and Fichte this is God, but Hegel seems to take the third postulate to be yet another form of consciousness, which at least appears holy. We
might call this third postulation that of the *sacred* consciousness; it is *the divine
within human nature.*

224. Cf. Kant's *Religion within the Bounds of Reason Alone,* III, Division 1, I:
Concerning the Ethical State of Nature, "In both [the ethical and judicial state of
nature], each individual prescribes the law for himself, and there is no external
law to which he, along with all others, recognizes himself to be subject. In both,
each individual is his own judge, and there exists no powerful *public* authority to
determine with legal power, according to laws, what is each man's duty in every
situation that arises, and to bring about the universal performance of duty,"
Akad., vi, 95.

has it for its purpose, for it wants to achieve. *Duty in general*, then, falls outside it into another essence, which is consciousness and the sacred law-giver of pure duty.[225] For the agent, just because he is agent, the other of pure duty is immediately valid; this duty, then, is the content of some other consciousness but is holy only mediately for that consciousness in that it is in this one.

172–608   Because it is posited in such a way that the value of duty as something holy *in and of itself* [330] falls outside of actual consciousness, the latter stands therefore altogether on one side as the *imperfect* moral conscious-ness.[226] Just as in terms of its *knowing*, moral consciousness thus knows itself as one whose knowledge and conviction are incomplete and contin-gent, so too in terms of its *willing* it knows itself as one whose purposes are affected with sensuality. Hence on account of its unworthiness, it can-not view happiness as necessary, but as something contingent, which it can expect from grace alone.

173–609   However imperfect is its actuality, duty still counts its *pure* will and knowledge as the essence; so, in the concept, inasmuch as it is opposed to reality, that is, in thinking, consciousness is perfect. But the absolute essence is precisely this thought and is postulated as beyond actuality; hence it is the thought in which moral knowing and willing, which are imperfect, count as perfect; as well, since it takes these as crucially impor-tant, it thereby bestows happiness according to worth, namely, according to the *merit ascribed* to knowing and willing.[227]

---

225. Kant says, "Hence only he [the superior being] can be thought of a high-est lawgiver of an ethical commonwealth with respect to whom all *true duties*, hence also the ethical, must be represented as *at the same time* his commands; he must therefore also be 'one who knows the heart,' in order to see into the inner-most parts of the disposition of each individual and, as is necessary in every com-monwealth, to bring it about that each receives whatever his actions are worth. But this is the concept of God as moral ruler of the world," *Religion within the Bounds of Reason Alone*, III, Div. I, *Akad.*, vi, 96.

226. The reference is to the one who has a *good will* and acts on moral disposi-tions alone, as opposed to the perfected moral consciousness of him who obeys the moral law as if it were a divine command. Only the latter is the true lawgiver. The former is *evil* in Kant's eyes because his will is determined according to the interests and drives of human nature, which is wholly corrupt and *radically evil*. In *Philosophy of Spirit* this is for Hegel the burgher whose disposition is governed by a sense of legal right—"seine Gesinnung [ist] Rechtschaffenheit"—and who trusts the state and its legal constitution. Beyond this level of commitment he has no moral identity. Cf. *GW*, viii, 268. The course of the dialectic proceeds through this imperfect self-consciousness, who knows that it is unworthy of blessedness.

227. The unity between perfected and imperfect consciousness is the segue to the Romantic school, especially the philosophy of Friedrich Schiller. Even for

Herein the world-view is completed; for in the concept of moral self- 174–610
consciousness both sides—pure duty and actuality—are posited in one
unity, and by virtue of this the one, as well as the other, does not exist in
and for itself, but exists as a *moment* or as sublated. In the final part of the
moral world-view this comes about for consciousness: consciousness posits pure duty in some essence other than itself, that is, consciousness
posits it partly as something *represented*, and partly as something that is
not valid in and of itself; in contrast, the nonmoral is valued as perfect.[228]
Equally, consciousness posits itself as one whose actuality that is discor-
dant with duty is sublated, and as *sublated*—in the *representation* of absolute essence—it no longer contradicts morality.

Nonetheless, for moral consciousness itself, its moral world-view does 175–611
not have the significance of consciousness developing its proper concept
in that world-view and making it into an object for itself; it has neither a
consciousness about this antithesis with respect to form, nor about the
antithesis with respect to content; it does not compare or connect these
parts among themselves, but in its development it rolls along without
having the coherent *concept* of the moments. For it knows only *pure essence*
(that is the object, in so far as it is *duty*, or insofar as it is an *abstract* object
of its pure consciousness) to be pure knowing or to be its own self. Therefore it conducts itself only as thinking and not as conceiving. Hence the
object of its *actual* consciousness is not yet transparent to it: it is not the
absolute concept that alone grasps *otherness* as such, or grasps its absolute
[331] opposite as its own self. Its own actuality, of course, just like all
objective actuality, counts as *inessential* for it; however, its freedom is the
freedom of pure thinking, in contrast to which, therefore, nature has
arisen at the same time as something equally free.[229] Since each of them—

Kant, however, there exists a means of reconciliation, which is found in the "aesthetic sense." The imperfect consciousness can and will appreciate the form of
reason in his aesthetical appreciation of the beautiful. Thus, aesthetical education
can overcome the natural boundary of our imperfect nature.

228. That is to say, the sentimental or emotive is valued as perfect. Hegel
probably has Schiller in mind. See Schiller's "Concerning the Necessary Bound-
aries with Using Beauty Forms" (1795) and "Concerning the Moral Use of Aesthetical Customs" (1795). Schiller denies that human nature is evil, and although
morality is the determination of the will under the laws of reason, it is also the faculty of taste as the harmony of reason and emotion that produces the conviction
that the good is to be enjoyed and evil detested.

229. Nature, according to Kant, is the dynamical unity of appearances; it
becomes "free" in that it obeys the moral law (i.e., laws of reason). Cf. Schiller's
"On the Sublime" (1801), "The whole of nature acts rationally; its prerogative is
simply that it act rationally along with consciousness and will." Schillers *Werke*

the *freedom of being* and the enclosure of being in consciousness—is in consciousness in the same way, its object comes to be something *existent,* which *at the same time* is only *thought of.* In this last part of moral consciousness's [world] view the content is posited essentially in such a way that its being is something *represented,* and this joining between being and thought, expressed as what it is in fact, is *representing.*

176–612   When we consider the moral world-view in such a way that this objective mode is nothing else than the very concept of moral self-consciousness, which it makes objective for itself, then, through this consciousness about the form of its origination, there results another shape to its presentation. —That is, the starting point from which it proceeds is the *actual* moral self-consciousness or in other words *there is one that is actual.* For the concept posits this determinately in such a way that for consciousness all actuality in general has only essence inasmuch as it conforms to duty; and the concept posits this essence as knowledge, that is, in an immediate unity with the actual self. Consequently, this unity is itself actual—it *is* a moral, actual consciousness. —Now the latter as consciousness represents its content as the object, namely, as the *final purpose of the world,* as the harmony of morality and all actuality. However, since it represents this unity as *object* and is not yet the concept that has power over the object as such, the unity is a negative of self-consciousness for it, or in other words the unity falls outside of self-consciousness as something beyond its actuality but at the same time as something that *also* is *existent,* though only in thought.

177–613   Thereby what remains behind for self-consciousness, which as self-consciousness is something *other* than the object, is the lack of harmony between actuality and the consciousness of duty, and this is indeed proper to it. So the proposition now runs: "*There is no morally complete, actual* self-consciousness"; but since what is moral in general only is insofar as it is complete, duty is the *pure* unsullied *in-itself,* and morality consists only in being concordant with this purity; thus in general the second proposition states that: "There is *no morally actual* self-consciousness."

178–614   But since in the third place self-consciousness is one self, it is *implicitly* the unity of duty and actuality; this unity, therefore, becomes object for it as completed morality—yet as something *beyond* its actuality, which nevertheless ought to be actual.

179–615   In this goal of the synthetic unity of the first two propositions, self-conscious actuality, as well as duty, is posited only as a sublated moment,

(Nationalausgabe), hrsg. von Benni von Wiese, Bd. 21, Teil 2 (Weimar: Hermann Böhlaus Verlag, 1962), p. 38. What nature cannot do is act spontaneously; it must follow rational law.

[332] for neither of them is singular; thus these two, in which the essential determination is to be *free from the other,* are each no longer free from the other in this unity, and hence each is sublated. Consequently, according to the content, they become the object as the sort of moments where *each may count for the other,* and according to the form they come to be such that this exchange on their part is at the same time only *represented.* —In other words, because the self-consciousness that is *actually not* moral is equally pure thinking and raised above its actuality, it is in the representation still moral and is taken for something completely valid. In this way the first proposition—that there *is* a moral consciousness—is established but bound up with the second—that there *is* none: that is, there *is* one but only in representation; or in other words there is none, but it is still allowed to count as such by an other.[230]

b. Misrepresentation[231]

In the moral world-view, on the one hand, we see consciousness *itself*   180–616 *engender* its object with *consciousness.* We see consciousness neither comes upon the object as something foreign, nor the object comes to be for it unconsciously; instead, it proceeds throughout in accordance with a ground out of which it *posits:* the *objective being.*[232] It thus knows the latter to be itself, for it knows itself to be the *agent* that engenders it. At this point, then, consciousness seems to reach its rest and satisfaction, since it can find them only where it no longer needs to go beyond its object because the object no longer goes beyond it. On the other hand, consciousness posits the object quite *outside itself,* as something beyond it. But what is here in and for itself is nonetheless posited as something that is not free of self-consciousness, but exists at the beck and call of the latter and comes about through it.

The moral world-view, therefore, is in fact nothing else but the cultiva-   181–617 tion of this basic contradiction in its various aspects. To use a Kantian expression here where it is most appropriate, it is a *whole nest* of thoughtless

---

230. Hegel continues with the notion that there is a destructive dilemma at work in this concept. The Antinomies of Practical Reason are not answered by Kant; now Schiller's attempt at unity through an "aesthetical sense" is being examined. Schiller's position seems to mark the second stage of the "nordic essence," namely, the moment of division.

231. *Verstellung.* Normally this term is translated as "misplacement" or "displacement," both of which are literally correct. However, Hegel has in mind a false idea that is masquerading as something true. We thought that "misrepresentation" captures this sense better than the traditional translations.

232. <*Wesen*>

contradictions.[233] In this development, consciousness behaves in such a
way that it pins down one moment, passes over from it directly to another,
and cancels out the first.[234] But as soon as it *has presented* the second
moment it *also misrepresents* it again, and makes the contrary the essence
instead.[235] Consciousness is [333] aware, at the same time, of its contradiction and *also* its *misrepresenting,* for it passes from one moment (and
directly in *connection with that very moment*) only to the opposite one.
Because one moment has no reality for it, consciousness posits the very
same moment as real$_2$; or, what comes to the same thing, in order to affirm
one moment as existing in itself, it asserts the *opposite* to be what is exist-
ing-in-itself. In this way it confesses that in fact it is not in earnest about
either of them. This must be considered more closely in the moments of
this cheating movement.

182–618   Let the presupposition that there is an actual moral consciousness rest
initially upon itself, since it is not made directly in connection with anything prior, and let us turn to the harmony of morality and nature, which
is the first postulate. It is supposed to be *implicit,* not to be for actual consciousness, not present; on the contrary, the present is only the contradiction of the two. In the present, *morality* is taken to be *at hand,* and
actuality is so presented as not to be in harmony with morality. The *actual*
moral consciousness, however, is one that acts, and yet this constitutes the

233. Kant's actual expression is "a whole nest of dialectical presumptions,
which the transcendental critique can easily detect and destroy," *Critique of Pure
Reason,* A609 = B637.

234. Hegel is explaining the problem inherent in the category of *Gesinnung*
(disposition), which defines the self-conscious commitment to *Recht.* In *Philosophy of Spirit* Hegel makes two comments that clarify what is happening: first, "just
as each singular being in its knowledge is free and thus has a diversity in its disposition, so too the powers, the singular sides of the whole or the abstract moments
(of labor and fabrication . . .) are free"; and "The *disposition* of each estate, its self-
consciousness, which is its being as pure knowing within itself, is immediately
torn from determinate being," *GW,* viii, 264ff. A separation and disruption within
the unity of this self-conscious identity is now occurring. The parts of the individual's own self-certainty, like the parts of the republican state, are being pulled
into separate spheres of identity. "Disposition," such as Schiller's "aesthetical
sense," cannot hold all aspects of the individual (or its collective identity)
together.

235. Hegel plays on the two German terms, *aufstellen* and *verstellen.* Literally,
these words would mean "assemble" and "dissemble." The "assemblage" is the
honest presentation of consciousness: it is what it shows itself to be. The "dissem-
blance" would both be the removal of the honest façade and the cloaking what
consciousness truly is. We have tried to preserve these meanings by using
"present" for *aufstellt* and "misrepresent" for *verstellt.*

actuality of its morality. But in the very *acting* itself, that presentation is immediately misrepresented, for acting is nothing else but making the inner moral purpose actual, nothing but the production of an *actuality determined through the purpose,* that is, the harmony of moral purpose with actuality itself. At the same time, the completion of the action is for consciousness; it is the *presence* of this unity of actuality and purpose. And because in this completed action consciousness is actualized as this singular, and sees determinate being turned back into it (this is what constitutes enjoyment), so too there is contained, at the same time, in the actuality of the moral purpose its very form, which is called enjoyment and happiness. —And so, in the deed acting immediately fulfills what was handed down as something not supposed to happen, and what was supposed to be only a postulate, merely a beyond. Through its deed, then, consciousness expressed the fact that it is not in earnest about the postulate, since the sense of its acting is rather to make present what is not supposed to be present. Now, since the harmony is postulated for the sake of the activity (namely, what is supposed to become *actual* through the activity must be *so implicitly,* otherwise the actuality would not be *possible*) then the interconnection between the action and the postulate must be so constructed that, for the sake of the action (i.e., for the *actual* harmony of purpose and actuality), this harmony is posited as *not actual,* as something *beyond.*

In that *action* comes about, consciousness is thus not at all in earnest   183–619
about the *incommensurableness* of purpose and actuality. On the contrary, it seems to be in earnest about the *action* [334] itself. But in the deed actual action is only the action of a *singular* consciousness, and hence is itself merely something singular, and the work is contingent. The purpose of reason, however, the universal, all-encompassing purpose, is nothing short of the whole world: an ultimate purpose that goes far beyond the content of this singular action and that is to be placed, therefore, above all actual acting. Because what is universally best[236] is to be performed, nothing good is done. In the deed, however, the *nullity* of actual acting and the *reality* of the *total* purpose alone, which are now presented, are once again misrepresented on all sides.[237] Moral action is not something contingent and limited, since it has pure *duty* as its essence. Duty makes up the *singular total* purpose; and, since the action is the realization of that purpose, it brings the total absolute purpose to fulfillment, no matter how limited the content is otherwise. Or again, if actuality is taken to be nature, which has

---

236. Or, "what is good in common . . ."

237. Literally this reads, "But in the deed the *nullity* of the actual action and the *reality* of *total* purpose, which are now assembled, are again displaced on every side." Hegel is again making a play on the words *aufstellen* and *verstellen.*

its *own* laws and is opposed to pure duty, so that duty cannot realize its law in nature, then, since duty as such is essential, the concern in the deed is not with the *fulfillment* of pure duty, which is the total purpose; for the fulfillment would not have pure duty as its purpose, but rather its opposite, *actuality.*[238] But the fact that the concern is not with actuality is once again misrepresented; for according to the concept of moral acting, pure duty is in essence *active* consciousness. So action should of course come about; absolute duty should be expressed in the whole of nature; and the moral law should become the law of nature.[239]

184–620   If we let this *highest good* be counted as essential, then consciousness is not in earnest about morality at all. For in this highest good nature has no other law than morality has. But with that, moral acting itself falls away, for acting occurs only under the presupposition of something negative that is sublated through the action. If, however, nature conforms with the ethical law, then such law would be violated by the acting, that is, by the sublating of what is. —Moreover, in assuming the highest good to be essential, a state of affairs is conceded to be the essential condition whereby moral acting is superfluous and does not take place at all. Hence from this side the postulate of the harmony of morality and actuality (of a harmony that is posited through the concept of moral acting, bringing both into agreement) is also expressed as follows: because moral acting is the absolute purpose, then it is the absolute purpose that moral acting not be present at all.

---

238. Hegel appears to be referring to Kant's third Antinomy in the first Critique, namely, the conflict between natural and free causes. In part, Kant's solution is to posit an *ought* for a possible world, "This *ought* expresses a possible action, the ground of which cannot be anything but a mere concept; whereas in the case of a merely natural action the ground must always be an appearance. The action to which the *ought* applies must indeed be possible under natural conditions. These conditions, however, do not play any part in determining the will itself, but only in determining the effect and its consequences in appearances," (A548 = B576). However, this moral action may fail to be effected; in fact there is no assurance that it will be: "Reason does not here follow the order of things as they present themselves in appearance, but frames for itself with perfect spontaneity an order of its own according to ideas, to which it adapts the empirical conditions, and according to which it declares actions to be necessary, even although they have never taken place, and perhaps never will," Ibid. In *Philosophy of Spirit* Hegel calls this the "ambiguous ought."

239. Hegel is referring to the second formulation of Kant's Categorical Imperative: "Act as if the maxim of your action were to become through your will a universal law of nature," *Grounding for the Metaphysics of Morals* (1785), *Akad.*, iv, 421. Cf. Kant's discussion of the "empirical character" of moral reason in *Critique of Pure Reason*, A449–50 = B577–8.

If we present these moments together, through which consciousness 185–621
continues on its way in its moral representation, it is obvious that it sublates each moment again within its opposite. It proceeds from the fact that
for consciousness, morality and [335] actuality are not in harmony, but consciousness is not in earnest about this, since *for it* there is the presence of
this harmony in the action. But it is no more in earnest about this *acting*
either, since it is something singular; after all, it has such a high purpose,
the *highest good*. However, this too is only a misrepresentation of the facticity, for in it all acting and all morality fall away.[240] That is, consciousness is not genuinely in earnest about *moral* acting; instead what is
absolute and most devoutly to be wished is that the highest good be
achieved and moral acting rendered superfluous.[241]

From this result consciousness must continue on its way in its contra- 186–622
dictory movement and once again necessarily misrepresent the *sublating*
of moral acting. Morality is the in-itself; if there is to be room for it, the
final purpose of the world cannot be brought about. Rather, the moral
consciousness must be *for itself* and confront *nature opposed* to it. However, it must be completed with respect to itself. This leads to the second
postulate of the harmony of morality and nature, which is immediately in
moral consciousness: sensibility. Moral self-consciousness presents its
purpose as so pure and independent of inclinations and impulses, with
the result that this purpose has eradicated the purposes of sensibility
within itself. —But having presented this sublation of the sensible
essence, consciousness once again misrepresents it. It acts, brings its purpose to actuality, and the self-conscious sensibility, which is to have been
sublated, is just this middle term between pure consciousness and actuality; it is the instrument of the former for its realization, or its organ, and is

---

240. This marks the return to the essential category of Reason, "facticity,"
which is itself duplicitous. Hegel remarks further in *Philosophy of Spirit* that this
category comes to the burgher's consciousness when he takes money to be the sign
of value. This is where the "moral category" of disposition (*Gesinnung*) leads us:
i.e., "The disposition of the commercial estate is therefore the understanding of
the unity between *essence* and thing; thus it is as real as his money. . . . This significance has immediate determinate being; the 'essence' of the fact [*Sache*] is facticity itself [*Sache selbst*]. The 'value' is the clinking coins. The formal principle of
reason is [now] present to consciousness," *GW,* viii, 269ff.

241. The purpose of existence is to obtain what one desires, and in this end a
newfound unity occurs within this "moral" disposition. Hegel comments on the
effect of this unity, namely, that "Spirit has come to be its own object in its
abstraction, that is, as the *selfless* inner. But this inner is the I-self, and this self is
its determinate being. The shape of the inner is not [just] some dead thing, i.e.,
money, but is equally the *I* . . ." *Philosophy of Spirit, GW,* viii, 270.

called impulse or inclination. Therefore, it is not in earnest about the sublating of inclinations and impulses, for they are just *self-consciousness realizing itself.* However, they are not to be *suppressed,* but only to *conform* to
reason. And they conform to it because moral *acting* is nothing else but
consciousness realizing itself and thus giving itself the shape of an
impulse; in other words, it is immediately the present harmony of impulse
and morality. In the deed, however, impulse is not only this empty shape,
which could have in itself a trigger other than itself to propel it. For sensibility is a nature that has its own laws and trigger springs implicit in it.
And so, morality cannot be in earnest about being the impelling trigger of
impulses, the angle of inclination for inclinations. For, since these have
their own firm determinacy and proper content, the consciousness to
which they were to conform would conform to them—a conformity that
moral self-consciousness disavows. And so, the harmony of the two [336]
is only something *in itself* and *postulated.* —In moral acting this *present*
harmony of morality and sensibility has only just been presented; but it *is
now* misrepresented.[242] It lies beyond consciousness in a cloudy distance,
in which there is nothing more to be distinguished or conceived with
accuracy, for nothing came of the attempt we just made to conceive this
unity. In this implicit [harmony], however, consciousness completely
abandons itself. This implicit [harmony] is its moral fulfillment, in which
the struggle between morality and sensibility has ceased, and sensibility
conforms with morality in a way that cannot be grasped. And so, this fulfillment is once again merely a misrepresentation of facticity; for, indeed,
in that fulfillment *morality* would instead be given up, since it is only consciousness of the absolute purpose as *pure* and hence *opposed* to all other
purposes. Morality is just the *activity* of this pure purpose inasmuch as it
is conscious of the elevation above sensibility, of the admixture of sensibility, and of its opposition to, and struggle with, it. The fact that consciousness is not in earnest about moral fulfillment finds immediate expression
in the fact that consciousness misrepresents fulfillment by projecting it
into *infinity* and asserting that it is never fulfilled.

---

242. The misrepresentation concerns the condition when what is only for
itself is also for the universal that constitutes the unity and identity between the
individual and the state. The burgher wants money because he feels that this will
satisfy him, but he is also committed to the legal stature of the state, since only
through the state and its corporations will the burgher have the opportunity to
gain money. He is *for the state* even though his "disposition" is only for himself.
Hegel represents this stance of identity as completely contradictory but nonetheless sufficient to unify the individual within the state's constitution: "to this spirit
[that is, the I-self] the state in general is the object of its doings, employments, and
purpose," *Philosophy of Spirit, GW,* viii, 270.

Rather, it is only this intermediate condition of nonfulfillment that is 187–623
valid for it—a condition, however, that is still to be at least an *advance*
toward fulfillment. Except that it cannot even be that, for an advance in
morality would be instead a moving on toward its demise. In other words,
the goal would be the above-mentioned nothingness, or sublating of
morality and of consciousness itself. But to come ever nearer and nearer
to nothingness is what is meant by *diminution*. Besides, *advance* in general,
as well as *diminution*, would adopt distinctions of *magnitude* in morality;
but, of course, in it there can be no talk of such. In morality, as the consciousness for which ethical purpose is *pure* duty, there can be no thought
of any variety whatever, least of all in respect to the surface feature of
magnitude. There is only *one* virtue, only *one* pure duty, only *one* morality.

Then, too, since consciousness is not in earnest about moral fulfill- 188–624
ment but rather about the intermediate condition (that is, as has just been
explained, about nonmorality), we return from another side to the content of the first postulate. That is to say, we cannot see how happiness may
be demanded for this moral consciousness on the basis of its *worthiness*.[243]
It is conscious of its lack of fulfillment, and therefore cannot in fact
demand happiness as something earned, as something of which it would
be worthy. Rather, it can only ask for it, that is, for happiness as *such* in
and of itself, as a free grace. It can expect it, not on the basis of the absolute ground previously mentioned, but as happening capriciously and by
chance. Nonmorality here expresses just what it is: [337] that it is not
concerned with morality, but rather with happiness in and for itself without connection with morality.

By means of this second aspect of the moral world-view the other asser- 189–625
tion of the first is nevertheless also sublated, the one in which the disharmony of morality and happiness is presupposed. For there will be an
experience that in this present world things often go badly for the moral
person, while things go well for the immoral one. Yet the intermediate
stage of morality unfulfilled, which has turned out to be what is essential,
makes it obvious that this perception and alleged experience is only a misrepresentation of facticity. For, since morality is unfulfilled or, in other
words, in fact is *not*, what can there be in experience according to which

---

243. We are turning to the imperfect consciousness who is aware of its unworthiness. Again, Hegel continues to play out the destructive dilemma of this entire
conceptual development. Each side of the dilemma is being played out, and each
one is proving to be self-contradictory or otherwise lacking. As we will eventually
see, the imperfect consciousness has the attitude of "faith," which was thwarted
back in the Enlightenment sections. For Hegel the "evil" being (in the Kantian
sense that it acts only on its "good will" and is directed by its own human nature)
is the most genuine form of self-consciousness.

things go badly for it? Since it has just emerged that consciousness is concerned with happiness in and for itself, it is manifest that in the judgment things go well for the immoral person; it does not mean that what here takes place is something unjust. Insofar as morality in general is unfulfilled, the designation of an individual as someone immoral falls away *of itself* and has only a capricious ground. The sense and content of the judgment of experience thereby comes just to this: that happiness in and of itself should not have happened to certain individuals, in other words, what is meant is that *envy* takes morality to itself as a cloak. The reason why others should partake of so-called fortune, however, is good friendship, which *grants* and *wishes* this grace, this chance, for others as well as itself.[244]

190–626   Thus morality is unfulfilled in moral consciousness. This is what is now being presented. But the essence of morality is to be *pure* and *fulfilled*. It follows that unfulfilled morality is impure; in other words, it is immorality. Morality, itself, then, is to be found in a being other than actual consciousness; this other is a holy moral lawgiver. —*Unfulfilled* in consciousness, the morality that is the ground of this postulating has *first of all* the significance that morality, insofar as it is posited in consciousness as *actual*, stands in connection with an *other*, with a determinate being, and so gets otherness or distinction even into itself, from which a manifold plurality of moral commands arises. But moral self-consciousness at the same time considers these *many* duties to be inessential; for the only thing at issue is the *one* pure duty, and they have no truth *for self-consciousness* to the extent that they are *determinate*. These duties can have their truth, then, only in an other, and they are the very thing they are not, in relation to actual self-consciousness: holy, through a holy lawgiver.[245] —But this is

---

244. Hegel, in the last lines of the *Phenomenology*, quotes Schiller's poem "Friendship," and he may be preparing us already for the denouement of the book. But more likely at this point he has more the Aristotelian "noble" virtue in mind than Romantic sentiment; as Aristotle says, "For without friends no one would choose to live, though he had all other goods; even rich men and those in possession of office and of dominating power are thought to need friends most of all . . ." *Nicomachean Ethics*, Bk. VIII, I, 1155a5–7. The idea that good fortune, or happiness, is desired for every friend is also Aristotelian, "[friendship] is more beautiful in good fortune, and so we also look for good men as our friends, since it is more desirable to confer benefits on these and to live with them. For the very presence of friends is pleasant both in good fortune and also in bad, since grief is lightened when friends sorrow with us," Ibid., Bk. IX, XI, 1171a24–30.

245. This looks to be a reference to Eschenmayer's *The Hermit and Orphan*. Eschenmayer, as part of his criticisms of Schelling's Identity Philosophy, contends that the "holy" is found and bound to simple, naive consciousness. Hegel is contending that this misrepresents the nature of facticity.

once again only a misrepresentation of the facticity. For to itself, moral self-consciousness is absolute, and duty is simply and solely what *it knows* as duty. [338] Now it knows only pure duty as duty. What is not holy for it is not holy in itself; and what is not holy in itself cannot be made holy by a holy being.[246] Hence, moral consciousness is not at all in earnest about letting something be holy *through a* consciousness *other* than itself; for quite simply what is holy for it is so only for it by virtue of *itself and within it*. And it is just as little in earnest in claiming that this other being is a holy one, because that would suppose that in this other being something has become essential that has no essentiality in itself—that is, for moral consciousness.

If the holy being were so postulated that in it duty would have its valid- 191–627 ity not as pure duty but as a plurality of *determinate* duties, then this, too, must again be misrepresented; and the other being alone must be holy insofar as only *pure duty* has validity in it. And in fact pure duty has valid- ity only in an other being, not in moral consciousness. Although pure morality alone seems to have validity in the moral consciousness, this must be framed in another way, for moral consciousness is at the same time a natural consciousness. In it morality is affected and conditioned by sensibility; hence it is not in and for itself but is a contingency of the free *will;* in it as pure *will*, however, it is a contingency of *knowledge; in and of itself*, therefore, morality is in an other being.[247]

Thus, this being is here pure fulfilled morality, for the reason that in it 192–628 morality does not stand in connection with nature and sensibility. But the *reality* of pure duty is its *actualization* in nature and sensibility. Moral consciousness locates its imperfection in the fact that in consciousness morality has a *positive* connection with nature and sensibility, because to have simply and solely a *negative* connection with them is for it an essen- tial moment of morality. On the other hand, because the pure moral being is exalted above the *struggle* with nature and sensibility, it does not stand in a negative connection with them. So there remains for it, in fact, only the *positive* connection with them, in other words, precisely what counted just now as the unfulfilled or the immoral. But were *pure moral- ity* completely separated from actuality, so that it would be just as much

---

246. <Wesen>

247. The juxtaposition of first sensuous and then pure willing as descriptive of moral consciousness is reminiscent of Jacobi's moral philosophy. The "other being" in this context is empirical consciousness, as opposed to Kant's transcen- dental Self. Hegel makes many comments about Jacobi in *Faith and Knowledge*, in respect to his practical philosophy: see *GW*, iv, pp. 380–82; Cerf and Harris trans- lation (Albany, NY: State Univ. of New York Press, 1977), pp. 142–6.

without positive connection with nature and sensibility, then it would be an abstraction, without consciousness and without actuality. In it, the concept of morality, which consists in thinking pure duty with a willing and doing, would be quite simply annulled. Such a pure moral being is, therefore, once again a misrepresentation of the facticity and must be given up.

193–629   In this purely moral being, however, the moments of contradiction, on which this synthetic representation turns, approach one another; so, too, do the opposing "also's" that consciousness lets follow one upon the other, without bringing these thoughts it has together, and continually, by means of the other, lets loose such an antithesis [339] that consciousness must here give up its moral world-view and take flight back into itself.

194–630   It recognizes this morality, therefore, as not fulfilled, because it is affected by a sensibility and nature opposed to it, which in part obscures morality as such, in part gives rise to a host of duties, and through these it gets into difficulty in the concrete case of actual activity. For each case is the concretion of many moral connections, just as an object of perception in general is a thing with many properties. And since the *determinate* duty has a purpose, morality has a content, and its *content* is a part of the purpose; so morality is not pure. —Therefore, pure morality has its *reality* in an other being. But this reality means nothing other than that morality is here *in and for itself: for itself,* that is, it is the morality of a *consciousness; in itself,* that is, it has *determinate being* and *actuality.* —In that first unfulfilled consciousness, morality is not carried out; it is there the *in-itself* in the sense of an *ens rationis.* For it is associated with nature and sensibility, with the actuality of being and consciousness, which makes up their content; and nature and sensibility are morally nugatory. —In the second consciousness, morality is present as *fulfilled,* and not as an *ens rationis* which is not carried out. But this fulfillment consists in just this: that morality has *actuality* in a *consciousness,* precisely as *free actuality,* or determinate being in general, which is not what is empty but laden with content. —In other words, the fulfillment of morality is posited in this: that what was determined precisely as morally nugatory is present in morality and in relation to it. —In the first instance, it is supposed to have validity simply and solely as a nonactual *ens rationis* produced by pure abstraction, yet, equally in this form, to have no validity. Its truth is supposed to consist in its being opposed to actuality, in being wholly free of it and empty, and yet again in being actuality.

195–631   The syncretism of these contradictions, which is articulated in the moral world-view, collapses into itself, since the distinction upon which it rests—the distinction of a thing that must necessarily be thought and posited, and yet at the same time is inessential—becomes a distinction that can no longer be expressed in words.[248] What is posited finally as something diverse, as the nugatory as much as the real, is just one and the same: determinate being and actuality. And what is supposed to exist absolutely as the *beyond* of actual being and consciousness, and just as much to exist only in actual being and consciousness, and as the beyond is supposed to be nugatory—this is pure duty, and the knowledge of duty as the essence. Consciousness that draws this distinction that is no distinction, asserts actuality to be something nugatory and real at the same time, [340] and asserts pure morality to be both the true essence and lacking essence—this consciousness enunciates together the thoughts that it had hitherto kept separated, and itself announces that it is not in earnest regarding this determination and the presentation of the moments of the *self* and the *in-itself* as outside of each other. On the contrary, it announces that what it declares to be the absolute *existent* outside consciousness, it rather contains enclosed within the self of self-consciousness, and that what it declares to be the absolute *object of thought* or absolute *it-itself,* just for that reason it takes to be something that has no truth. —Consciousness becomes aware that the presentation of these moments as outside of each other is a misrepresentation, and it would be *hypocrisy* if it continued to adhere to this misrepresentation. But as pure moral self-consciousness, it flees from this nonequivalence between its *representation* and what is its *essence,* flees from this untruth that asserts as true what it holds as untrue, flees in aversion back into itself. It is *pure conscience,* which scorns such a moral representation of the world.[249] It is *within itself* simple spirit certain of itself, which acts directly and conscientiously without the mediation of

---

248. The use of the word "syncretism" implies that Hegel has in mind the philosophy of W. T. Krug, especially Krug's attempt to blend the "eternal truths" of religion and morality with the empiricism of Kantian philosophy, while all along denying the transcendental Self. Krug called his synthesis of the pure and the empirical "transcendental syncretism." Fichte, Schelling, and Hegel all thought Krug's philosophy to be fallacious; see Hegel's article "How the Ordinary Human Understanding Takes Philosophy," *GW,* iv, 91–115. There is an English translation of this piece in *Between Kant and Hegel,* trans. and ed. by George di Giovanni and H. S. Harris (Indianapolis: Hackett Publishing Co., 2000), pp. 292–310.

249. In *Philosophy of Spirit,* this is the third moment of the nordic essence, namely, "mistrust." It is a mistrust in unity, of the identity between state and individual, and even a mistrust in identifying with the separate divisions among the singular aspects of conscious being. It rejects abstract right; it rejects our disposition for unity in any external object, including money and the state's own good. It is concerned only with knowing the "pure Self." Hegel is, however, preparing us for the conclusion that this form of consciousness also falls into contradictions.

those representations and possesses its truth in this immediacy. —But if this world of misrepresentation is nothing different from the development of moral self-consciousness in its moments and thereby is its *reality,* then, by its retreat into itself, consciousness will become in its essence nothing distinct. Rather its retreat is within itself just the *achieved consciousness* that its truth is a simulated one. It *would* still always *have to give out* this truth as *its* truth, for it would have to express and present itself as an objective representation, but it *would know* that this is merely a misrepresentation. It would thus be hypocrisy in fact, and the former *scorn* of that misrepresentation would already be the first expression of hypocrisy.

c. Conscience, the Beautiful Soul, Evil and Its Forgiveness

196–632   The antinomy of the moral world-view—that there is a moral consciousness and that there is none; or that the validity of duty both lies in a realm beyond consciousness and, conversely, takes place only in consciousness—this antinomy had been comprehended in the representation in which the nonmoral consciousness [341] assumed moral validity, its contingent knowing and willing were accepted as having full weight, and happiness was allotted to it as a matter of grace. Moral self-consciousness did not take this self-contradictory representation upon itself but rather passed it off on to a being[250] other than itself. But this placing outside of its very self of what it must think of as necessary is as much a contradiction in form as was the former a contradiction in content. But because precisely what appears to be contradictory, and what the moral world-view goes about trying to separate and then to resolve once more, is inherently one and the same (that is, pure duty as *pure knowing* is nothing other than the *self* of consciousness, and the self of consciousness is *being* and *actuality*), and also because what is supposed to lie beyond *actual* consciousness is nothing other than pure thinking, and thus is in fact the self—for these reasons self-consciousness *for us* or *in itself* retreats into itself and knows that being to be its very self, in which the *actual* is at once both *pure knowing* and *pure duty.* It takes itself to be something that is completely valid in its own contingency and that knows its immediate singularity as pure knowing and acting, as true actuality and harmony.

197–633   This *self of conscience,* spirit that is immediately certain of itself as absolute truth and being, is the *third self,* which has come to us out of the third world of spirit and which should be compared briefly with the preceding

---

250. <Wesen>

ones.[251] The totality or actuality that presents itself as the truth of the ethical world is the self of the *person;* its determinate being consists in *being
recognized.* Just as the person is the self void of substance, so too its determinate being now is, similarly, abstract actuality. The person has *validity,*
indeed has this immediately. The self is the point that is immediately at
rest in the element of its being; this point is without the separation from
its universality, and thus the two are not in movement and in connection
with one another. The universal is in it without differentiation; neither is
it the content of the self nor is the self fulfilled through its own self. —The
second self is the world of culture that has arrived at its truth, in other
words, spirit that has recovered itself from diremption: absolute freedom.
In this second self, the immediate unity of singularity and universality in
the first comes apart; the universal, which in the same way remains a
purely spiritual essence—being recognized or a universal actuality. But it
does not have the form of determinate being that is free from the self; it
thus attains in this self no fulfillment and no positive content, no world.
Moral self-consciousness indeed lets its universality go free, so that universality becomes a nature of its own; and equally, self-consciousness
holds it fast within itself as something sublated. But it is only a play of
misrepresentation that consists in exchanging these two determinations.
[342] Only as conscience does it come to have, in *self-certainty,* the *content*
for the duty that has previously been empty, as well as the empty right and
for the empty universal will; and, because this self-certainty is equally
something *immediate,* it comes to have determinate being itself.

Now that it has attained this stage of its truth, moral self-consciousness
relinquishes, or rather sublates, the separation within itself from which
misrepresentation had arisen—the separation between the *in-itself* and the
self, between pure duty (as pure *purpose*) and *actuality* (as a nature and sen-
suousness that is set over against pure purpose). It is thus returned into
itself, it is *concrete* moral spirit, which in the consciousness of pure duty

198–634

---

251. This person is a Romantic, e.g., a member of the "Jena Circle." Hegel is
thinking of the Schlegels, Tieck, Novalis, Fichte (who was a frequent visitor),
Schleiermacher, and to some extent Schelling, who was a close associate of the
Schlegels until about 1801. The Romantic notion of the Self is a continuation of
the aesthetical idea of unity through a "common sense," but unlike Schelling the
emphasis here is on our imperfect human nature. The fire and passions of love
and loss (*Sturm und Drang*) heighten supposedly our moral and religious sentiments. The reference to the three Worlds should remind us, as is intended, of
Novalis's three ages of redemptive religion (Catholicism, Protestantism, and the
ecumenicalism of the Romantics themselves), which he presents in *Christendom or
Europe* (1800), and of Eschenmayer's three stages of history that prove the truth of
Christianity, which he presents in *Hermit and Orphan.*

does not give itself pure duty, and similarly nature that is set against it; these are sublated moments. Spirit is, in an immediate unity, a *self-actualizing moral* essence, and action is an immediately *concrete* moral shape.

199–635   A case of action presents itself: it is, for the knowing consciousness, an objective actuality. Consciousness as conscience knows it immediately and concretely, and at the same time it only is as consciousness knows it to be. Now knowing is contingent, insofar as it is something other than its object. But spirit, which is certain of itself, is no longer a contingent knowing of this sort, nor an internal creation of thought distinguished from actuality. Rather, since the separation between the *in-itself* and the *self* is sublated, the case of action is immediately, in the sense-*certainty* of knowing, the way it is *in itself;* and it is *in itself* only the way it is in this knowing. —Action, as actualization, is thus the pure form of willing: the simple conversion of actuality as a *given*[252] case into a *performed* actuality, the conversion of a mere mode of *objective* knowing into a mode of knowing this *actuality* as something produced by consciousness. Just as sense-certainty is immediately taken up, or rather converted into the in-itself of spirit, so too this conversion is simple and unmeditated, a transition by means of the pure concept, without alteration of the content. The latter is determined by the interest of consciousness knowing itself. —Furthermore, conscience does not split apart the circumstances of the case into diverse duties. It does not behave as a *positive, universal medium* in which the many duties, each on its own, would acquire an unshakable substantiality. For in that instance *either* no action whatsoever would be possible— because every concrete case included opposition in general and, in the case of morality, included the opposition of duties, so that in defining an action, *one* side, *one* duty, would be constantly *violated—or else,* if there were action, then a violation of one of the opposed duties would surely ensue. [343] Conscience is rather the negative one of the absolute self that destroys these diverse moral substances. It is simple, dutiful action, which does not fulfill this or that duty, but knows and does what is concretely right. It is thus above all else just moral *action* as action, into which the preceding inactive consciousness of morality has passed. —The concrete shape of the deed may be analyzed into diverse properties by the differentiating consciousness, that is, in this case into diverse moral connections; and each of them may be either affirmed as absolutely valid (as it must be, if it is to be duty), or else they may be compared and tested. In the simple moral action of conscience, duties are so mashed together that there is an immediate *breakdown* of all these singular essences, and in the

---

252. <*seiende*>

unwavering certainty of conscience there is no place at all for a testing and sifting of duty.

Neither is there present in conscience the dithering uncertainty that, in one moment, posits the so-called pure morality outside itself in the other, holy essence and deems itself to be unholy, but, in the next moment, also posits moral purity within itself once again and posits the connection between the sensuous and the moral in the other essence.   200–636

It renounces all these positions and misrepresentations of the moral world-view when it renounces the consciousness that grasps duty and actuality as contradictory. According to this consciousness, I act morally when I am *conscious* of fulfilling pure duty alone and *nothing else* whatever, and this means, in fact, *that I do not* act. But when I actually act, I am conscious of an *other*, an *actuality;* both one that is present and one that I want to bring forth. I have a *determinate* purpose and fulfill a *determinate* duty: there is something *else* to it than pure duty, which should have been the sole consideration. —Conscience, on the contrary, is the consciousness that if moral consciousness declares *pure duty* to be the essence of its action, this pure purpose is a misrepresentation of the matter. For the fact of the matter[253] is that pure duty consists in the empty abstraction of pure thought and obtains its reality and content only in a determinate actuality, an actuality that is the actuality of consciousness itself (understood not as a *ens rationis* but as something singular). Conscience has its truth *for its own self* in the *immediate certainty* of itself. This *immediate* concrete self-certainty is the essence. When this certainty is considered in accordance with the antithesis of consciousness, certainty's immediate *singularity* is the content of the moral deed; and the *form* of this deed is precisely this self as pure movement, that is, as *knowing* or as *its own conviction*. [344]   201–637

Considering this more closely, in its unity and in the significance of its moments, moral consciousness grasped itself only as the *in-itself* or as *essence;* but as conscience it grasps its being-*for-self* or its *self:* a simple *self*, which is both *pure* knowing and a knowing of itself as *this singular* consciousness. Hence, this self constitutes the content of the previously empty essence; for it is the *actual*, which no longer has significance of being an independent nature, alien to the essence and having laws of its own. As the negative, it is the *distinction* of pure essence, a content, and indeed one that is valid in and for itself.   202–638

Further, this self, as pure, self-equivalent knowing, is the *universal pure and simple*, so that precisely this knowing, *as the self's own* knowing, as conviction, is *duty*. Duty is no longer the universal confronting the self,   203–639

---

253. <Sache>

but is known to have no validity in this separateness. It is now the laws
that exist for the sake of the self, rather than the self existing for the sake
of the law. Law and duty, however, consequently have the significance not
only of *being for itself* but also of *being-in-itself;* for knowing is, on account
of its self-equivalence, precisely the *in-itself.* This *in-itself* also separates
itself, in consciousness, from that immediate unity with being for itself; in
this confrontation, it is *being, not being for other.* —At this point, as duty
that has been abandoned by the self, duty is now known to be only a
moment. It has sunk from the significance of being absolute essence down
to the level of the being that is not a self, not *for itself,* and that is thus
being for other. But this *being for other* remains an essential moment precisely because the self, as consciousness, constitutes the antithesis of
being for itself and being for other, and now duty is itself something
immediately *actual,* and no longer merely abstract pure consciousness.

204–640   This *being for other* is thus the substance that subsists *in itself* and is distinguished from the [conscious] self. Conscience has not surrendered
pure duty or the *abstract in-itself;* on the contrary, duty is the essential
moment of relating to others as *universality.* It is the communal element of
the self-consciousnesses, and this element is the substance in which the
deed has *stability* and *actuality:* the moment of *coming to be recognized* by
others. Moral self-consciousness does not have this moment of recognized
being—of *pure consciousness* that *is there*[254] and is therefore not in the least
active or [345] effective. *What is in-itself* is for it either the abstract *nonactual* essence, or *being* as an *actuality* that is not spiritual. But the *subsistent
actuality* of conscience is such a one that is a *self,* that is, a determinate
being conscious of itself, the spiritual element of *coming to be recognized.*
The deed is thus only the transition of its *singular* content into the *objective* element in which it is universal and recognized; and it is precisely its
being recognized that turns agency into actuality. Agency is recognized
and thereby actual, because the actuality that is there is immediately
bound to conviction or knowing, that is, because the knowing of one's purpose is immediately universal recognition, the element of determinate
being. For duty, the *essence* of agency consists in the *conviction* of conscience about it; this conviction is just the *in-itself;* it is the *implicitly universal self-consciousness,* the state of recognition and thereby the actuality.
What is done with conviction of duty is thus something immediate that
has standing and determinate being. So there is no talk now of the good
intention not coming to fruition, or things going badly for the good man;
rather, what is known as duty fulfills itself and attains actuality, because
precisely what is dutiful is the universal for all self-consciousnesses, what

---

254. <*Daseyn*>

is recognized, and, hence, what is.[255] Without the content of the self, however, this duty, taken separately and alone, is *being for other,* which can be seen through and has only the significance of an essentiality in general without material content.

If we look back at the sphere wherein general *spiritual reality* first came 205–641 on the scene, our concept was that the expression of individuality *should be* what is *in and for itself.* But the shape that immediately expressed this concept was the *honest consciousness,* which busied itself with the *abstract facticity.* This *facticity* was there the *predicate,* but in conscience it is for the first time *subject,* which has posited all the moments of consciousness in it, and for which all these moments—substantiality in general, external being,[256] and the essence of thinking—are contained in this certainty of itself. *Facticity* has substantiality in general in ethical life, determinate being in culture, self-knowing essentiality of thinking in morality; and in conscience it is the subject that knows these moments in itself.[257] Whereas the honest consciousness only grasps at the *empty facticity,* conscience, in contrast, achieves it by the fulfillment that conscience gives to it all by itself. Conscience is this power, because it knows the moments of consciousness as *moments* and dominates them as their negative essence. [346]

When we consider conscience in connection with the singular determi- 206–642 nations of the antithesis, which appear in action, and because it is *its own* knowing, which it has about their nature, we see that conscience behaves primarily as a *knower* in relation to the *actuality* of the *case* in which it is to act. So far as there is the moment of *universality* in this knowing, it is incumbent on the knowing [moment] in conscientious action to grasp, without limitation, the actuality that lies before it, and thus to know all the circumstances of the case exactly and take them into consideration. This knowing, however, since it is *aware* of the universality as a *moment,* is thus a sort of knowing of these circumstances, which is conscious to itself of not grasping them and of now being conscientious in this regard, that it does not in fact really grasp them. The true universal and pure connection of knowing would be a connection with something and not opposed to it—a

---

255. <Seyende>

256. <Daseyn>

257. Facticity as subject is when the identity of the Self is formed through its own business activity, that is, its own self-selected work. Supposedly nothing outside of "its business" matters. Hegel can speak of the Romantic this way because the Romantic genius lives through art and aesthetical appreciation of the beautiful. The deception here (there is always deception with facticity) is that this spirit is caught in its own emotive struggles. It lives for "storm and stress" and thus its "own business" cannot sustain it.

connection with its very self. But, because of the antithesis, which is essential to it, *action* connects with a negative of consciousness, with an actuality that *has being in itself.* In contrast to the simplicity of pure consciousness (the absolute *other,* or the manifold in itself), this actuality is an absolute plurality of circumstances, which splits up and spreads out endlessly—backward into their conditions, sideways into their surroundings, forward into their consequences. —The conscientious consciousness is conscious of the nature of this facticity and of its own relation to it; and it knows that it is, but is not aware (in the universal way that is required) of the situation in which it is acting, and this pretense of weighing out consciously all the circumstances is in vain. Yet, this awareness and weighing out of all the circumstances is not entirely absent, but it is present only as a *moment,* as something that is only for *another;* and this incomplete knowing counts for conscientious consciousness as adequate and perfect.

207–643   Conscience behaves in the same way with respect to the universality of *essence,* that is, the determination of the content by pure consciousness.[258] —As it goes into action, conscience becomes connected with the many sides of the case. The case breaks apart, and so does the connection of pure consciousness with it; hence the manifold of the case becomes a manifold of *duties.* —Conscience knows that it has to choose from among these duties and make its decision; for none of them is absolute in its determinacy or in its content: only *pure duty* is so. But this abstraction has attained, in its reality, the significance of the self-conscious *I*. Spirit certain of itself is at rest within itself as conscience, and its *real* universality, its duty, lies in its pure *conviction* of duty. This *pure* conviction is, as such, just as empty as pure *duty*—pure in the sense that nothing in it, no determinate content, is duty. But there should be action; there must be something *determined* by the individual; and self-certain spirit, in which the in-itself has attained the significance of the self-conscious *I*, knows that it has this determination and content in the immediate *certainty* of its own self. As determination and content, this certainty [347] is *natural* consciousness, that is, the drives and inclinations. —Conscience acknowledges no content as absolute for itself, for it is the absolute negativity of everything that is determinate. It determines *from its own self;* but the circle of the self, in which determinacy as such falls, is so-called sensibility: there is nothing ready at hand other than sensibility that can supply a content out of immediate certainty.[259] —Everything that presents itself in

---

258. We take this sentence to refer back to the first sentence of ¶206–642.

259. For the Romantic hero, the direction of a course of action is always decided by feeling. Goethe's *Egmont* (1786), whose hero is torn by conflicting duties, might be thought of as a case in point.

previous shapes of spirit as good or bad, or as law and right, is something *other* than the immediate certainty of its self; it is something *universal,* which is now a being-for-other; or considered in another way, it is an object, which as it mediates consciousness with itself, steps between consciousness and its own truth, and separates consciousness from itself rather than being the immediacy of consciousness. —But for conscience, certainty of its self is the pure, immediate truth; and this truth is thus its immediate certainty of its self represented as *content*; that is, in general, the wilfullness of the singular and the contingency of its nonconscious natural being.

This content counts, at the same time, as moral *essentiality,* or as *duty.* 208–644 For pure duty is utterly indifferent to all content (as it turned out to be earlier in the testing of laws), and will put up with any content. Here duty has the essential form of *being for itself* as well, and this form of individual conviction is nothing else but the consciousness of the emptiness of pure duty and that pure duty is only a moment; the consciousness that its substantiality is a predicate, which has its subject in the individual, whose wilfullness gives pure duty its content. It can bind any content to this form and can fasten its conscientiousness to it. —An individual increases his property in a specific way: it is everyone's duty to care for the support of himself and his family too, and no less to care about the *possibility* of becoming useful to his fellow humans and of doing good for those in need of help. The individual is consciously aware that this is duty, for this content is immediately contained in the certainty he has of himself; he has the insight moreover, that he is fulfilling the duty in this case. Others, perhaps, take this specific way to be deceit: *they* hold to other aspects of the concrete case, whereas *he* holds fast to this aspect, that is, that he is consciously aware of increasing his property as pure duty. —Thus what others call violence and lawlessness fulfills the duty of asserting one's independence from others. What they call cowardice fulfills the duty of preserving one's own life and the possibility of being useful to one's fellow humans. But what they call courage only violates both these duties. But cowardice cannot be so inept as not to know that the preservation of life and the possibility [348] of being merciful to others are duties—it cannot be so inept as not be *convinced* by the dutifulness of its action and not to know that duty consists in *knowing*: otherwise, it would commit the ineptitude of being immoral. Since morality lies in the consciousness of having fulfilled duty, this will no more be lacking for the action labeled cowardice than for the action labeled courage. The abstraction called duty, since it is capable of any content, is capable of this content also. Thus abstract duty knows what it does to be duty; and since it knows this, and since the conviction of duty is just what is dutiful, it is thus recognized by others: thereby action has validity and actual determinate being.

209–645   It is no use asserting—against this freedom that puts any content whatsoever, each one as good as the next, into the universal passive medium of pure duty and knowing—that another content should be introduced. For whatever the content may be, each one has the *stain of determinacy* upon it, from which pure knowing is free and which it can disdain—just as it can accept any determinacy. Every content, because it is determinate, stands on the same level as [every] other, even if it seems to have precisely the characteristic that particularity is sublated in it. Since in the actual case duty is divided up into *antithesis* quite generally, and therefore into *singularity* and *universality*—it may seem that this duty, whose content is the universal itself, possesses the nature of pure duty in it, so that form and content become wholly concordant to one another. Thus, it may see, for example, that action for the universal good[260] is to be preferred to action for the individual good. But this universal duty is what is present overall as substance, which subsists in and for itself as right and law, and it is valid *independently* both for the single [agent's] knowledge and conviction and for his immediate interests: thus, it is just the *form* against which morality in general is directed. As for its *content,* however, that is a *determinate* one, too, inasmuch as the universal good is *opposed* to the singular good. Hence, its law is one from which conscience knows itself to be utterly free; and conscience gives itself an absolute warrant to add or to subtract from it, to neglect it as such as to fulfill it. —But then, moreover, by the very nature of antithesis generally, that distinction between duty toward the singular and duty toward the universal is nothing fixed. On the contrary, whatever the singular does for himself makes a contribution to the universal. The more he has taken care of himself, the greater is not merely his *possibility* of being useful to others; but his very *actuality* is nothing but this: to live and to be in solidarity[261] with others. His singular enjoyment has essentially [349] the significance of surrendering what is his to others, and [therefore] helping them to obtain their own enjoyment. So, in the fulfillment of duty to the single agent, and thus to oneself, duty to the universal gets fulfilled as well. The *weighing* and *comparing* of duties, which could come in here, would lead to the calculating of the advantage that the universal derives from an action. But, thereby, morality would in part succumb to the inevitable *contingency* of *insight;* it is in part just the essence of conscience to *cut out* all such *reckoning* and weighing and make decisions by itself, without grounds of this kind.

---

260. <allgemeine Beste>
261. <Zusammenhang>

In this way, then, conscience acts and maintains itself in the unity of 210–646
being in itself and *being for itself*, in the unity of pure thinking and individuality: it is spirit that is certain of itself, which has its truth in respect to
itself, with its own self, [that is,] in its knowing, and [precisely] as the
knowing of duty therein. Spirit maintains itself in this unity precisely
because what is *positive* in action—just as much the content as the form
of duty, and the knowledge of it—belongs to the self, to self-certainty.
But, whatever claims to be a *proper in-itself* that *confronts* the self counts as
nothing true, or only as sublated, [that is] only as moment. What counts
is not the *universal knowing* in general but rather *its awareness* of the circumstances. The knowing self puts the content, which it draws from its
natural individuality, into duty, as universal *being in itself;* for this is the
content present to the knowing self. This content, by virtue of the universal medium wherein it exists, becomes the *duty* that the self carries out;
and empty, pure duty is *eo ipso* posited as sublated, or as a moment: this
content is duty's sublated emptiness, that is, its fulfillment. —But, at the
same time, conscience is free of any content at all: it absolves itself from
every determinate duty that is supposed to count as law.[262] In the
strength of its own self-certainty it has the majesty of absolute autarchy—
to bind and loose. Hence, this *self-determination* is immediately sheer
dutifulness: duty is knowing as such. But this simple selfhood is the in-
itself; for the *in-itself* is pure self-equality, and self-equality is [found] in
this consciousness.

This pure knowing is immediately *being for another:* for as pure self- 211–647
equivalence, it is *immediate* or being. But this being is at the same time
universal, the selfhood of all: in other words, the action is recognized and
hence actual. This being is the element whereby conscience stands immediately in a connection of equality with all self-consciousnesses, and the
significance of this connection is not the selfless law but rather the self of
conscience. [350]

But because this right done by conscience is at the same time *being for* 212–648
another, an inequality seems to befall it. The duty it fulfills is a *determinate* content. It is, to be sure, the *self* of consciousness and, so, its *knowing* of itself, its *equality* with its own self. But once completed, once
installed in the universal medium *of being,* this equivalence is no longer
knowing, no longer the differentiating that just as immediately sublates

---

262. As it should be clear from the context, Hegel is still speaking of a member of the lower estate whose sense of self and duty to the state is subject to doubt.
In *Philosophy of Spirit* the members of the lower estate are listed more specifically
as the commercial estate, the learned or scholarly estate, and the military estate.
So Hegel is speaking of their respective senses of duty. Cf. *GW,* viii, p. 266.

its own differentiations. Rather, in *being,* the difference is posited as permanent, and the action is a *determinate* one, not equal to the element of everyone's self-consciousness, and therefore not necessarily recognized. Both sides, the conscience that acts and the universal consciousness that recognizes this action as duty, are equally *free* from the determinacy of this deed. On account of this freedom, their connection in the communal medium of interdependence is rather a relation of complete inequality; and as a result, the consciousness, which is aware of the action, finds itself in a state of complete uncertainty regarding the spirit that acts in self-certainty.[263] Spirit acts; it posits a determinacy in being;[264] others hold onto this *being* as its truth, and are certain of it therein. In this being, it has declared *what* counts for it as duty. However, spirit is free from any *determinate* duty; it has moved away from where the others think it actually is; this medium of being itself counts for spirit as a moment and so too does duty, which has being *in-itself.* What spirit presents to others, therefore, it misrepresents again as well—or rather, it has immediately misrepresented it. For spirit's *actuality* is, to spirit, not the duty and determination that has been outwardly, but rather that which it has in the absolute certainty of itself.

213–649   The others, therefore, do not know whether this conscience is morally good or evil; or rather, not only can they not know it, but they must also take it to be evil. For just as conscience is free from the *determinacy* of duty, and from duty which has being *in itself,* so too are the others. What conscience presents to them, they themselves know how to misrepresent. It is something which expresses only the *self* of *another,* not their own; not only do they know themselves to be free from it, but they must dissolve it in their own consciousness, and nullify it through judging and explaining in order to maintain their own selves.

214–650   The action of conscience is, however, not just this *determination* of being that has been abandoned by the pure self. What is supposed to be valid and to be recognized as duty is so only through the knowing and conviction of it as duty, through the knowing of its self in the deed. If the deed ceases to have this self in it, it ceases to be what alone constitutes its essence. The determinate being of the deed, which is abandoned by this consciousness, would be a common actuality, and the action would appear to us a consummation of one's pleasure and desire. What ought to *be there*[265] is an essentiality here only because it comes to be *known* as self-

---

263. *selbst gewissen.* Hegel plays on the equivalence between self-certainty (*Selbstgewißheit*) and conscience itself (*Gewissen sich selbst*).

264. <als seyend>

265. <*Daseyn*>

declaring individuality; [351] and this *being known* is what is recognized and what should *as such* have *determinate being.*

The self enters determinate being *as self.* Spirit, which is certain of   215–651
itself, exists as such for others; its *immediate* action is not that that has validity and is actual: what is recognized is not the *determinate,* not *what has being in itself,* but only the self-knowing *self* as such. The element of stability is universal self-consciousness. What enters this element cannot be the *efficacy* of action: this does not endure in it, this can achieve no stability; but only self-consciousness is what is recognized and gains actuality.

So here again we can see *speech* to be the determinate being of spirit.   216–652
Speech is the self-consciousness that subsists *for others,* which is immediately present as such and is universal as [a] *this.* It is the self, splitting itself apart, which becomes objective to itself as the pure *I = I,* maintaining itself as *this* self just as much as it fuses immediately with others and is *their* self-consciousness. It hears itself just as it is heard by others, and the hearing is precisely *determinate being that has become a self.*

The content, which speech has gained here, is no longer the inverted,   217–653
inverting, and torn self of the world of culture. Instead, it is sprit that has returned into itself and is certain of itself (certain in its own self of its truth or of its recognizing) and is recognized as this knowing. The speech of ethical spirit is the law and the simple command, as well as the complaint, which is more [than] a tear shed over necessity. Conversely, moral consciousness is still *mute,* shut away by itself in its inner life. For consciousness, the self does not yet have determinate being; but rather, determinate being and the *self* stand initially in an external connection with one another. But speech becomes prominent only as the middle [term] between independent and recognized self-consciousnesses; the *self* that has *determinate being* is immediately universal; it is plural and is simple recognized being in this plurality.[266] The content of the speech of conscience is *the self that knows itself as essence.* This alone is what speech declares, and this declaring is the true actuality of the doing, and what makes the action count. Consciousness declares its *conviction,* and it is in this conviction alone that the action is duty; also, self-consciousness is *free* from the *determinate* action that *merely subsists.* What counts for self-consciousness is not *the action* as *determinate being,* but rather the *conviction* that it is duty: this is actual in speech. —The performing of the action [352] does not mean here translating its content from the form of

---

266. In the circle of friends each Self is recognized by others as a Self and is esteemed by them. We could think of groups such as the Jena Circle, the Bloomsbury Group, the Existentialists in their cafés, and the "Vienna Circle," to grasp Hegel's point that the individual's identity is tied to the group and its speech.

purpose or *being-for-self* into the form of *abstract* actuality, but rather translating its content from the form of the immediate *certainty* of the self (which knows its knowledge or being-for-self as essence) into the form of the *assurance* that consciousness is convinced of its duty, and knows duty to be conscience that *comes from its own self.* Thus this assurance assures that consciousness is convinced that its conviction is the essence.

218–654   Whether the assurance of acting from conviction of duty is *true?* —Whether it is *actually* the *duty* which is done?—these questions or doubts have no meaning for conscience. —To put the question, Whether the *assurance* is *true?* would presuppose that the inner intention is distinct from what is alleged; that is, the volition of the singular self could separate itself from the duty or from the will of the universal and pure consciousness. The latter would be put into speech, but the former would in fact be the true incentive for action. However, it is precisely this distinction—of the universal consciousness and singular self—that has sublated itself, and this sublation is conscience. The immediate knowing of the self-certain self is law and duty; its intention, by virtue of being its intention, is what is right. All that is demanded is that it know this, and that it state the conviction that its knowing and willing is what is right. The declaration of this assurance sublates into itself the form of its particularity; it recognizes therein the *necessary universality of the self.* In calling itself *conscience,* it calls itself a pure self-knowing of itself and pure abstract willing; that is, it calls itself a universal knowing and willing, which recognizes others, it is equal to them (for they are just this pure self-knowing and willing) and is thereby also recognized by them. In the willing of the self that is certain of itself, in knowing that the self is the essence, there lies the essence of what is right. —Thus, whoever says that he does what he does out of conscience, speaks truly, for his conscience is the knowing and willing self. However, it is essential for him to *say* this, for this self must be at the same time the *universal* self. There is no universal self in the *content* of the action, for this content is indifferent to itself on account of its *determinacy;* rather universality lies in the form of action. This form is to be posited as actual; it is the *self* that as such is actual in speech, which declares itself to be true and precisely therein recognizes all selves and is recognized by them.

219–655   Thus conscience, in the majesty of its sublimity over the determinate law and every content of duty, puts into its knowing and willing what content it likes. It is that character of moral genius,[267] which knows the inner voice of its immediate knowledge to be the divine voice, and since in this knowing it knows determinate being in an equally immediate way, it is the

---

267. <Genialität>

divine creative power that has living force in its concept.[268] [353] In the same way, the character of genius is within itself worship, for its acting is the intuiting of its own divinity.

This solitary worship is, at the same time, essentially the worship of a *community*, and the pure inner self-*knowing* and self-perceiving goes on to become a moment of *consciousness*. The intuition of itself is its *objective* determinate being, and this objective element is the declaration of its knowing and willing as a *universal*. By virtue of this declaration the self becomes a self that counts, and the action an accomplished deed. The actuality, and the sublating of its act, is the universal self-consciousness. But the declaration of conscience posits the self-certainty as pure self and thereby as universal self; the others let the action count for the sake of this talk in which the self is expressed and recognized as the essence. Thus, the spirit and substance of their bond is the reciprocal assurance of their conscientiousness, good intentions, the rejoicing over this mutual purity, and the basking in the splendor of knowing and declaring, of caring and cherishing such excellence. —Insofar as this certainty of its *abstract* consciousness is still distinguished from its *self-consciousness*, the life of conscience is only *hidden* in God. God is indeed *immediately* present in its spirit and heart, in its self; but what is revealed, its actual consciousness and the mediating movement of it, is for conscience something other than that hidden inner life and the immediacy of the essence that is present. Only in the perfection of conscience does the distinction between the abstract consciousness and self-consciousness sublate itself. Conscience knows that this *abstract* consciousness is precisely *this self*, this self-certain being on its own account; it knows that in the *immediacy* of the *connection* between the self and the in-itself (which when posited outside the self is the abstract essence and what is hidden from it) precisely this *diversity* is *sublated*. For the same connection is a *mediating* one, in which the connected [terms] are not one and the same; rather, each is an *other* for the other, and only in a third are they one. But the *immediate* connection means in fact nothing else but their unity. Consciousness, having risen above the thoughtlessness that holds distinctions, knows the immediacy of the presence of the essence within it as the unity of the essence and its

220–656

---

268. Most likely a reference to Schelling's view that in and through artistic genius there is unity with the absolute. Despite human imperfections the very act of artistic genius transcends human limitations. In a word the genius is an *Übermensch*. For example, Schelling claims, "The postulated product [of identity] is nothing else than the product of genius, or since genius is possible only in art, [it is nothing else than] the *product of art*," *System of Transcendental Idealism* (1800), *SW*, iii, p. 617.

[own] self; thus it knows itself as the living in–itself and knows this know-ing as religion. As intuited knowing or knowing that has determinate being, religion is the speaking of the community concerning its spirit.[269]

221–657   What we see here is self-consciousness returned into its innermost [being], for which all externality as such has disappeared, [that is] returned into the intuition of the [354] I = I, where the *I* is all essentiality and determinate being. It sinks into this concept of itself, for it has been driven to its furthest extremities, and, in such a way that the distinct moments (whereby it is real or *consciousness* still) are not for us only these pure extremes. Instead, what it is on its own account, and what is *intrinsic* for it, and what is *determinate being* for it have [all] evaporated into abstractions that no longer provide support or substance for this con-sciousness itself, and everything that was essence for consciousness until now, has returned into these abstractions. —Refined to this purity, con-sciousness takes its poorest shape, and the poverty, which constitutes its sole possession, is itself a disappearing. This absolute *certainty*, in which substance is dissolved, is the absolute *untruth* that collapses into itself; it is the absolute *self-consciousness* into which *consciousness* sinks.

222–658   If we consider this sinking within itself, then *substance*, which is *in itself*, is, for consciousness, *knowing* as *its* [own] knowing. As conscious-ness, knowing is separated into the antithesis of itself and its object, which is the essence for it. But [now] this very object is something completely transparent; it is *its* [own] *self*, and its consciousness is only the knowing of itself. All life, and all spiritual essentiality has returned into this self and has lost their distinction from the I-self. Hence, the moments of con-sciousness are these extreme abstractions, none of which stand firm, but rather each loses itself in an other and produces it. It is the exchange of the unhappy consciousness with itself, but one that for consciousness itself goes on within it; it is consciously aware of being the concept of rea-son that the unhappy consciousness is only *in itself.* Thus the absolute cer-tainty of itself directly strikes up as consciousness into a sound that dies away, turns into the objectivity of its being- for-self; but this created world is its *talk*, which it hears just as immediately, and the echo of which returns to it. Hence, this return does not mean that in talk consciousness is *in* and *for itself*, since for consciousness the essence is not something *in itself* but is consciousness itself. Nor does it have *determinate being*, for the objective does not come to be a negative of the actual self, just as the

---

269. Although several Romantics held to this view, the most articulate propo-nent of the idea that the truth of Christian religion is found in the individual's own heart is Schleiermacher in his *Speeches to the Despisers of the Christian Reli-gion* (1799). Hegel might well be thinking of these speeches.

actual self does not come to be actuality. It lacks the force of externalization, the force to make itself into a thing and endure being. It lives in
dread of sullying the splendor of its inner being through action and determinate being. In order to preserve the purity of its heart, it flees from the
touch of actuality and persists in its stubborn powerlessness.[270] It cannot
renounce the self, which has been sharpened to the point of ultimate
abstraction and cannot give itself substantiality, transform its thinking
into being, and entrust itself to the absolute distinction. The hollow
object, which consciousness produces for itself, fills consciousness, [355]
thereby, only with the consciousness of emptiness. Its doing is the yearning, which only loses itself as consciousness itself comes to be an object
devoid of essence, and, falling back to itself beyond this loss, it finds itself
only as *lost*. In this transparent purity of its moments, an unhappy, so-
called *beautiful soul*, it grows dim within itself and wastes away like a
shapeless mist that dissolves in air.[271]

But this quiet confluence of the pithless essentialities of the evaporated 223–659
life has still to be taken in the other meaning of the *actuality* of conscience
and the *appearance* of its movement; conscience is to be considered as acting. —The *objective* moment in this consciousness determined itself
above as universal consciousness. The self-knowing that knows is distinct
from other selves, as *this* self. Speech (this universal equivalence, in which
all selves recognize themselves reciprocally as acting conscientiously) falls
apart into the nonequivalence of singular being-for-self; similarly, out of
its universality each consciousness is simply reflected into itself. Hence,
there enter necessarily the antithesis of singularity against other singulars
and against the universal; this relationship and its movement is now to be
considered.[272] —In other words, this universality and the duty have the

---

270. Hegel is describing both literary heroes, such as Goethe's Werther and
Jacobi's Woldemar (1779), but also certain Romantic thinkers who lived lives like
the literary heroes. Both Friedrich Schlegel and Novalis suffered from the throes of
passion and yearnings. Schlegel's problem was resolved when he married (this is the
basis of his novel, *Lucinde*) but Novalis's longings proved futile, since his beloved
died. Novalis in his *Hymns to the Night* (c. 1799) believed that such fruitless yearnings could lead to a spiritual awakening and recognition of religious revelation.
"Yearning" as a sign of redemption now becomes the subject of Hegel's inquiry.

271. The term "beautiful soul" comes from Goethe's *Sufferings of Young Werther* (1776). It refers to a perfect soul mate. But the reference to "wasting away,"
i.e., consumption, means Hegel is thinking of Novalis and his soul mate,
Sophie von Kühn.

272. Hegel appears to be referring to a dispute between Goethe and Jacobi on
the nature of romantic love and redemption. Jacobi, after reading *Werther*, wrote a
novel, *Woldemar*, in which the hero's spiritual yearnings for love save him from a

strictly opposite [i.e., inverted] significance that the determinate *singularity* that exempts itself from the universal; for this singularity, pure duty is only the universality that comes to be *surface* and is turned outward; duty lies only in words and counts as a being for another. Conscience, being at first only *negatively* directed toward duty as *this determinate presence,* knows itself to be free from it. But since it fills the empty duty with a *determinate* content *out of its own self,* the positive consciousness, which conscience has, constitutes the content of *this* self. As empty knowing, its pure self is what has neither content nor determination. The content, which conscience gives it, is taken from its [own] self as *this* determinate self, from itself as natural individuality. In the speaking of the conscientiousness of its acting, it is, to be sure, conscious of its pure self; in the *purpose* (the actual content) of its acting, however, it is conscious both of itself as this particular singular [agent] and of the antithesis between what it is for itself and what it is for another—the antithesis between universality or duty and its reflectedness out of universality.

224–660   If the antithesis that conscience comes into when it *acts* is expressed thus in its inner being, then it is, at the same time, the outward nonequivalence in the element of determinate being; the nonequivalence of its particular singularity as against another singular [agent]. Its particularity consists in this: the two moments [356] that constitute its consciousness, the self and the in–itself, have unequal validity in it, specifically with the determination that the certainty of itself is the essence *as against the in-itself* or the *universal,* which counts only as a moment. Over against this inner determination, therefore, there stands the element of determinate being or universal consciousness, for which rather the universality, duty, and essence have validity, and in contrast the singularity, which is on its own account in opposition to the universal, counts only as a sublated moment. For [the consciousness that] holds fast to duty, the first consciousness counts as *evil,* because it is the nonequivalence of its *being within itself* with the universal; and it counts as *hypocrisy,* too, since, at the same time, it declares its action, as equivalent with itself, to be duty and conscientiousness.[273]

_____

death not unlike Werther's. The very profession of love, conveyed through the written word, is sufficient to bring the soul mate to rescue the hero from what seems to be death. Goethe, after reading this rubbish, detested the novel so much that he wrote a short parody of it, *The Secret of Woldemar* . . . (1779), in which the Devil appears at the death scene to carry Woldemar away to Hell, but not before he explains that passion alone, which is really a passion for oneself, is merely a conceit of the heart. It is both pride and vanity. Jacobi supposedly never spoke to Goethe again after the parody appeared. Hegel sides with Goethe in this dispute.

273. It is also possible to read this line as, "since, at the same time, it declares

The *movement* of this antithesis is, first of all, the formal₂ setting up of   225–661
the equivalence between what evil is within itself and what the first consciousness declares. It must come to light that the first consciousness is
evil; thus its determinate being must become equal to its essence, *hypocrisy* must be exposed. —This return of the nonequivalence present in
hypocrisy, in equivalence, is not established just because hypocrisy, as is
commonly said, demonstrates its respect for duty and virtue by the very
fact that it puts on the *show* of them and uses them as a mask for its own
consciousness no less than for an alien consciousness, and equivalence
and agreement are contained in this recognition of its opposite in itself.
But, at the same time, hypocrisy is just as much reflected out of this recognition of speech and into itself; and its use of what has being *in itself,*
only as a *being for another,* is rather hypocrisy's own disrespect for it and
the displaying of its essence for everyone. For what allows itself to be used
as an external instrument shows itself to be a thing that has no inner
weight of its own.

Also, this equivalence is not established either through the one-sided   226–662
insistence of the evil consciousness upon itself [i.e., its conscientiousness]
or through the judgment of the universal consciousness. —If the evil consciousness denies itself in the face of the consciousness of duty and claims
that what the universal consciousness proclaims to be wicked and the
absolute nonequivalence with the universal is an acting according to its
inner law and conscience, then there remains in this one-sided assurance
of equality its inequality with the other, for, of course, this other does not
believe it and does not recognize it. —Or, if the one-sided insistence dissolves itself as the *one* extreme, then evil in the process would, of course,
admit to being evil, but by so doing it would *immediately* sublate itself, and
would no longer be hypocrisy nor be exposed as such. It does in fact admit
to being evil through the assertion that it acts in accordance with *its* own
inner law and conscience, in opposition to the recognized universal.²⁷⁴ For
if this law and conscience were not [357] the law of its *singularity* and

its deeds to be equivalent with itself, duty, and consciousness." The identity of
the Self with passion, yearning, and longing for the beautiful other is "evil"
because it is a sign of what Hegel calls the "frenzy of self-conceit." Goethe's criticisms of Jacobi's exaltation of subjective feeling seem to be the basis for these
dire protestations.

274. Daniel Jarmos believes that Hegel is likely referring to Friedrich Schlegel and his portrayal of youthful sexual license, the sign of strong passion, as being
for the "good." Schlegel's *Lucinde* was one of the first novels to speak openly of
the "virtue" of a esthetical passion. Hegel, who had personal experience with sexual misadventures, sees such passion as a vice. Cf. "'The Appearing God' in
Hegel's *Phenomenology of Spirit*," *Clio,* 19:4 (Summer 1990), 353–65.

whim, then it would not be something inner of its own, but rather what is universally recognized. So, whoever acts according to *his* laws and conscience vis-à-vis the other says in fact that he mistreats the other. But the *actual* conscience is not this insistence on knowing and willing, which opposes itself to the universal; on the contrary, the universal is the element of its *determinate being*, and its speech declares its doing to be *recognized* duty.

227–663   Nor is the insistence of the universal consciousness upon its judgment the exposure and dissolution of hypocrisy. —Since it denounces hypocrisy as bad, contemptuous, and so on, it is appealing to a law of *its own* in these judgments just as much as the *evil* consciousness appeals to *its own* law. For the first law enters in the antithesis against the second, and thus emerges as a particular law. Thus, it has no advantage over the other but rather legitimizes it, and its zeal does precisely the opposite of what it means to do: namely, it shows that what it calls true duty, what should be *universally* recognized, is something *not recognized;* and so it concedes to the other the equal right to be on its own account.

228–664   But the judgment [of the universal consciousness] has another side too, which becomes the first step in the dissolution of the present antithesis. —Consciousness *of the universal* does not behave toward the first [consciousness] as an *actual* [being] and *agent,* for it is the first that is actual instead; on the contrary, it is opposed to the first as one that is not biased by the antithesis of singularity and universality, that is involved in acting. It remains in the universality of *thought*, behaves as *apprehending* consciousness, and its first action is only the judgment. Now, as we have just noted, through this judgment it places itself *beside* the first, and *through this equivalence* the first comes to the intuition of itself in this other consciousness. For the consciousness of duty behaves *as passive apprehension,* but by doing so it is in contradiction with itself as the absolute will of duty with itself, the strictly self-determining will. It has kept itself good in its purity, because it does *not act;* it is the hypocrisy of wanting judgment to be taken for an *actual* deed and proves its righteousness by the declaration of fine sentiments instead of through action. So its whole structure is just like that of the consciousness against which the reproach is leveled that it makes duty into mere talk. In both of them, the side of actuality is equally distinguished from talk: in the one through the *self-serving purpose* of action, in the other through the *lack of action;* the necessity of acting lies in speaking about duty itself; for duty has entirely no meaning at all without a deed. [358]

229–665   But judging is also to be considered as the positive action of thinking, and has a positive content; on this side the contradiction, which is present in the apprehending consciousness, and its equivalence with the first

[conscience] become more complete than before. The acting consciousness declares its determinate deed to be duty, and the judging consciousness cannot deny it that; for duty itself, being the form with content, is
diverse in its many-sidedness, has the universal side in it, which is the one
taken to be duty, just as much as it has the particular that constitutes the
share and interest of the individual.[275] The judging consciousness does
not stand still at the [universal] side of duty and, thereby, at knowing the
agent, [namely] that this is his duty, the necessary condition and relationship of his actuality. Rather, it holds to the other side, plays the action over
in the inner realm, and explains it on the basis of the selfish *motive* and the
intention that are different from the action. Just as every action can be considered under the aspect of its conformity to duty, so too it can be considered under the other aspect of *particularity;* for, as an action, it is the
actuality of the individual. —Thus this judging places the action apart
from its determinate being and reflects it into the inner realm, that is, in
the form of its own particularity. If the action is accompanied by fame,
then the judging knows this inner realm to be a *craving* for fame. If it is in
harmony with the status of the individual generally, without going beyond
this status, and is so constituted that individuality does not have the status
hung on it like an external determination, but fills out this universality
with itself and precisely by so doing shows itself to be fit for a higher status, then the judgment knows its inner aspect to be ambition, and so on.
Since in action, generally the agent attains the intuition of *his own self* in
his objectivity, or of the feeling of this own self in his determinate being,
he attains enjoyment; so that the judgment knows the inner aspect as the
drive for its own happiness—even though this may consist only of inner
moral vanity, enjoyment by consciousness of its own splendor, and the
foretaste of the hope of a future happiness. —No action can escape from
such a judgment, since the pure purpose of duty for duty's sake is what is
nonactual, the purpose has its actuality in the deed of individuality, and
the action has thereby the side of particularity in it. There are no heroes
for the valet, not because the hero is not a hero, but rather because the
valet is a valet with whom the hero has dealings, not as hero, but in the singularity of need and representation generally, or as one who eats, drinks,
and dresses.[276] Similarly, there is for the judging consciousness no action

275. In both *Werther* and *Woldemar* the "hero" writes letters to other characters in the novel. In *Werther,* the person who receives the letters acts as the "judging consciousness." This is true especially of Charlotte, namely, the "beautiful
soul" for whom Werther has such longing.

276. Supposedly based on a French saying. Jarmos points out that on occasion
Goethe spoke this line.

in which it cannot set against [359] the side of the singularity of individuality the universal side of the action, and act the part of the moral valet toward the agent.

230–666   Hence the judging consciousness is itself *contemptuous*, because it divides the action, bringing forth the action's nonequivalence with itself and holding fast to it. This consciousness is *hypocrisy* as well; for it labels its judging, not as an *other manner* of being wicked but as the *just consciousness* of the action; in all of its inactuality and vanity of knowing what is good, it sets itself up above the deeds it decries, and it wants that its words, though without deeds, are accepted as a superior *actuality.* —Thus having made itself equal to the agent who is being judged, the judging consciousness is recognized by him to be the same as himself.[277] The agent finds himself not only comprehended by it, as something both alien and unequal to it but also finds himself equal to it according to its consciousness's own constitution. Because he intuits this *equality* and *admits* it openly, he makes *confession* to it and since the other has made itself equal with him in the deed, he expects that it will also reproach his words, will admit its *equality* openly and enter the state[278] of recognition. His confession is not an abasement, a humiliation, or degradation in relation to the other. For this open admission is not the one-sided kind in which he posits his *nonequality* with it; on the contrary, it is only because of this intuition *of the other's equality* that he declares himself. From his side he openly admits their equality in his confession, and he does so because speech is the *determinate being* of spirit as an immediate self. So he expects that the other will contribute its part to this determinate being.

231–667   However, to the avowal of the one who is evil: "I am so," there does not follow this *reproduction* of a similar confession. This is not what the judging consciousness meant; quite the contrary! It repels this community and is the hard heart that is for itself and that rejects any continuity with the other. As a result the scene is turned around. The one who made confession finds himself repulsed and sees the other to be in the wrong: because it disdains the emergence of his inner self into the determinate being of words and sets the beauty of his soul against the one who is evil, against the confession it sets the stiff neck of the character who remains equal to itself and the silence that keeps to itself and will not throw away its self for another. What is posited here is the most far-reaching insurrection of spirit certain of itself; it beholds itself as this *simple knowing of self* in the other and in such a way that the outer shape of this other is not a

---

277. The Devil in *The Secret of Woldemar* . . . makes this point against Henriette, the "beautiful soul" who attempts to save Woldemar through a pure passion.

278. <Daseyn>

thing like wealth, something without essence. On the contrary, what is maintained against him is thought, knowledge itself; it is this absolutely fluid continuity of pure [360] *knowing* that disdains for its part to establish communication *isolated being-for-self,* posited himself as a sublated particularity, and hereby posited himself as this continuity with the other, that is, as universal. With respect to the one who confesses, however, the other claims its uncommunicative being-for-self. With respect to the confessing consciousness, it is maintaining the very same being-for-self that the former had already thrown away. It thereby shows itself to be a spirit-forsaking and spirit-renouncing consciousness; for it does not recognize that spirit, in the absolute certainty of itself, is master over every deed or actuality and can throw them away and make as if they never happened. At the same time, it is not cognizant of the contradiction it is committing by not letting the rejection that takes place *in words* count as the true rejection, whereas it has itself the certainty of its spirit, not in an actual action, but in its inner being, and finds this inner being to be there in the *words* of the judgment. Thus it is the judging consciousness itself who hinders the other's return from the deed into the determinate spiritual being of the words and into the equality of spirit, and which, through this hardness of heart, produces the inequality that is still present.

Since self-certain spirit, as a beautiful soul, does not now have the strength of alienating the self-knowledge that is holding onto itself, it cannot attain equality with the repulsed consciousness and thus cannot attain the intuited unity of itself in the other; [that is] it cannot attain determinate being. Hence, equality comes about only negatively, as spiritless being. Lacking actuality the beautiful soul is caught in the contradiction between its pure self and the necessity that the self, by alienating itself and turning into actuality, has being. It is caught in the *immediacy* of this firmly held antithesis (an immediacy raised to its pure abstraction, and which is pure being or empty nothing). Thus, as consciousness of this contradiction, the beautiful soul, in its unreconciled immediacy, is deranged to the point of madness and pines away in yearning consumption.[279] So, in the deed, it gives up holding hard and fast to *its own being-for-self,* yet it brings forth the spiritless unity of being.

232–668

---

279. Here the reference seems to be the poet-philosopher Novalis, who died of consumption in 1802. Novalis is himself identified as the "beautiful soul" in the person of the judging consciousness. Hegel may be thinking of how Novalis in his *Hymns to the Night* describes the overcoming of his longing for the dead Sophie von Kühn; he turns away from the grave and looks to heaven from where his love appears as a goddess. Yet, the description of judging consciousness as "hard-hearted" does not actually apply to the character of Novalis, who if anything was

233–669   The true equalization, namely, the one that is *self-conscious* and has *determinate being*, is, due to its necessity, already contained in the foregoing. This breaking of the hard heart and its elevation to universality is the same movement expressed by the consciousness that confesses. The wounds of spirit heal without leaving scars. The deed is not imperishable but rather is taken back into itself by spirit; the side of singularity present in it, whether as intention or as the deed's existent negativity and [361] limit, is something that immediately vanishes. The actualizing *self,* the form of its action, is only a *moment* of the whole; so is the knowledge that determines by judgment and fixes the distinction between the singular and universal side of action. The one who is evil posits this externalization of itself or posits itself as moment in that, through the intuition of itself in the other, it has been drawn forth into the determinate being that confesses. But just as the one who is evil must break down the one-sided, unrecognized determinate being of its particular being-for-self, so the other must break down its one-sided, unrecognized judgment. And just as the former displays the power of spirit over its actuality, so the latter displays spirit's power over its determinate concept.

234–670   But the judging consciousness renounces the divisive thought and the hard heart of a being-for-self that holds fast to it, because in the deed it intuits itself in the agent. This one who throws away his actuality and makes himself into a *sublated this* thereby displays himself in the deed as something universal; from his external actuality he returns into himself as essence. Thus universal consciousness has cognition of itself therein. —The forgiveness, which it allows the agent to experience, is the renunciation of itself, of its *nonactual* essence; it makes this essence equal to that other one, which was *actual* action. It recognizes as good what was called evil in the determination that action received in thought; or rather, it lets go of this distinction between determinate thought and its self-subsistent, determining judgment, just as the other has let go of its self-subsistent determining through action.[280] —The word of reconciliation is spirit *being determinate,* which intuits the pure knowing of himself as *universal* essence in its contrary, that is, in the pure knowing of

---

too soft-hearted, but more to the "kinds" who are members of the scholarly estate—such as poets, writers, and philosophers. They love their "business" more than they do their families, friends, and even their lovers. Their state of mind, Hegel tells us in *Philosophy of Spirit,* is set for the universal as universal, which is only an empty concept. Cf. *GW,* viii, p. 273.

280. Self-forgiveness is the first sign of a return to the religious self-consciousness. But in self-forgiveness there is also the recognition of evil within, otherwise there would be nothing to forgive.

himself as *singularity* that has being absolutely within himself: a reciprocal recognition, which is *absolute spirit*.[281]

Absolute spirit steps into determinate being only at the summit upon   235–671
which its pure knowledge of its own self is the antithesis and alternation
with itself. In that it knows that its *pure knowledge* is the abstract *essence,*
absolute spirit is this [self] knowing duty in absolute antithesis to the
knowledge that knows itself to be the essence as the absolute *singularity* of
the self. The dutiful knowing is the pure continuity of the universal,
which knows the singularity that knows itself as essence to be in itself a
nullity, to be *evil.* But this is the absolute discreteness that knows itself
absolutely in its pure oneness and knows that universal as something nonactual that is only *for an other.* Both sides are refined to this purity, in
which there is no longer any selfless determinate being, nothing negative
of consciousness left in them; rather that *duty* is the consistently self-same
character of its self- knowledge, and this evil has likewise its purpose in its
being-within-self and its actuality in its words. The substance of its subsisting is the content of these words; it is the assurance of the certainty of
spirit within itself. —Each of these self-certain spirits has no [362] other
purpose than its pure self. But they are still diverse, however, and the
diversity is absolute because it is posited in this element of the pure concept. And it is not only for us, but also for the very concept that stands in
this antithesis. For these concepts are indeed *determinate* vis-à-vis one
another, but, at the same time, they are in themselves universal, so that
they fill out the whole range of the self, and the self has no other content
than this very determinacy, which neither goes beyond it nor is more
restricted than it. For the determinacy, the absolute universal, is just as
much the pure knowledge of itself as the self, the absolute discreteness of
singularity, and both of them are nothing but this pure self-knowing.
Thus, both determinacies are pure, knowing concepts whose very determinacy is immediate knowledge; in other words, whose *relation* and
antithesis is the *I.* Because of this they are out-and-out opposites to *each
other*—it is the completely *inner word* that has confronted itself in this way
and stepped into determinate being. The opposites constitute *pure knowing,* which is posited as *consciousness* through this antithesis. But it is still

---

281. In *Philosophy of Spirit,* Hegel makes a note concerning this moment of
Spirit's development. He remarks that "the *ethical life* of spirit certain of itself [is]
when self-certainty has made the *heart* the grave of the heart, [i.e.,] all joys and
sorrows of its heart, all sins and crimes of its own are put aside, and what was done
is as if it was never done . . ." *GW,* viii, 277, n3. This is what is occurring here
when religious consciousness reemerges as the Unhappy Consciousness that forgives itself in its own recognition of a self-deluded conceit.

not *self-consciousness*. It receives this actualization in the movement of this antithesis. For, in addition, this antithesis is the *nondiscrete continuity* and *equality* of the $I = I$; and each "for itself" sublates itself with respect to itself precisely because of the contradiction of its pure universality that, at the same time, still strives against its equality with the other and cuts itself off from it. Through this externalization, the knowledge that is divided in its *determinate being* returns into the unity of the *self*. It is the *actual I*, the universal *of its own self* in its *absolute contrary*, that is, in the knowledge that is *within itself*, which, on account of the purity of its isolated being-within-self, is the universal come to completion. The reconciling *yes*, in which the two *I*'s let go of this opposed *determinate being*, is the *determinate being* of an *I* expanded into duality, wherein it remains equal to itself and has the certainty of itself in its complete externalization and in its contrary. It is God appearing in the midst of those who know themselves as pure knowing.

A COMMENTARY ON HEGEL'S "SPIRIT"

PRELUDE

The chapter on Spirit is Hegel's demonstration that the philosophical Concept of Self and World is reconciled within his philosophical system. This chapter, then, becomes the crucial test for the philosophical project that Hegel has undertaken to overcome the difficulties inherent in the system that Schelling first proposed at Jena. Hegel appears to accept Eschenmayer's criticism against Schelling's construction of the system, and in reply to that criticism Hegel provides the historical proof that was previously lacking.[1] We should think that the problem concerning historical proof applies not only to Schelling's system but also includes Hegel's own drafts of the system, which he composed from 1803 to 1806 (the so-called Jena Projections).

Hegel's present concern in this chapter is to answer the question of how the self-deception manifest in the facticity of self-consciousness is overcome. We know from the concluding section of the preceding chapter, "Reason," that the solution lies in the universal laws that Reason itself provides and tests. But these laws are in reality "abstract," or independent of the human experience, even though Reason accepts them as universal and inherent in experience. Indeed, Hegel makes a point of quoting Sophocles' *Antigone*, when Antigone declares that the laws of the gods are "not something of now or yesterday, but they live forever" (Miller, ¶437). The reference to Antigone in "Reason" is the first sign that we will be looking at a Universal History to discover if the laws that bind self-consciousness and transcend the limitations of facticity are in fact true. Hegel's comment on the laws is that they belong to the universal essence

---

1. See the Introduction, p. xvff.

of life or the essence of self-consciousness itself. These laws, he tells us, are articulated into the masses of life. In terms of the pure laws, this articulation is for the clear consciousness of the lawgiver, which is undivided, and which considers itself to be an unspoiled heavenly shape. (Hegel notes in the *Philosophy of Spirit* [1806] that the Greek leader Solon is a lawgiver and Plato is a "law tester.") The differentiations in custom, belief, social behavior, and so forth, in the masses are ignored by clear consciousness in its appeal to the universality and "truth" of the rational laws, because this consciousness attempts to retain its native innocence simply by obedience to them: eternal rightness is its creed. Such universality ignores all distinctions.

The shape of the laws functions to reconcile differences, but as long as Reason encloses itself in the purity and simplicity of its own rightness, it will never understand the truth in the articulation of the masses of life. It will not see, as Antigone did not see, from whence the laws come and have meaning. The history of Spirit is to provide this understanding but not simply to provide it. Reason in its self-declared purity is *not* the heavenly shape that clear consciousness presumes it to be. The history of Spirit is the history of sin and redemption. It provides the evidence that proves the deception of Reason when it isolates and abstracts itself from the essential differentials of life. It presents the lesson that will teach Reason to acknowledge its own essence. The masses themselves are first observed in an elemental progression of nature as it produces human life.

The masses are initially the four elements that make each individual a real material being. We are all composed of "air," "fire," "water," and "earth." (Or, if you prefer, gas, plasma, liquid, and solid.) In the body they are in balance, forming a unifying connection through which the body subsists and sustains itself. Not only is the body maintained, but the mind is as well. These elements can also be represented as "humors," which, if kept in balance, forming a unifying connection, result in the healthy mental state (*mentis compos*) of the individual. If they are set against each other, then the mind is upset, torn apart, and the result is delirium. Finally, in "Spirit" they become symbols of an ethical order that represent the classes, or estates, of the *ancien régime*. As with the individual's body and mind, the social organism, if it has a unifying connection among the elemental masses, has a social body that remains healthy. If, on the other hand, a misalignment occurs producing collisions and conflicts, then the corporation itself becomes ill (producing social discord) or mad (producing state terror). In either case, insurrection occurs.

The *mentis compos* of the "old regime" depended on the unity and identity of each "element" in society. This "element" is the estate (*Stand*).

The masses form the collective identity of each estate.[2] They represent the shape of an infinite arrangement—that is, an organization of the whole through all of its individual parts, like a body subsisting through all of its cells and organic systems—that defines the *essence* of self-consciousness. Self-consciousness, belonging to a world-historical individual, has its shape determined in and through its membership in the corporation. It is an element partaking in the infinite arrangement. It has its identity in and through the essential connections that have taken shape. The articulation of the masses and the identity of self-consciousness in and through them are both the material causes of rational law and its content. This is what clear consciousness, which relies only on abstract Reason, has failed to recognize, or, if it has recognized its social place, it has not yet acknowledged its own essence as part of the infinite articulation of the masses; thereby it divorces Reason from its own material causal form.

In Chapter 3, "Force and Understanding," Hegel likens the apparent shapes of rational law to "the soul of the World, the universal blood" (Miller, ¶162). We do not actually see what he means by this description, however, until the full emergence of Spirit in Chapter 6. The point to recognize here is that nature itself provides the first glimpse of the articulation of the elemental progression, and our natural associations—as members of a family, as parts of a social organization, as subjects under state rule, and even as moral agents connected to others as friends and lovers—show the articulation of the masses as the *principle of identity* for self-consciousness. This identity of the Self is in and through the particular spheres of being in which the law of Reason appears, and this is how Hegel approaches "Spirit." The identity of the Self is *not* determined in and through the Self's own abstractions but in the identity framed by the associations that it has within the natural and social World. The spheres of identity and the conflicts within them propel the dialectic onward.

The object of the development is to gain the determination of the Self as a unified, complete being. In this unity, the law of Reason will finally enable the world-historical individual to gain insight into itself, and from that insight it can separate itself from the "Way of the World."[3] At that

---

2. There are two privileged estates, the Church and the nobility, one unprivileged estate, the bourgeoisie, and then one that is "declassed" in the modern world; that is, it is not recognized by the others, namely, the peasants, etc. Hegel believes, however, that the fourth class is the "earth," in which the other three have their foundation.

3. Self-determination versus worldly determination is just one of the conflicts inherent in the development of rational self-identity. This theme is presented by Hegel in his chapter "Reason." Reason is itself a dual process; even as we strive to form ourselves as autonomous self-defined beings, this movement is countered by

moment the truth of abstract Reason's deception can be acknowledged: we see and declare our essential Self to be hypocritical, that is, a failure on the path of *self*-justification. In this insight religious truth will inevitably follow, namely, that we are redeemed not by our limited identity within the spheres of the World but with the absolute identity of the Self that occurs in religious practice. The law of Reason is itself part of a higher sphere of law, which belongs in a Spinozistic fashion to the sempiternity (*sub quadam aeternitatis specie*) of the divine presence in humanity itself. The law of Reason can bind and heal self-consciousness because it has already divine redemption within it: the law of Reason is itself the appearance of divine law in the World.

The history of Spirit does not then provide us with the solution to the problem of facticity. It provides us with the pathway to reach the solution. "Spirit" comes after the chapter on Reason to show us the articulation of the rational law in the spheres that define the essence of the self-consciousness life. It comes before "Religion" because religion represents the solution to sin and hypocrisy. "Spirit" is the "middle term," and as such it is the *media res* by which we come to understand ourselves as having both levels of unity and crises of self-identity. Without "Spirit," the truth of the Concept could not be known. In terms of the other parts of the system, "Spirit" is also important. It, of course, gives us insight into Hegel's *Philosophy of History*, but more importantly it gives a tangible content to his abstract logical categories: *Dasein* (determinate being), *Ansichsein* (being-in-itself), and *Wesen* (essence), just to name a few, all of which have a determinate human content within "Spirit's" development. There are no "pure categories," whose meaning lies in abstract sense (*Sinn*)—that would be the conceit of abstract Reason. "Meaning" (*Bedeutung*) is always shown in the concrete form that the category has, and even though "Spirit" is not the only reference point for understanding a logical category, it is the most significant reference point. The shapes of "Spirit" present the fulcrum for understanding Hegel's logical categories. What becomes clear the more one understands "Spirit" is that the lawfulness of categories is proven in the experience of self-consciousness itself, which belongs to how the Self is formed in and through the World's appearance.

---

the realization that the World and its ways strive to make us contingent beings, subject to the whim of the state power. Under the "Way of the World" we are subject to the power of a destiny that is alien to our rational choices and self-conscious behavior. The conflict cannot be resolved at the level of Reason itself but is resolved in and through a testing of Reason's resolve to establish self-identity in moral-religious autonomy. The World presents the test, and more often than not the world-historical individual fails in the face of it. Cf. "Die Tugend und der Weltlauff," in *Phänomenologie des Geistes, GW,* ix, 208–14.

(The Self does not appear for-itself without there also appearing the World in which the Self is determined. Hegel's idea is that we are worldly beings, but we are worldly beings whose existence is defined through our own agencies and is thus defined against the World.)

INTRODUCTION

Let us consider Hegel's chapter. He begins with an introduction of the Concept. He contends that Spirit is the truth of abstract Reason, which has only achieved the formal category of the *Sache selbst*, or the facticity of individuality (cf. ¶1–438). Reason sees itself as a spiritual essence divided against itself. It has realized that its truth lies in its own lawfulness, but that the actual world-historical individual has not fulfilled the law. In the concept of facticity the universal truth of the Self qua Spirit has been grasped intellectually but not yet as actualized in the World; that is to say, the content of self-actualization has not been proven in worldly action. We see, indeed, that the content of consciousness does not agree with its formal truth. It still remains something singular, kept apart from the essential Self. *Spirit,* the subject of this chapter and Hegel's name for the world-historical individual, addresses itself to the question of the Self qua substance and shows the development of its self-identification within the World.

If we were to take a look at the general features of Hegel's chapter, it would present what we see as the actuality of Reason in stages. These stages define the world-historical individual through its worldly experiences. The chapter is thus a Universal History, but more importantly it shows a philosophical Concept of what the world-historical individual has undergone in order to acknowledge first its guilt, then its self-estrangement, and finally its worthiness to be redeemed. These three moments constitute the central themes for the divisions of the chapter. Thus we would see that Hegel presents three epochs of Spirit's World in this chapter. Each epoch presents at some point a basic conflict between the dominant culture and an individual's sense of right. Eschenmayer's objection to the system of Transcendental Idealism is thus answered through this presentation of the world-historical individual's own realization of the actuality of Reason.

Hegel begins with ancient Greek society prior to Athens's Golden Age. He calls this stage "True Spirit." It presents the age of the World that Sophocles describes in his plays on Oedipus and his family. In it the moral and religious bonds of life center on kinship, and even the state power acknowledges the right and importance of blood ties in forming civil society. However, this is also the World where positive law makes its first appearance opposite to the divine and familial laws. The conflict emerges in ancient Thebes when the representative of positive law, Creon, imposes a sentence on his dead nephew, Polynices, because the nephew had attacked the city, but by so doing Creon comes to oppose the duties of the familial obligations to the dead. Creon's niece, Antigone, acts against his injunctions and appeals instead to the laws of the underworld and the rights of the household gods. She represents the divine power centered on family and religious values.[4] In this conflict between the two laws and their representatives, the power of positive law prevails but with dire consequences for the family and the city. We see the outcome for positive law in the last age of this epoch, when the legal conditions are formed in Roman jurisprudence. Here there is a supposed assurance that citizens have rights and that there is a legal process to protect those rights. However, the fact that these rights are subject to the whim of tyrants and undercut by social decadence belies the belief that they are secured in practice. The "True Spirit" of the ancient World is annulled by power, appetite, and conceit. The world-historical individual acknowledges these failings and takes them upon itself, informing itself on the consequences of this conceptual development. What has to occur for its satisfaction is a reconciliation between king and citizen, between the spiritual and temporal powers of the state, and in this attempted reconciliation, "good" and

---

4. Hegel relies on Sophocles' plays to illustrate the moral and personal conflicts involved in this section; most likely he used Friedrich Hölderlin's version of *Antigone* as the dramatic representation. In Hölderlin's version both Creon and Antigone appeal to Zeus' law: Creon to "sky Zeus" and Antigone to "underworld Zeus." Creon's appeal justifies his own "divine appointment" as ruler of Thebes, which ended the original conflict between the gods and Oedipus. *His* sense of divine sanction is openly rational and presents what we might call "philosophical Reason." But Antigone counters his authority by appealing to Hades, who judges each individual and guards the sacred laws of the household. This is the god of blood ties, and his authority is accordingly "higher" to her than Creon's. By making these distinctions in the tragedy Hölderlin appears to show the limitation of Creon's practical sense of divine authority. Positive law, which resides solely in the legitimate authority of Creon's will, *should* represent the divine sanction, but what will eventually become clear to him, as he sees his entire family perish as a result of his decree, is that his rational world-view, while "just" in human terms and appropriate to god on high, fails to encompass fully the values and rights of the family. Ultimately he errs and suffers more than Antigone. He comes to know his error as part of a self-deception on what constitutes the universal will. So the conflict that Hegel is presenting between human and divine law is in reality *a conflict between two visions of divine law*. Both visions are "true," but only Antigone's understands the full significance of what is more important to the survival of the Ethical Life.

"bad" ought to be seen clearly in terms of what brings felicity to the state power and its estates. Yet, even as this occurs, there will be an impediment to any good outcome. Hegel's "facticity of the individual," which in the chapter on Reason was shown to be self-deceived and in need of a spiritual law to raise it to the level of universal Reason, still operates here as an inherent fault in the character of the world-historical individual. This essential fault becomes the Original Sin in the World, and it will propel Reason in all of those epochs that follow the demise of "True Spirit."[5]

It should be noted again that Hegel's history in this chapter is a spiritual journey that demonstrates the truth of Reason; for this is the world history of Reason acting out the concept of the facticity of the individual. "Spirit" is the witness to the Godforsakenness that Reason has already formally addressed in the preceding chapter, but in "Spirit" the solution to the problem lies in the development of the relationship between the individual and her World. Reason, because of its worldliness, comes to acknowledge this problematic relationship and makes as one of its philosophical demands that we look at world history to provide the objective resolution to our deceptions and errors. Reason, however, also knows what the resolution will be, even before it looks to history. Reason alone provides the motif of redemption in history, and it alone provides the outcome as the act of forgiveness of all sin and the reconciliation among people in their Godforsakenness.

Hegel's history is a narrative of individual trials and sufferings, and it is filled with horrors and human monsters committing great atrocities. Hegel's sense of world events is guided by Voltaire's dictum that history is a slaughter bench, and we should appreciate that Hegel wants us to

---

5. "Self-Estranged Spirit" is where the attempt at reconciliation is spoiled by self-deception: what "good society" declares to be "good" is in fact "bad." "Culture," which should make one worthy to be a member of the good society, is the condition that spoils any virtue and brings the individual to ruin through vice. To overcome Culture there is a need for both a spiritual cleansing, which Hegel likens to the Israelites raising the Seraph in the desert, and to a political revolution, which, while killing off the old order, only fulfills the downward path to cultural self-destruction. "Morality" is the conceptual remedy for the failings of the World. It is the level of the Concept that acknowledges the failings both of Culture and of the entire identity between the temporal and spiritual powers. But it, too, will suffer a particularly devastating fault. Morality is either too abstract or too emotional. It presents a false pride in its own sense of the good, which ultimately defeats its rational justifications concerning what is morally right. Its moral visions Hegel likens to the "beautiful soul," which, when faced with the realities of the World, can only wither and die, like a consumptive character from a Thomas Mann novel, or destroy itself, like Werther in Goethe's novel of romantic "moral" sentimentality.

acknowledge the full extent of the evil that has invaded the World through time; but the purpose of understanding the trials and suffering is that history also shows us a religious purpose to all of this (even if the horrors are not justified by it). The pageantry of moral evil and human sorrow is displayed as part of Hegel's presentation of the Concept of the world-historical individual as promulgating the fact that in all suffering redemption is implicit. Hegel's "divine comedy" includes devilish characters (such as Caligula and Robespierre) in opposition to divine Providence. But even their acts point to a recognition that there is a need for mercy and that evil can be forgiven in a purely moral perspective. What is being forgiven is the "evil" inherent in the Self. Spirit's identification with each World epoch is ultimately the identification that it, along with the World it has created and in which it is created, is redeemed in and through humanity's divine nature. The truth of Reason is that we learn to acknowledge human redemption through conflict and suffering. Divine Providence is only the recognition of this fact—a recognition that belongs to the subsequent stage of Spirit that Hegel calls "Absolute Spirit."

Let us now turn to the main sections of the text. For each of these sections I will first give a general overview, which will be followed by a more precise presentation of the content of each subsection. There will be some overlap between the general overview and the more detailed presentation, but I believe one might get a better perspective by approaching the text in this fashion. I will also be stressing the historical dimension of Hegel's argument because, at least initially, the historical dimension provides a clearer and more coherent account of what Hegel is attempting to do.

A. TRUE SPIRIT, THE ETHICAL LIFE

Hegel explains in this first section how the dialectic of Reason as the world-historical individual will proceed. The facticity of individuality will be considered in practice, which will break apart the simple substance of consciousness. This breaking apart is a practical judgment that leads to action, but the formal reason for the division is to further the category of Reason's unity. The abstract nature of the facticity will consequently be divided as well: one side will be seen as its substance and the other side as the essential Self.[6] By "substance" Hegel means the essentiality of

---

6. Hegel's concept of Self undergoes a number of transformations. Its first appearance in "Spirit" is as an ethical being that exists for-itself, and thus it considers itself distinct from nature and natural impulses. Hegel's Concept is

abstract Reason, which, as seen in the previous chapter, is determined by law. The substance, Hegel contends, is antithetical to itself, and it divides into two realms of law, namely, the human and the divine laws. Each one comes into conflict with the Self's drive for certainty of life, that is, its drive for self-knowledge and self-satisfaction. The self-certainty of life constitutes the character of self-consciousness, and thereby self-consciousness comes to act ethically only vis-à-vis its substance, but in this relation the Self will break apart as well, because its substance is already divided. Self-identity is subsumed into the essential differences of life (that is, family, citizen, and later, subject, burgher, and so forth). This all occurs within the concept of Reason as a practical judgment.

Hegel is speaking speculatively here on Reason's development as facticity in practice, but it is easier to follow his thought if we think of the historical references in this section. The first subsection is "The Ethical World," which centers on family life. In the family the rational division of the Concept is between man and woman, by which the man rules the house even as the woman manages its affairs. This rational division will account for how the family functions and even how initially the state sees itself as an extension of the household's rule. The man has the power of the will—the basis for positive law—to make binding decisions, and he is free, by virtue of this power, to act for himself both in the house and in public life. The man represents the positive freedom of self-consciousness to act willfully and for what Hegel calls Reason "in the daylight" (cf. ¶37–474). The woman is equal to the man, however, in terms of the household. She is his continual helpmate in all things but especially in her performance of religious obligations, that is, through her obsequies to the Lares and Penates—the shades of the ancestors and the household gods. In this World *her* duties are seen to be crucial for the survival and prosperity of the family, and since the state is itself formed through clans or *demes*, based on kinship, it survives and prospers through her actions. In this "Ethical World" there are harmony and unity among the various elements of society: the individual, the family, the state, and all segments of society are tied together by the underlying domestic or religious law that the woman safeguards. This bond is the unity of the Concept that belongs to

---

Spinozistic, especially when we realize that the "substance" referred to is an "ethical substance," which generates the mode of ethical action from itself. Later the concept of Self becomes the "universal Self" of the ethical being to whom the family and nation appeal for their own self-understanding. Oedipus seems to be the archetype for this version of the Concept. Still later the Self is determined by a legal status, and it becomes the "person." The point to bear in mind is that Self undergoes transformations of its definition according to the epoch of the Concept. *The identity of the Self is always to be seen in terms of its historical World.*

Reason, and it is this same unity that will be dissolved by logical divisions inherent in it.

The second subsection, "Ethical Action," centers on when the logical division in the family becomes an open conflict, wherein the state's will (represented by the man's free will) is opposed to familial rights and duties (represented by the woman's obligations). In this conflict the respective roles between men and women are at odds. The development of Reason is seen in two opposing practical judgments, both of which are perfectly valid given the presumptions of law that are being appealed to. The state is founded on civic Reason, or Reason of the daylight, and thus, on the authority of a leader's will (either a prince or an assembly), it decides what is the good for the city and for its citizens independently of any concerns expressed by individual subjects. Hegel's example is Creon's decree that the rebel prince will not receive the obsequy of burial. The ruler's judgments present the legal right that seeks to protect and promote civic good. The family, however, is founded on divine or subterranean Reason, and thus it relies on the authority of the domestic gods' will. It decides what is good for the family and for its members, independently of any concerns expressed by civil authorities. Its judgments present the moral right of Reason that seeks to protect and promote the good of the family, which *it* sees as the civil basis of society. The collision between these two equally valid rights destroys the harmony of the family and society. The ethical life of clanship is destroyed, as is the status of the woman within the Concept.[7] The woman and the subterranean law of the gods are sublated (that is, they are suppressed but nonetheless preserved), even though the concerns for the family and the divine law remain as an undercurrent throughout the rest of the chapter.

Canceling out one side of the Concept will reestablish unity through the effectiveness of the positive law. The civic law itself is to supply the articulated concept of Self solely in terms of Reason's own insights. This will become the concept of "person" in jurisprudence. However, by canceling out the role of subterranean Reason, the reality of its power and worth will reemerge, at least at a subconscious level, and it will reemerge with vengeance in the mad egoism and lust for power of the state government.

The last subsection of "True Spirit" perverts the descriptive value of

---

7. Woman, or what Hegel calls the "female principle," falls into the subterranean level of Reason. Her sense of religious obligation and private right is sublated (negated but still preserved) in the advance of Reason "in the daylight." Hegel's point is descriptive: this is what happens. He is not evaluating what occurs in Greek Ethical Life.

the name. "The Condition of Right" is almost an entirely negative development of the Concept of Reason as a practical resolution to the dissolution of the Ethical Life. The *formal* condition of right as a legal measure comes from the philosophical schools of Stoicism and Skepticism. In terms of law, the legal process of Roman jurisprudence advances the Concept by establishing that the Self is a "person," which is a category free of either any natural condition or family status. "Persons" are legal, not natural, beings. This advance, however, is more *in mente* than *in factum*, since the power of positive law resides in the will of the prince, who presents himself as a god on earth. The condition of positive law abrogated by individual power is a profanity against Reason and its eternal lawfulness, even though this condition is produced by Reason as the logical outcome of human (especially male) rule. The fate of Creon, to see his family and city destroyed, will recur continually in Rome as well, because the hubris and appetites of the emperors precipitate the decline and fall of "True Spirit" and the death of the "Ethical Life." Thus what was supposedly gained by the suppression of subterranean Reason is only a short-lived advance for the formality of Reason in the daylight. What civic Reason sought to gain by its own power—to protect the good of the city—is actually lost, and what was suppressed returns in the full expression of self-deception.

For this last subsection Hegel relies on Gibbon's history of Rome for his factual interpretation of imperial government, but the underlying moral tone for Hegel's interpretation comes from Augustine's *City of God*, which criticizes both the moral decadence of Rome and the invalidity and ineffectiveness of the philosophical schools to offer moral direction for Roman society. Hegel's "divine comedy" combines these two unlikely components—secular Enlightenment historiography and Christian morality—to show that the concept of Reason advances through the "Condition of Right" in spite of the impotence of philosophical Reason to secure the actual rights of persons in this spiritually impoverished culture.

The development of Reason, as we can see from the historical references used, is not a simple formal articulation of the Concept. On the contrary, the "development" is governed only by a pattern of Reason that seeks moral self-sufficiency. The human and divine sides of Reason, which became separated and opposed in the second subsection, require a reunification, one which will not be truly accomplished until the "Morality" section at the end of the chapter. It is only in this last section that self-identity in and through eternal law returns completely to the Self.

With the role and development of the Concept understood in general, let us look at how Hegel treats it in the individual subsections.

a. The Ethical World, Human and Divine Law, Man and Woman

Within the first World of Spirit lie the two realms of law. Self-consciousness comes to know these laws through its own essence, namely, the power of human law, represented in the will of the government, which can free the world-historical individual through its *de facto* rule, and the power of custom, religious belief, and so on, which binds the individual's will to the underlying (family) values of a society. Initially, the first law frees only the Self to become a willful power. It declares that it grants freedom and sets down universal justice, but this declaration conflicts with the underlying domestic values of the society. The second law points out the unethical nature of human law, and it strives to bring the "free" individual to conform to divine justice. The power of the first law, that is, the will of the government, opposes the possessive nature of the divine, and it seeks to punish the representatives of it by appealing to the common good and the universal will for its ground. The power of the second law, that is, the fear and passion of the household gods (the Penates), lies in the ethical substance of society, namely, in the family and its blood ties. It claims specific rights for individuals against the so-called common good, especially the rights of caring for the dead and the honor of the individual, so, for it, even a traitor who is a family member has the right to be treated honorably by being buried according to Greek custom.

Each side has its representatives. The realm of the divine law is represented by the woman, who cares for the private interests of the family. It is through her that the family has prospered and multiplied its members. It is through her that the blood relations of the family are sustained and kept "pure." The realm of the human law, on the other hand, is represented by the adult male, who has left the family unit and entered into public life. The man is the one who sets himself free and becomes the arbitrator of the public will. It is he, for instance, who makes war to protect the "public good," and it is he who ultimately turns against custom supposedly to free us all from its "bonds," but in reality he is turning against the recognition of the singular individual as such, and thus in his practical actions he destroys the domestic unity of the society. The "beautiful concord" that held all together, *as if* all citizens had kinship with each other, perishes (¶39–476). The Ethical Life itself is thought to reside in the family and the bonds of matrimony, and thus, as the bond of blood is sacrificed for the public good, the ethical life dies.

In this section we see that the question of the Ethical Life also includes the practical decisions of family members, who must decide if marriage comes prior to religious duties.[8] Even though Hegel is describing what the Ethical Life is in general, at the pinnacle of this section is the decision of Antigone to oppose the will of Creon, her uncle, her ruler, and her future father-in-law, for the sake of her dead brother, Polynices. It is Antigone's practical judgment to defy the legitimate power of Creon, which will elicit his judgment against her, and hence bring about the tragedy for the entire family. In this reciprocal effect, the practical judgment destroys the ethical substance of the "beautiful" society.

b. The Ethical Action, Human and Divine Knowledge, Guilt and Destiny

As the shade of the family member and the honored citizen of the state, the world- historical individual is raised to universality. The character of the individual is divided in this World, and Hegel tells us at the beginning of this subsection that the singularity of the individual has not yet come forth. He means that the individual in his or her own particularity has not yet been developed. This required advance occurs in the individual's encounter with destiny. "Destiny" is Hegel's term for the relationship between the individual and her ethical substance. As we have already seen, the conflict between the two valid forms of law will precipitate a clash of principles, and this now emerges as a tragedy within the kingdom of the Ethical Life.

"Ethical Action," Hegel's name for this subsection, applies to men and women who make free practical judgments based on their rationalized desires and prudential goals. But here we also see that the action is predicated on their ethical substance—the basis of law and source of virtue. On it, the individuals are simply accidents, or modes, of existence whose actions are determined as part of their being. The conflict is between the sexes as they identify themselves with different aspects of the ethical substance. In this conflict over duties and identities, each gender finds the other guilty of some crime, because the laws themselves have become polarized. Even in the case where the "ethical action" is done unconsciously—violating the law unintentionally—the person whose action it is has violated his ethical substance and thus is a criminal. The case of Oedipus is featured, since his "ethical action" shows both the full extent of "sin" and guilt. He elicits retribution on himself, his family, and his

---

8. This is shown as a conflict within the woman, or the "female principle," since her life's goal is to become a wife and mother, but her role as the equal partner to her husband is to serve the gods of the household. Thus her religious duties conflict with her personal goals. In terms of Greek Ethical Life her destiny is to pursue her religious duties and sacrifice her personal goals.

community. It is Antigone, however, who is the prophet of this epoch. Her pronouncement, "Because we suffer, we recognize that we have erred," is a death sentence on both herself and her community (cf. ¶ 33–470). These tragedies unfold within the inherent flaw of the world-historical individual. The hubris of the individual is simply the expression of Reason's self-deceptive unity, which Hegel described in the previous chapter.

The tragedy of the Greek ethical life becomes part of the greater narrative of divine redemption, since the "sin" of the individual—to be torn from her substance—permits the Concept to shift from the individual as such to the community as a people. The advance makes possible a freedom of the law from substance; now the people themselves create the notion of freedom and law as constitutive of moral reconciliation, and for a moment this notion puts an end to the tragedy.

The "free state" that bears witness both to the tragedy of the individual and to the promise of rational reconciliation through law is Athens. (The Athenians are present at Colonus where Oedipus is redeemed, and there they turn Creon—and the old order—away.) The Golden Age of Athens represents the idea of a people who belong to the "beautiful concord," in which identity and unity is founded on the sense of agreement between the rational god (Athena) and the self-knowing people. Here divine and human law coincide, at least speculatively. This is, however, a short-lived moment of the dialectic. No sooner is the concord recognized and declared valid than the community is beset by war and eventually destroyed. The war that Hegel refers to is the Peloponnesian War, in which not only Athens falls but the entire kingdom of the Ethical Life perishes (cf. ¶38–475). In this war the universal self-determinacy that all Greeks are one under divine justice is lost. In a war of all against all, only the brute force of nature remains, and the character of a free and just Spirit is sacrificed.

What remains from this stage is the concept of law, or to be more precise, the "right" (*jus, Recht*) on which the law is thought to be just and virtuous. The world-historical individual will adopt this Concept and take it as its founding idea that the *jus genitum* (the right of the people) replaces the ethical substance as it applies to all. By such a law the notion of a "person" will arise. Hegel will tell us in the final subsection of this epoch that the rise of a universal law occurs within Roman jurisprudence, and in it the Concept takes its next step.

What we should bear in mind through this section is that Hegel sees the dialectic of "true spirit" as running parallel to the dialectic of the "thing and its properties" in Chapter 2 of the *Phenomenology*. In that chapter the thing was dissolved, and the properties became detached from their substance. But even the properties, having no substance in them, dissolved into "many things," namely, atoms, which only adhere to each other by the effect of natural forces. As Spirit parallels that development, we see a dissolution of the entire universal substance of the ethical life, leaving behind only living atoms, that is, persons, in a void. Here they are governed only by the natural forces of appetite and will. Such a condition returns us to a universal materialism or, for the social unit, the basic drives for power, wealth, sex, and enjoyment without caring for the absolute character of Spirit. The "divine being" is transposed from the gods to the state and the imperial government.

c. The Condition of Right

In the previous section, "The Ethical Action," we witnessed the destruction both of clan society in the civil strife of one brother attacking another and of the "universal community," which thought that the ideal of the Ethical Life would suffice to constitute the national community. All civil ties are broken in war. War shatters the identity of universal relationship between the individual and the society. What remains are individuals pursuing their own being-for-self. "Being-for-self" becomes thus an atomic "point" in the shading of the whole. This point has no dimension: it is without substance, since the kingdom of the Ethical Life has ceased to exist. We are now in the Roman World after the end of the Greek Golden Age. We see the return of the Stoics and the Skeptics, as they appeared in Chapter 4, "Self-Certainty," but here the development of Stoicism and Skepticism has a decided social and political function: they serve to establish that these "points" are people with legal status. We might look to Cicero and Seneca as Hegel's models of the Skeptic and Stoic who pronounce the condition of legal right as sufficient to bring order and harmony to society.[9]

---

9. Gibbon mentions both Cicero and Seneca in passing in his first chapter of *History of the Decline and Fall of the Roman Empire* (1776–88). Cicero is taken as the skeptic whose work *De Natura Decorum* shows god to be nature and the popular civic deities to be false. Seneca and Marcus Aurelius are presented as the stoical consciousness. Seneca's *Consolatium ad Helviam* is explicitly mentioned by Gibbon. "Legal status" was intellectually promoted by the Stoics and Cynics, but Gibbon credits the "good" emperors for establishing it as part of the mores of this society. He says, "The progress of manners was accelerated by the virtue or policy of the emperors; and by the edicts of Hadrian and the Antonines, the protection of the laws was extended to the most abject part of mankind. The jurisdiction of life and death over the slaves . . . was taken out of private hands, and reserved to the magistrates alone," *Decline and Fall of the Roman Empire*, vols. I–II, ed. by Oliphant Smeaton (NY: The Modern Library, n.d.), I, p. 36.

Cicero has a conception of individuals as atoms under the determination of a "natural law," but nature is subordinate to the duties and legalities of the state. It is the state that has a "divine" function, and the citizens serve it as if it were a god. The state is in actuality a *res publica*, that is, a "public thing," in which all share, just as atoms share in nature's composition. Thus each citizen receives from the state its substance, its protection, and its legal recognition.

What belies this virtuous but material conception of society is the power of the prince and the general corruption of civic morals. The prince takes the next logical step; if the state is divine and he is the state, then he must be divine as well. Hegel follows Gibbon's the account of Rome's legal condition. Beginning with Augustus, the source of power and authority lies in titles, modes of flattery, and craftiness. The prince has two roles and two distinct names: on the one hand, as a virtuous member of the state and servant of the republic, he is the "censor," and he acts supposedly only as the chief magistrate of the state, leaving legislation to the assembly; but, on the other hand, the prince is an absolute despot whose private will is public law, and his role as the absolute monarch is known by the name "imperator."[10] Hegel clearly refers to Elagabalus in this subsection, since this is the prince who proclaims himself god of the World. Elagabalus believes himself to be the sun god (which foreshadows Louis XIV's conceit in the next section of the text), forming his own religious cult to worship him, and he behaves just as if his every whim were a divine right.[11] His most noteworthy "sovereign

---

10. Gibbon refers to the so-called reforms of Augustus: "The reformation of the senate was one of the first steps in which Augustus laid aside the tyrant, and professed himself father of his country. He was elected censor; and . . . he examined the list of senators, expelled a few members, whose vices or whose obstinacy required a public example, persuaded nearly two hundred to prevent the shame of an expulsion by voluntary retreat . . . and accepted for himself the honourable title of Prince of the Senate. . . . But whilst he restored the dignity, he destroyed the independence of the senate. The principles of a free constitution are irrevocably lost, when the legislative power is nominated by the executive. . . . The respective advantages of monarchy and a republic have often divided speculative inquiries; the present greatness of the Roman state, the corruption of manners, and the licence of soldiers, supplied new arguments to the advocates of monarchy. . . . After a decent resistance [to the senate's offer of the crown], the crafty tyrant [Augustus] submitted to the orders of the senate; and consented to receive the government of the provinces, and the general command of the Roman armies, under well-known names of Proconsul and Imperator," I, pp. 53–55, *passim*.

11. Gibbon tells us that this emperor, whose real name was Belissus Antonius, took the name "Elagabalus" from the name of the sun god: "The Sun was worshiped at Emesa, under the name Elagabalus, and under the form of a black

acts" are his orgies and murders, his rapes, and his wearing of female attire.[12]

Hegel is showing that in the ancient society that has lost the "beautiful concord" there enters on the scene only two courses of action: either you become a philosopher and renounce the World and its ways, or you enter into a mad orgy of life, believing literally in youthful Elagabalus' *carpe diem* (¶44–481). In the second instance you become bestial, returning to the most primitive and virtually irrational moment of self-consciousness—pursuing only egoistic passion and sexual self-gratifications. In either case you are likely to be murdered, as both philosopher and emperor were, and your "legal right" will not help you. The Stoical or Skeptical conceptions, which advanced "legal right" as a moral concept, fall under the actuality of the *carpe diem* and fail because of it. Cicero's and Seneca's imperially imposed suicides show the futility of self-enclosed certainty, and in place of it the *carpe diem* of the adolescent beast is seen to be the lord and master of all actions. In the end the irrational beast will also die, but only because the privileged estates, the nobles of the senate and the elite guards of the imperium, can no longer suffer it to live. One of the first actions of the estates, exerting their power and privilege, is to kill their hereditary prince and, then, envelop one of their favorites with the mantel of an

---

conical stone. . . . To this protecting deity, Antonius, not without some Reason, ascribed his elevation to the throne. . . . The triumph of the God of Emesa over all the religions of the earth, was the great object of his zeal and vanity; and the appellation of Elagabalus (for he assumed as pontiff and favourite to adopt the sacred name) was dearer to him than all the titles of Imperial greatness," p. 126. Belissus Antonius became emperor by luck and craftiness. He was lucky because the previous emperor, Macrinus, fled the field of battle, even though he was winning, and thus his cowardice undid him. He was crafty because Antonius sent letters to the Roman senate persuading them falsely that he was related to Marcus Antonius and that he was committed to similar virtues. Cf. Gibbon, I, p. 125. The senate was gullible enough to believe him. (Notice the theme of fortune continues from the previous subsections. Hegel deliberately picks his references to continue his motifs.)

12. Gibbon writes, "whilst Elagabalus lavished away the treasures of this people in the wildest extravagance, his own voice and that of his flatterers applauded a spirit and magnificence unknown to the tameness of his predecessors. To confound the order of seasons and climates, to sport with passions and prejudices of his subjects, and to subvert every law of nature and decency, were in the number of his most delicious amusements. A long train of concubines, and rapid succession of wives, among whom was a vestal virgin, ravished by force from her sacred asylum, were insufficient to satisfy the impotence of his passions. The master of the Roman World affected to copy the dress and manners of the female sex," I, p. 127ff.

emperor.[13] This act can have one of two effects. Civil disharmony will result if a weak man is raised to the imperium. According to Gibbon this is what happened when Caligula was murdered by his guard and Claudius was made emperor;[14] or, when the estates act to protect and promote virtue and a virtuous prince is selected, then not only is the harmony of society hoped for, but privilege is recognized to have honor.[15] According to Gibbon this is what occurred when Elagabalus was murdered and Alexander was picked as the prince. But even honor does not suffice to produce and protect "ethical action," which, when free of an ethical substance, cannot sustain virtue, civic harmony, and reconciliation in the world order.[16] The series of purges and murders continues virtually unabated, that is, as long as the spiritual ineffectiveness of this World remains. War and death are the constant companions of the self-deceived material society. Lust, avarice, and power are the

---

13. Hegel says, "their self-consciousness is the powerless wrapping and the field of their tumult," ¶45–481.

14. This is the case where the estates are divided in their common interest, and thus they choose the weakest leader. Gibbon comments, "When the throne was vacant by the murder of Caligula, the consuls convoked the assembly in the Capitol, condemned the memory of the Cæsars, gave the watchword *liberty* to the few cohorts who faintly adhered to their standard, and during the eight and forty hours acted as independent chiefs of a free commonwealth. But while they deliberated, the Prætorian Guards had resolved. The stupid Claudius, brother to Germanicus, was already in their camp, invested with Imperial purple, and prepared to support his election by arms. The dream of liberty was at an end; and the senate awoke to all the horrors of inevitable servitude," I, p. 64.

15. Gibbon gives an account of how Alexander routed a rebellion by shouting to his troops, "'*Citizens!* Lay down your arms, and depart in peace to your respective habitations.' The tempest was instantly appeased; the soldiers, filled with grief and shame, silently confessed the justice of their punishment and the power of discipline," I, p. 136. The name "citizens" is one of *dishonor*, removing from the soldiers their nobility and privilege.

16. Gibbon tells the story of the prefect Ulpian, under the rule of virtuous Alexander: "the wise Ulpian, was the friend of the laws and of the people; he was considered as the enemy of the soldiers; and to his pernicious counsels every scheme of reformation was imputed. Some trifling accident blew up their discontent into a furious mutiny; and a civil war raged, during three days, in Rome, whilst the life of that excellent minister was defended by a grateful people. Terrified, at length, by the sight of some houses in flames, the people yielded with a sigh, and left the virtuous, but unfortunate, Ulpian to his fate. He was pursued into the Imperial palace, and massacred at the feet of his master, who vainly strove to cover him with the purple, and to obtain his pardon from the inexorable soldiers," I, p. 134. Alexander himself meets a similar fate at the hands of his own troops. Cf. Gibbon, I, p. 149.

driving motives for actual action. The virtuous emperor, such as Alexander Severus, is just as likely to be murdered by his guards as was the vice-ridden beast, Caligula.

This restlessness ends suddenly in the next section, "Self-Estranged Spirit." What must occur to end the strife is a recognition of mutual trust between the estates and the prince, and this only occurs when pledges and oaths become symbols of trust—when *words* replace deeds. The assurance of "one's word," used as a pledge of honor, embodies social harmony and civic unity. The shift is obviously to a conception of feudal allegiance, the system of vassalage, and the moral code of chivalry. In terms of the historical reference, the shift is from Rome to the kingdom of the Franks, that is, to France. (Gregory of Tours notes that Clovis, king of the Franks, takes for himself the purple mantel of the imperium to show that his authority is a continuation of the Roman emperor.) For the Concept there is an advance toward reconciliation and unity. The promise is that a "natural unity" of honor will be forged between the temporal and spiritual powers, which will reunite the Self and return it to its substance. The promise fails, however, because the bonds of unity are not the real source of strength. The World in which Spirit has created the promise is profane, and in it the Self does not remain true to its own promises of honor and duty.

B. Self-Estranged Spirit; Culture

Hegel introduces us to the second section of "Spirit," which is both a continuation of the earlier section, "True Spirit," and a departure from it in terms of what constitutes the basis for the rational unity and identity of the world-historical individual. In the earlier section the basis of the Concept was in the "natural associations" of family and the sovereign's will. "Nature," unified through blood kinship and self-identity, was tied to the family and local custom. Even in Rome, nature—understood either through Stoicism as atoms in a void or through the *carpe diem* of world power—governed the unity and identity of the individual. In this section Spirit makes itself estranged from nature, at least estranged from the "simple connection" that formed the beautiful concord in "True Spirit." Nature's elements are set loose and enter into a new articulation of the "masses" (cf. ¶55–492). Hegel, when he speaks of "masses," is referring to the establishment of social classes, or estates, which are based on a "natural" hierarchy. These classes form the social unity of the Estates General that constituted (in theory) the government of the *ancien régime*.

In this articulation of the masses nature has evolved into what we might
call a "social organism," wherein the individual's own being is defined by
either his allegiance to or contempt for the natural order of social privilege. Hegel focuses on the "being" of the world-historical individual, thus
leaving aside the social-political issues that affected feudal society. We get
only a faint hint that the political arrangement is under stress, when, for
instance, the "haughty vassal" (Prince de Condé at the time of the
Fronde) acts contemptuously to the state power (cf. ¶68–505).[17] The
uprising of the Fronde is, however, just background to Hegel's analysis of
the determination of being in which the social organism is divided and in
conflict. Hegel is concerned not with the literal events of the seventeenth
century but with the nature of the political organization as it involves conflicts and divisions in the spiritual unity and identity of the classes. Rome,
France, and the Holy Roman Empire (that is, the German and Italian
states as they existed until 1806) have a similar foundation of elemental
unity—that is what Hegel's Concept is attempting to analyze.

What divides "being" is, on one side, religion and, on the other side,
the political power. The unity of the Estates General presupposes fidelity
and trust between the two privileged estates (the Church and nobility)
and the submission of the third estate (the bourgeoisie or burghers) to this
unifying idea. In such a condition what holds this entire array together is
the labor of the declassed "mass" of peasants—or what Hegel refers to as
the *Knechten*[18] in Chapter 4, "Self-Certainty." The function of this class
is ignored by the acknowledged estates. This unity is chiefly a spiritual
accomplishment, since it is the Church that anoints the king as the
supreme state power and it asks the nobility of their lives in sacrifice. The

---

17. The Fronde was the time when the Paris *parlement* and nobility rose
against the boy-king, Louis XIV (c. 1648–52). The uprising was directed not so
much against him as against his mother and Cardinal Mazarin, who ruled in
Louis's name. Hegel appears to allude to the events of the Fronde when Prince de
Condé demands to be paid for his service to the king. The account in given in Voltaire's *Histoire du Parlement de Paris* (1769), in *Oeuvres Complètes*, t. 34 (Paris: Baudouin Frères, 1878), p. 313: "Le prince de Condé demanda hautement le prix des
ses services"—"The prince of Condé asked haughtily the price of his services."

18. The *Knechten* are servants who are bound to a master's will; colloquially,
the term refers to "boys" who work for their livelihood on ships and in shops. In
his earlier writings Hegel sometimes uses the word *Slav* instead of *Knecht*. The
two have different meanings. *Slav* is a slave or a person who has no actual legal or
moral standing in the ethical community. His status is similar to any beast in the
stable yard. But a *Knecht* is recognized as "someone," who though inferior to a
person of privilege has nonetheless some moral and legal legitimacy. In "Spirit"
Rameau's nephew is a *Knecht;* he is not a *Slav.*

character of these beings whose lives are in service to spiritual unity is called "honorable," and Hegel might well be thinking of the "knight of virtue" as the kind of being who identifies himself with the social organism.[19] In terms of this "kind" we could think of one example that Hegel surely knew from literature, the Crusader Cacciaguida of Florence, who states in Dante's *Paradise,*

> I served with Conrad in the Holy Land,/ and my valor so advanced me in his favor/ that I was knighted in his noble band./ With him I raised by sword against the might/ of the evil creed whose followers take from you/ . . . what is yours by right./ There, by that shameless and iniquitous horde,/ I was divested of the flesh and weight of the deceitful World, too much adored/ by many souls whose best hope it destroys;/ and came from martyrdom to my present joys (Canto XV, 139–49).[20]

Nobility and honor account for the identification of this self-consciousness, and with it the feudal estates are completed to form the unity that was lacking in the previous stage of spirit. The key to this identification is the love and adoration of God in his Church and the recognition of his Providence in the World. The prince and the two privileged estates both acknowledge this as the foundation for social unity; as long as this identification suffices then the "beautiful concord" exists in principle. Even those whose lives are sacrificed to sustain this concord have the promise of the other World, what Hegel calls the "beyond," which is true to them as an actuality *more real* than the profane World, or what Hegel calls "this-sidedness" (cf. ¶49–486). They believe, as Cacciaguida says, that they are undergoing martyrdom, escaping from a "deceitful World" and entering into God's World of eternal joy.

Discord enters into this concord from two sub rosa traits inherent in the outward worldly character of even the virtuous knight: namely, that the entire unity of the Estates General cannot be sustained without money, and so *wealth* becomes the means to attain honor and privilege (¶58–495ff.); and that the monarch in his decrees and in the flattery of the court has to be acknowledged as the absolute power of the World, and with this identification the *être suprême* becomes identified with the state

---

19. The "knight of virtue" is one shape of the rational Concept that appears in Chapter 5, "Reason." Cf. *Phänomenologie des Geistes, GW,* ix, pp. 317–29. Hegel seems to refer there to the Marquis d'Posa, who was a knight in service in Philip II's court.

20. *The Divine Comedy,* trans. by John Ciardi (New York: W. W. Norton and Co., 1970), p. 485.

itself (cf. ¶75–512). As these two traits rise and become dominant, the honorable vassal becomes haughty and contemptuous (unless he becomes the favorite of the absolute power and for his service he receives not only esteem but great prizes). Once wealth becomes the identifying trait for having an honorable character, then the shift in unity and identity between Self and World is underway. From what was once the "nobility of the sword" there now appears the "lesser" nobility of the robe. The privilege of class distinction is recognized as honorable by the old guard, but the new nobility who simply buy their offices are contemptuous of them and all honor. The third estate, because of its wealth, exerts *its* power over all and receives privileges from the state (cf. ¶75–572ff.), but then the true extent of the fraudulent "spiritual" unity shows itself. The bourgeoisie has only money, and it becomes in this identification both the contemptuous class (against the privileged estates) and the object of contempt for those few who have a sense of honor and self-worth. The lesser nobility and bourgeoisie are only members of the *espèce,* the kind of being that is contemptible (cf. ¶52–489, ¶87–524).

What characterizes and differentiates the so-called honorable classes is the "kind" of person who belongs to "good society." Hegel deliberately uses the ironic term *"espèce"* to designate them. Hegel takes the name from Diderot's satire, *Rameau's Nephew* (c. 1762), and he believes, as did Diderot, that "culture" has the effect of estranging character: to be raised and trained in a World where "religion" is almost wholly political, where the "good" and "bad" have opposite meanings from what they should, and where money is the only thing that really counts means that a kind of social schizophrenia is being produced in the bourgeoisie's character.[21] This lunacy is shown in the speech of Rameau—a tutor of music and parasite on the wealthy bourgeoisie (cf. ¶85–522).

"Culture" has no reference to virtue that comes either from natural associations or from positive law. It is only a collection of fashion, "witty" repartée, and the recognition that who invites whom to what *soirée* determines one's place in society. The lunacy of such differentiae affects all aspects of society, and only two forces appear to oppose it: the simplicity of Jansenist faith, which decries the vanity of the Self and its contemptible World (¶89–526); and the consciousness of "pure insight," which is

---

21. The sense that "Culture" eviscerates our social and moral character comes from Rousseau's discourse "On the Origin of Inequality," which Diderot helped to edit and promoted among the *philosophes.* Hegel seems to refer to this essay in the penultimate section of the chapter on Reason, in the part called "The Spiritual Kingdom of the Animals . . . ," *Phänomenologie des Geistes, GW,* ix, pp. 216–32.

embodied in the *philosophes'* call for a return to nature and individual liberty. "Nature" is the symbol of Reason, and "a return to nature" is a call to self-interested pleasure and utility, which not only focuses on the ethical concern of the individual to pursue happiness but attempts to defrock the religious establishment of the first estate by showing it to be built on despotism and superstition (¶106–542).

These two "spiritual" forces, both born from the contempt against the state power and its "religious" supporters, *begin* as allies, but, as Hegel notes in the Enlightenment section, they succeed only to wage war against each other. Their success is to destroy the pretensions of the other, so that "on one fine morning . . ." one side gives "its comrade a shove with the elbow and bash! crash! the idol lies on the floor . . ." (¶109–545). Spirit resides in this contest of forces, in which only one side can be victorious. Hegel notes that the freethinker will lie about the position of faith, but that does not matter, because in the end it is the freethinker who presents the *quality* of the Concept as a determination of human right and as the espousal of freedom. Only one side will be victorious in securing a determination of the Self in this "Age of Reason," and it is the freethinker who succeeds in raising the banner of the Academy of the Arts and Sciences as synonymous with the Concept of Reason in the World.[22]

It is not until the "Truth of Enlightenment" section that Hegel discloses that the values of the freethinker have virtually succeeded in defending the metaphysical Concept of Spirit. They have recognized the "musty weave" of Spirit as forming a great web that ties both mind and society together. As Diderot explains in *D'Alembert's Dream* (c. 1769; publ. 1782),

> Upset the center of the web and you change the nature of the whole creature, whose entire being seems to be concentrated there, sometimes dominating outlying threads, sometimes being dominated by them. [. . .] The center of the network issues orders and the rest obeys. Then the animal is master of itself, *mentis compos*. . . . It is the epitome of a weak political administration in which each one usurps the authority of the ruler. There is only one way of curing this that I know of . . . it is for the center of the sensitive network, the part

---

22. Hegel does not favor the freethinkers in his account of the Enlightenment. He sees them as snakes, but he does credit them with developing the concept of Reason as enclosing human values, especially the value of liberty. The freethinkers take from the religious side what was implicit there but never actualized. They actualize "freedom" but only by lying about the true nature of religious value, which always concerns self-redemption.

which constitutes the Self, to be given some powerful motive for
regaining its authority. . . .[23]

Humanity and nature both have a materialistic base, but it is not nature
itself that forms this bond; it is the mind (*esprit*), as an inventive assemblage of ideas, that has created a society of manners. Nature itself is just a
perfectly operating machine that must be considered distinct from
"mind." Hegel notes that the freethinkers have reached the penultimate
stage of the Concept. What is lacking to them, of course, is that in their
worldliness the true value of religion has no place. Instead they have created a Religion of Man, a religion in which Reason is worshiped without
regard for either the humanity or the fragility of it. The highest achievement of this philosophical advance is to attain "absolute freedom," and
that also marks the collapse of the idea of the Enlightenment. The "freedom of the Self" that the philosophical community advocated becomes
the absolute freedom of the Reign of Terror; the return to nature becomes
the return of the Lord of the World, which is Death; and the attempt to
annul the spiritual ties of the social organism becomes revolution, war,
and the murder of the *être suprême*. The hope for a rational community
governed by an "enlightened" despot all goes crashing to the ground, just
as the guillotine chops off heads "with no more significance than the
chopping off of a cabbage head or a gulp of water" (¶154–590). What was
to be the actuality of a worldly reconciliation that unites the universal will
to the common citizen, in fact, is just a return to the mad egoism of positive law that destroyed the ancient bonds and annulled legal right. The
distinction here seems to be that it is the citizen himself (at least represented by the citizens on the Committee of Public Safety) who becomes
the tyrant. Death to anyone who actually "thinks freely."

Despite this drive to self-destruction, Hegel sees this phase of Spirit as
making great strides in determining the Concept of Reason. It should be
noted that the Jansenists make the most significant contribution to how
the Concept of Reason is to reacquire a sense of value and unworldliness
true to itself. Hegel's mission, as stated in the essay *Faith and Knowledge*
(1802), was to establish the "speculative Good Friday," by which he
means, at least in part, to establish the fact that the material World is itself
Godforsaken.[24] This insight is what the Jansenist recognizes within faith:

---

23. *D'Alembert's Dream* (c. 1769; publ. 1782), trans. by Leo Hancock (Middle-
sex: Penguin, 1966), p. 204ff. I have Americanized the English spelling.

24. "the pure concept or infinity as the abyss of nothingness in which all
being is engulfed must signify the infinite grief purely as a moment of the
supreme idea and no more than a moment. Formerly, the infinite grief only

the World itself has no inherent value, only we who seek to find in the ways of the World amusements, which release us from boredom and make the World and nature significant. The "true" value of life lies within, and Hegel sees that the concept of Reason must turn inward, to the source of the Self. Nature does not supply us with this source; only humanity itself, shaped through its culture and through the process of self-estrangement, supplies the source. Thus, the Jansenists, even more than the freethinkers, recognize the way to truth, and with the claims against the vanity of the world-historical individual, they also recognize that the "fault of facticity" continues, no matter the advances in science, art, and philosophy. The human being ultimately must face this essential fault, and that requires a development in the critical power of the mind to discern moral good from evil, and how "right" comes from Reason itself. The Jansenists do not triumph in the Age of Reason, however, but their insight into the worth of the Self will eventually be reaffirmed in the moral stance of pure Reason.

We are presently just taking an overview of the section. Let us now look more closely at what Hegel asserts to be the moments of estrangement.

I. The World of Self-Estranged Spirit

There are two subsections in this section: a) Culture and Its Realm of Actuality and b) Faith and Pure Insight. The first subsection presents the World of social culture in the development of self-consciousness during the rise of the *ancien régime*. Hegel focuses on the development of contempt in both vassal and burgher. This is the story of the *espèce:* the kind of being who conforms to social manners and mores, and thus adapts his or her ego to belong to "good society." Opposite to the "espèce" is the "contemptuous consciousness," who decries the so-called virtues of good society and looks upon the "espèce" as vile. The "contemptuous consciousness," as we will see, appears under various guises: the "haughty

---

existed historically in the formative process of culture. It existed as the feeling that 'God himself is dead,' upon which the religion of more recent times rests; the same feeling that Pascal expressed in, so to speak, sheerly empirical form: 'la nature est telle qu'elle *marque* partout un Dieu *perdu* et dans l'homme et hors de l'homme.' By marking this feeling as a moment of the supreme idea, the pure Concept must give philosophical existence to what used to be either the moral precept that we must sacrifice the empirical essence or the Concept for formal abstraction. Thereby it must re-establish for philosophy the idea of absolute freedom and along with it the absolute Passion, the speculative Good Friday in place of the historical Good Friday. Good Friday must be speculatively re-established in the whole truth and harshness of its Godforsakenness," *Faith and Knowledge, GW,* iv, p. 413ff.

vassal" (Prince de Condé), the journeyman artist (Jean-François Rameau), the *philosophe* (Denis Diderot), and the reform-minded Jansenist (the follower of Pascal). These individuals have in common a contempt for the hypocrisy of society and the belief that living the life of a member of "good society" is the worst sort of life. Their story concerns the loss of essence but also the insight that their individuality, as an inversion of the *espèce,* is itself honorable and good. Or, we could also say that the story concerns the self-identification of individuals according to class distinction and social division, which lead to insurrection and ultimately to revolution, but this is a revolution in morals, which advances the philosophical Concept to legitimize human rights and personal liberties.

The second subsection presents two sides of the *ancien régime* as it confronts the dawning Age of Reason or the Enlightenment. On one side we find the pure simple soul of the Jansenist, who knows that his Catholic faith is the source of truth. "Faith" is the actuality of Self-Certainty, that is, it combines the Skeptic, who denies the material connections of society and pursues instead desires of Unhappy Consciousness, and the moral certitude of the Stoic, who rejects the "this-sidedness" of the World as a vain and empty amusement. This individual accepts only his thoughts as true, and especially the thought that "all is vanity" (¶89–526). What contradicts this individual's sense of truth is that he must both engage the World and be separate from it, so that his beliefs are opposed by the freethinkers, deists and atheists alike. The Jansenist attempts to use the instruments of the World against them, but such an "instrumental use" of Reason only belies his faith in the beyond. Publicly, Jansenism is successful on this world stage; its views triumph in the Paris *parlement,* which forces the freethinkers to flee France for Germany and England. But philosophically, the Jansenist is defeated by "pure insight."

The Concept of Reason in this cycle first acknowledges the primacy of nature and the importance of science and the liberty of conscience. Thus on the side of "determinate being" (Hegel's category of qualitative existence) it sides with the endeavors of the *philosophes,* most notably their materialism and declarations that the people deserve to know the truth about religion. The freethinker belongs to the society of science, art, and letters. He identifies himself with the newly formed Academy of Science; as such his thought comes into the World to act, and to see the World purely in terms of science and public law. Hegel will allude to a long list of *philosophes* in this division and the next, but chief among them are Diderot and D'Alembert, who were responsible for the *Encyclopédie* (1751ff.), the first compendium of philosophical science, and who brought to Prussia and into the court of the Frederick II the cultural values of the Enlightenment. Under the cycle of the material weave, the singular individual is seen as a person of rights, a legitimate member of the estates, and a member of a greater humanity. However, this cycle, as we will see, is also a perversion of Reason since it treats nature as the source and object of Reason, when in fact we already know that this is not true. Reason resides in the simplicity of thought that only religious piety provides.

Hegel's dialectic from the outset is centered on the "singular individual," especially the "torn" consciousness of the artist and philosopher. Throughout this division and the next, the comments of *le Philosophe* (*"Moi"* in the dialog and Diderot's alter ego) from *Rameau's Nephew* appear as a description of a social pathology within the individual who is torn between his cultural sense of Self and his own spiritual essence identified with his work.[25] Rameau is the key person for this diagnosis. In him, the crisis of identity is explicitly portrayed. He is in a state of turmoil because his conflicting values concerning work, family, talent, and society remain unresolved in a perpetual state of flux. The irony of the dialog is that we hear from this lunatic that the resolution to all such conflicts

---

25. In 1805 Goethe published his translation of Diderot's second satire. He saw it as a satirical presentation of the "culture of understanding"; a Culture that tears itself apart. The two characters, "I" who is the *philosophe* and "he" who is Rameau, both stand opposed to this Culture, even though it is the "fool" who rants and raves against it. "Rameau" is Jean-François Rameau, the nephew of the court composer Jean-Philippe Rameau. He is considered a fool because, although he supposedly has talent as a musician, he is forced to be a music tutor to an especially untalented family and to perform at the dinner parties which his patron, M. Bertin, regularly has. Rameau is made into a servant (a *Knecht*), is deprived of his ability to express his talent, and is torn between keeping up his livelihood—he has a son whom he is supporting—and keeping true to his art. It is this tearing of consciousness that seems to destroy his sanity. Diderot, who is supposedly the "I" in the dialog, finds himself in similar circumstances. He has lost his position as publisher of the *Encyclopédie*. He has had to sell his library just to have food on the table. He, too, has a young child whom he is trying to support. The difference seems to be that Diderot adopts the attitude of the Stoical consciousness, while Rameau adopts the Skeptical consciousness (both forms of consciousness have appeared in Hegel's Chapter 4, "Self-Certainty"). The Stoical attitude presents the case for acceptance of the status quo. Near the end of the dialog the character "I" gets Rameau to admit that the Culture of privilege and vulgarity is itself understandable and even necessary. "The cranes," he says, "fly above, and we stand here below."

Goethe tells us the circumstance under which the satire was written. During the reign of Louis XV, in 1759, Diderot's works were condemned by the Paris *parlement;* the Jansenists sought an indictment against him for the theological articles in his *Encyclopédie*. In May of 1760 the Catholic playwright Palissot, who supported the Jansenist cause, brought out a satirical play called *Le Philosophe*, in

resides in a return to simplicity (represented in purity of musical tonalities), which is not unlike the simplicity of soul that the Jansenist seeks. Throughout the presentation of the Concept we see the "deception" of Culture, which arises in speech, social standing, and most especially in music. "French opera" becomes the *cause célèbre* for the resolution of internal strife—the "quarrel of the *buffoon*"—because in this musical form there is a return to musical tonality. Hegel believes the simple tones reintroduced to society are actually a spiritual awakening, which itself allows us a return to simplicity in thought. Rameau's "tonal heaven" is the "natural attitude" of a pious consciousness.[26]

---

which the main character is Diderot. In the play, the *philosophes* are thieves and rakes. Diderot is their ringleader. Voltaire openly attacked the play, which only made it more popular, and wrote to Diderot advising him to leave Paris. Diderot did leave but only for a short vacation, during which time he began to write this satire. Supposedly a draft was completed in 1761, but he continued to work on it, making different drafts, until approximately 1775. The satire, then, is a response to Palissot's play but more generally it addresses the "cultural wars" of the day, especially concerning French versus Italian opera. It is also interesting to know that one version of the dialog got into the hands of the publisher Melchoir Grimm, and it is that draft that Goethe received. Diderot never published this work. The first French edition (1821) comes from a French translation of Goethe's translation (1805). Goethe's original copy was lost, as were all other copies, except one that was discovered later in St. Petersburg. Hegel most likely read Goethe's translation when it appeared in 1805. It becomes the dominant background piece for the "Culture" section of "Spirit," and it is the most often cited work in *Phenomenology of Spirit*.

26. Diderot makes much of the conflict concerning music in the dialog, and Goethe, in his editorial remarks, points out that the quarrel over music (between "natural" French music, as found in Rameau's compositions, and "artificial" Italian music) is at the heart of the dialog's discussion of discord and tonality. They are referring to what is commonly called the *quarrel of the buffoons*. Hegel, however, might also be thinking of Rousseau's *Confessions*, where Rousseau recounts the debate over musical form that precipitates social strife and even his own attempted murder. Rousseau recounts, "The buffoons acquired [for] Italian music very warm partisans. All of Paris was divided into two parties, the violence of which was greater than if an affair of state or religion had been in question. One of them, the more powerful and numerous, composed of the great, of men of fortune, and the ladies, supported French music; the other, more lively and haughty, and fuller of enthusiasms, was composed of real connoisseurs, and men of talent and genius. This little group assembled at the Opera-house, under the box belonging to the Queen. The other party filled up the rest of the pit and the theater. . . . The dispute, as it became more animated, produced several pamphlets. [Rousseau authored the *Lettre sur la musique* on behalf of Italian music.] . . . [T]he *Lettre sur la musique* was taken seriously, and incensed against me the whole nation, which thought itself offended by this attack on its music . . . [T]he

a. Culture and Its Realm of Actuality

In the first subsection of "Estranged Spirit" we see that the natural order is transformed: the vital elements of earth, air, fire, and water enter into a fourfold array, which moves the Concept with its bipolar divisions into a unity of four class distinctions (¶55–492). In place of the ancient Roman order of the *res publica,* in which people were only atoms in a spiritual void, comes the energy of the universal will (which is traditionally rendered as the General Will) and the Estates General. This universal will obliges the privileged classes to serve and protect the whole, and it constitutes the positive order of society as such. *Noblesse oblige* is the self-legitimating value of this society, and with it the feudal order perpetuates itself. Nonetheless we are witnessing the twilight of this social system. Hegel is looking at the end of the order, not at its beginning, to show the moral decline and ultimate fall of this empire of the universal will. French society imitates the death throes of the Roman empire. Where the Sun Emperor, Elagabalus, marked the precipice before the Roman fall, the Sun King, Louis XIV, and his court of flattery mark the edge of the abyss for the *ancien régime.* The structure of this rational society is outwardly spiritual but inwardly materialistic: what is called "good" is to be a member of the *bonne société,* which only values the "bad," namely, money.

In order to demonstrate this "good society's" worth, Hegel presents it in three stages of its development. In the first stage, we see the emergence of actual self-consciousness as belonging to universal self-identification in the Estates General. Then a split occurs in the Estates General as the nobility serves for honor and the bourgeoisie serves for the prize of nobility. In the second stage, we see the division of this identification developing into two opposing essences: the good and the bad. In this stage the individuals of the *ancien régime* will take sides against each other. Honor is initially the "good," while those who seek status through wealth are the "bad," but the honorable cannot sustain themselves or this World. Wealth

---

perilous state of French music was the only thing [that engaged] the attention of the public, and the only insurrection was against myself. . . . At Court, the Bastille or banishment was absolutely determined on, and a *lettre de cachet* would have been issued had not M. de Voyer set forth in the most forcible manner that such a step would be ridiculous. . . . Although no attempts were made on my liberty, I suffered numerous insults; and even my life was in danger. The musicians of the Opera orchestra humanely resolved to murder me as I went out of the theater. . . . I did not learn until a considerable time afterwards, that M. Ancelet, officer of the musketeers, and who had a friendship for me, had prevented the effect of this conspiracy by giving me escort, which, unknown to me, accompanied me until I was out of danger," *Confessions,* trans. by A. S. B. Glover (NY: George Macy, 1955), Pt. II, Bk. viii, p. 367ff.

takes precedence, and with it what was "good" is now "bad." For wealth, the "good" citizens live lives of manners, which seem to consist mainly in attending dinner parties and speaking wittily. To have a good wit, to have fashionable manners, means that a wealthy member of society may obtain stature and be accepted in the *bonne société*. He or she enters the *noblesse de robe*, which is granted to the burghers simply because they are wealthy and buy their offices from the state power.

Hegel sees in this development a shift away from the alliance between Church and nobility to the point where only the privilege of wealth prevails as the principle of unity and order. Wealth becomes the guarantee of entrance into "good society," and those who have no taste, no appreciation of either wit or art, will gain admittance to it because they are honored for their money. This shifting of unities produces in the Concept the "realm of actuality." The "realm of actuality" is self-contradictory however: the virtuous are considered fools, the "nobles" are sycophants and bullies, and a madman, the music teacher Rameau, speaking to another social outcast, the *philosophe* Diderot,[27] conveys more wisdom and "pure insight" than the whole court of cardinals, chamberlains, knights, and bankers. It is not surprising then that Hegel uses Diderot's satire as the vehicle for rational agency in this milieu; only in jest and irony can one appreciate self-contradiction.

In the third stage we see the Concept of self-estrangement played out within the viewpoint of the alienated artists, philosophers, and pious believers. Their views belong to this society in the sense that they, too, value wit and manners, but they also see the hypocrisy of the age. Their values and self-identity do not allow them to conform to the monotonous tune of wealth and privilege. Instead the artist and philosopher posit a core value of simplicity, which brings us back to the self-certainty of the Stoic and Skeptic. Here a "spiritual" insight is attained to which both Jansenist and freethinker agree: oppose the values of this World, express the freedom and identity of the Self, and look to the beyond as the source of truth. By the next subsection the Jansenist will adopt in his position of faith that truth is only in the "beyond" of God's kingdom, while the materialistic freethinker finds truth only in nature that lies beyond Culture.

---

27. Goethe in his translation of *Rameau's Nephew* remarks that Diderot was made into an abject fool on stage and in *parlement* by his enemies. By the time Diderot wrote this satire, he had lost control of the *Encyclopédie* and was able to survive financially only because Catherine the Great bought his library. Diderot's nemeses were the playwright Palissot and the members of the fashionable salon of the Marquise de la Mark. Many of his jibes are directed at the members of "good society," who frequented the theater and the salons.

If we look carefully in this subsection, we see that Hegel sides with the assumptions of the freethinkers in respect to "human value," even though he will oppose them on the question of the "truth of faith." He believes with them that there are materialistic connections in society that bind us together. Diderot is the spokesperson for this stage of Reason, and it is his theory of the "molecule" that ties the corporate society together, which Hegel sees as forming the natural bonds of the social fabric. Hegel also accepts that the piety of Pascal's Jansenism is correct, namely, that the vanity of this entire period is just another sign of Culture's self-deception. Only in religion are there the humanistic values that redeem us from this form of deception but religious value is in the form of "ennui"—world-weariness. We should think of Pascal as speaking for the religious consciousness who has contempt for the pretense of worldly self-fulfillment. As Pascal says, "Qui ne voit pas la vanité du monde est bien vain luy mesme. . . . Mais, ostez leur divertissement, vous les verrez se sécher d'ennuy; ils sentent alors leur néant sans la connoistre: car c'est bien estre malheureux que d'estre dans une tristesse insupportable, aussytost qu'on est réduit à se considérer et à n'en estre point diverti."[28] The poverty of worldly culture, because it proves itself to be vain and wearisome, eventually leads us to religion.

b. Faith and Pure Insight

At the end of the previous subsection the remedy for the torn consciousness was to return to lucid talk and "simplicity" of mind. For the religious being—who all along has sought to maintain honor in society—simplicity is the attitude of "faith": a faith that rejects the vanity of the World and is resolved to remain true to its pure and simple thoughts. This is the faith that unites Unhappy Consciousness with scientific Reason. For the freethinker—who is cynical about any honor in society as well as what faith has to offer—simplicity is the sole position of scientific intuition, that is, the "pure insight" of secular Reason. This insight recognizes the fact that Culture has corrupted moral values, and society needs to return to nature in order to find the true essence of the Self. Mettríe speaks on behalf of this simple insight: the "Self" is itself a mechanism, a machine that talks and thinks; it is the machine that is the essential Self. In the face of Culture and the Self as a machine, the resolution of the freethinker is to

---

28. The French reads approximately: "He who does not see the vanity of the world is himself empty. . . . But take away their amusements and you will see them perish of boredom; then they will feel their nothingness unconsciously; for it is truly unhappy to become unbearably sad, because you have been reduced to consider yourself without recourse to amusement," *Pensées*, ed. H. F. Stewart (NY: Pantheon Books, 1950), p. 50.

remain true to its thoughts of actuality: namely, to accept fatalistically that our atomic lives are in a void but also to declare that Reason alone tells us the truth, not faith with its spiritual thoughts of the World.[29] The essential determinacies of faith must be scrutinized in the pure light of secular Reason.

Even though both sides of Reason attain "purity" and attempt to establish the character of consciousness in simplicity, and even though both live in the World of manners but reject its ways, neither side can identify with the other. They recognize that they are the "same" in that they are contemptuous of the *espèce* and are equal in the "purity" of consciousness. (They are the same by virtue of their "negativity.") Between themselves, however, they are divided. The religious side raises the negation of the "world of actuality" into a spiritual realm and is content to remain within this realm. It accepts its own vanity even as it declares everything vain to be worthless. The scientific side, however, moves back toward the "Spiritual Kingdom of the Animals" (the penultimate section of Chapter 5, "Reason"), where prudence and self-interest reside. It sees itself as the true unrestricted concept of the World in which all must be judged according to the standard of pleasure and material enjoyment. Its code of conduct, described by Helvétius in his *De l'esprit* (1758), is to avoid boredom and take pleasure in finer things of life. In this return to self-interest it becomes duplicitous, recalling the condition of facticity that betrays its true contempt for the World and religion. In this transcending of the "world of actuality" the two sides will begin fighting, the goal of which is to establish once and for all the supreme good of the Enlightenment. (The war is fought out in the *parlement* of Paris, in the theaters and opera houses, and at the *soirées* in the great houses.)

In this nascent struggle between faith and science the Concept will develop from the uniform and static representation of identifying with, and then against, the social organism and the status quo, to the recognition that the World itself (as the great machine) creates our identities for us, and finally to the knowledge that "mind" is distinct from the World: the pinnacle of this development is Descartes's "I think, therefore I am," identifying the Self as distinct from nature and its causal order (¶142–578). The movement of the Concept occurs both on the side of faith and pure insight simultaneously and with the same pattern; the objective of this movement is toward an inward recognition of the Self and, ultimately,

---

29. There is a fairly explicit reference to Mettrie's *Man: a Machine* (1748), but the section seems to reflect more on the values expressed in Diderot's *Jacques, the Fatalist*. For Hegel the fatalistic freethinker and the pious Jansenist have the "same consciousness" in terms of their respective self-identities.

as we will see, to metaphysical dualism where nature and mind are both unified in one Concept but as distinct moments of it. Hegel considers this development necessary because it both dissolves the facticity of the individual, which thus shows that there is no genuine "simplicity," and brings the Self to be the object of scientific insight, which thus raises the Self beyond the limits of Culture and the World of Actuality. This development is thus necessary in order to advance the freedom and identity of the Self as belonging to the inwardness of the Concept.

II. The Enlightenment

The unity between the two sides of consciousness, as the "sameness" of faith and pure insight, will be dissolved into warring sides. Notwithstanding this dissolution, "sameness" remains, since for each side the object remains the same as before, namely, to retain the simplicity and purity of self-consciousness, which makes consciousness a "free" determinate being. As we will see, only religion succeeds in this endeavor, or, to be more precise, only the side of religion that embraces the extreme of inwardness—the Jansenist—succeeds in retaining its purity and freedom. This development occurs because simple piety knows its own vanity, and thus even when confronted by the allegations of materialistic Reason, which proclaims its opposition to religion because of religion's deceptions and alliance to despotism, the simple soul can deny the validity of the opposition with respect to the true object of faith. The faithful know that the simplicity of self-consciousness in its devotion and service is the only true object.

The case against religion is made in the name of Reason by the side of pure insight that rejects even deistic thought. It is the thoroughgoing materialists—D'Holbach and Diderot—who attempt to show that the system of Reason is only a material system, that the advancement of education, science, and art depends on the freedom to speak and think without recourse to religious belief or practices. On their side they have "human right," against which the "divine right" is seen as only the power and privilege of despotism. They have the "truth" as far as rational insight allows it to appear to us. However, they also deceive themselves. This occurs in their descriptions of faith, which remove the religious significance from religious acts, thus reducing them to being so much "hocus pocus." Faith knows that these descriptions are lies (cf. ¶114–550), but it cannot defend itself until it understands the rationale of pure insight. Faith recognizes that materialistic Reason has falsely identified the purpose of human existence, placing it in enjoyment and pleasure. Only when faith recognizes this deception will it come forth from its inwardness and express its desire for a pure World, one where poverty and chastity (namely, the Evangelical Counsels) govern the spiritual bonds of society. By so doing, it shows that it has *true* faith and that it alone sustains the purity and simplicity of consciousness.

Hegel contrasts the truth of faith with the "Truth of Enlightenment," which he characterizes as the "dank weave of spirit" that crawls serpentine on the earth.[30] On the one hand, in its positive appearance, the truth of the Enlightenment is the absolute truth of Reason, since both in our *compos mentis* and within the body politic all parts are tied together in and through material affections, self-interested desires, social utility, and a chain of natural causes. However, the unity and identity of individuals are left in this weave to be simply dry husks that no longer belong to the advancement of spirit (cf. ¶143–579). The weave is *only* the material connection; that is, what nature provides to spirit. Nature appears to the Enlightenment as the god of Reason, but this god is only an idol of material self-conceit. (It has no moral or spiritual power; it is the *name* "supreme being" that designates nothing.) The adherents to this god proclaim a Religion of Man, but this "religion" has no spiritual cohesion outside of negative disposition toward faith. Without such a bond the advocates of secular religion immediately fractionalize, and in their hunger to attain only the social and political good, but without attaining virtue, they fall apart, attack each other, and initiate social revolution.

Since we are now aware of what Hegel's objective is, let us turn to how he makes the argument in the various sections of the text.

a. The Struggle of the Enlightenment with Superstition

"The Enlightenment" is the Age of Reason, and it belongs to the "pure insight" of the freethinking *philosophe*. Although it was not initially opposed to the religious identification of the Concept, it accepts it only in terms of the World and its materiality. Thus the Christian religion is considered to be misguided, delusional, and only a side of materiality that has effaced its overt materialism. The Enlightenment, on the other hand, thinks itself free from the restrictions of Culture and the power of the estates. In this way it comes to oppose any form of religion that understands the object of faith to be outside of nature. It contends that only in the genuine opposition to religion will the "universal mass"— that is, the common people—become educated, and only in this opposition will they become free from false representational belief. The Enlightenment shows itself, by virtue of its attack on religion, to be an

---

30. The metaphor of the serpentine as false wisdom comes from the books of Genesis (3:1–7) and Numbers (21:4–9). Hegel is identifying the Enlightenment's materialism with the venomous saraph snakes that afflicted the Israelites in the march through the Sinai desert.

infection in the spiritual World; one which cannot be stopped by its opponents who fail, at least initially, to understand the misguided values and lies of the Enlightenment.

Throughout this section the process by which Reason identifies itself with material forms occurs through the conflict between faith, which keeps to its spiritual World, and the scientific community, which seeks freedom of knowledge and expression. There are several phases to the conflict. In the first phase the deism of most Enlightenment *philosophes* prevails. Its natural theology has, even for the religious community, the "fragrance" of rational insight: an insight freed from the beastly *espèce* and their vice-ridden manners. Soon, however, the *philosophes* turn against religion itself, accusing it of "priestcraft," idolatry, and abusive immoralities. By so doing, the Enlightenment shows itself to be a venomous snake that is poisoning Reason itself; it is the Seraph of Wisdom, a false idol of materialistic Reason. At this point religion is impotent to fight materialistic Reason because religious thought has already conceded that the Enlightenment represents truth and insight. The religious parties are paralyzed by their own stance regarding the World and Reason in the World. For instance, the Jesuits share in the decadence of Culture, identifying themselves with wealth and the state power; the Jansenists, despite their reformist motives, oppose the rights of human freedom; and the deists have already conceded to the opponents of religion that human purpose is only fulfilled through material satisfactions.[31] So, in the second cycle religion has to learn what is the cause of error, that is, what has led to the false identifications and accusations. At this level, religion acknowledges that the atheist has defined the Concept of Spirit but also sees that the Concept so defined contains error. According to the Concept, defined through materialistic Reason, man is a machine (Mettrie), nature is the system of Reason, and in it god is nature (D'Holbach); morality is a social construction created by taste, manners, and social utility (Helvétius). In the atheists' world-view the religious are fanatical liars; to speak the "truth" is to expose superstition and attack the political order; and the deists, who believe that God created nature according to a rational plan, are merely dreamers.

---

31. Hegel's line from *Rameau* refers to the smashing of idols and seems to be an allusion both to Jansenistic iconoclasm, which was directed against the Jesuits' institutions and their "worldliness," and perhaps to the biblical account of Moses smashing the idol of the golden calf. This is *not* what Diderot intended by the reference, which was an allusion to the Jesuit missionaries smashing the pagan idols in China and Japan. Diderot deplored the intolerance of the missionaries. Hegel is, however, thinking of the vengeance that the Jansenistic faction took against both the Jesuits and the freethinkers.

The "God" of materialism is a new Trinity, which is enunciated by Rameau in Diderot's dialog. In place of the Father, Son, and Holy Spirit are now the Good, as the social utility; the True, which denounces religion as superstition; and the Beautiful, which is exemplified in the natural tones of French opera. However, with these determinations of God, Reason, Self, and World as all belonging exclusively to materialistic Reason, the religious side of the Concept comes to understand its enemy and to redefine its own standard of worldly wisdom. It shows itself committed to the absolute essence of life, which is devoid of materialism and embraces instead the Evangelical Counsels (poverty, chastity, and obedience). In this redefinition, religion shows that it is capable of indicting the Enlightenment as the snake; it shows the "evil" within materialism. The only weapon that the religious have for their cause is the knowledge that the true expression of faith is a self-justifying form of consciousness, the essence of which is to become a virtuous spirit. "Faith" has nothing to do with "hocus pocus," the material criteria of evidence, or rational justifications through the forms of nature.

On the standard of material criteria and on the assumption that rational justifications are defined through nature, the atheist wins the battle against faith. So long as the naiveté of the believer is secure in its faith and rejects such claims, however, the best the secular opposition can do is to maintain its own position. It shows that the religious side also embraces wealth and, despite its vows, remains for the most part unchaste. The Enlightenment concedes nothing to faith, but in terms of the ideal social order it is forced to claim that religion represents the true human value of simplicity in paradise. So, the Enlightenment takes from the religious Concept *its* version of what shall attain "heaven" in and through private and public Reason.[32] The Enlightenment acknowledges that there is a true equality among all people, that we are all born free, and that as part of our social good we seek universal fraternity. From this position of a secular religious outlook a "positive" result emerges, one that will promote human rights, the good of social utility, and the

32. "Practical Reason" is Reason that produces moral action. It aims always for the supreme good, and the means it takes should be virtuous. "Private Reason" is practical Reason that is restricted and resigned to the authority of another. "Public Reason" is practical Reason that produces governmental action. It *should* be in agreement with the tenets of Practical Reason and is always "free," since it serves the common good. Kant makes this distinction in his essay "The Answer to the Question: What Is the Enlightenment?" *Akad.*, viii, pp. 33–42. All references to Kant's works are to the Critical Edition of the *Preußischen Akademie der Wissenschaften* (1902); rpt. Walter de Gruyter & Co., 1968. Citations are to the volume and page numbers in the reprinted edition.

advancement of individual freedoms. But such an "advance" only creates a new idol to replace the one of the *ancien régime*. Gone are the values of the *espèce*, but in turn the "material" values of a sensuous life become absolute. Thus, the "positive" result is to establish a heavenly kingdom on earth, but the kingdom of God has only profane meaning within this sphere. The Evangelical Counsels are altered to reflect this belief, and now instead of obedience to God comes obedience to absolute freedom. Figuratively the Church's assembly will be replaced by the National Convention. Because public Reason has created its own idol, which strips the concept of the Self of its genuine religious value, public Reason is doomed to failure. It will also bring about the collapse of the Enlightenment's humanistic values by surrendering the goods of life for the cry of liberty.

b. The Truth of the Enlightenment

Hegel begins his analysis of the "Truth of Enlightenment" by saying that it consists of "the relation of singular essences to the absolute essence, the connection of the first two moments" (¶123–559). That analysis led to the conclusions that faith lost its content and that Reason has sunk to the "dank weave of spirit," which is nothing else than the reappearance of the *serpent of pure insight*. Beginning with this section we come to appreciate the "truth" of the serpentine, whose God is Rameau's blessed Trinity, but these are only understood through "nature." Thus, the "true" is the scientific understanding of the human machine, which itself is governed by passions; the "good" is social utility that increases pleasures and eliminates pains; and the "beautiful" is the satisfaction of desire in the evenings of theater and dinner. Faith has been swallowed up in this "truth"; although it can indict the Enlightenment for having false values, it cannot deny that "pure insight" and the God of the Enlightenment have redemptive qualities. Of course, this "truth" is a fraud, and Hegel tells us as much by using the metaphor of the snake's weave. The fraud, however, cannot be corrected until the entire World of the Enlightenment with its "faith" in a benevolent Estates General is overturned. "Morality," in the guise of Robespierre's pure consciousness, is the cure for the fraud, and his cure is the terror that leads to the death of this so-called God.

III. Absolute Freedom and Terror

This section has a descriptive and an evaluative part. The descriptive part is a declaration that in the modern state there is freedom, especially when the third estate assumes the power of government. Hegel follows Abbé Sieyès's argument in *What Is the Third Estate?* (1789). In that work Sieyès contends that the third estate is nothing, yet it demands to be something.

It is this movement from nothing to something that Hegel believes shows the dialectical progression of the Concept that reaches beyond the spiritual bonds of the old regime and establishes the new political and spiritual order. It is the spiritual order that is most important to Hegel, because in this political climate, the god of Reason is supposed to come to earth. "Heaven" is heard in the harmonious tones of the French Republic singing the "Marseillaise" from the steps of the cathedral of Notre Dame. The revolutionaries represent the deity as Liberty. In one of his most famous speeches, Robespierre, dressed in a tricolor banner and speaking from the steps of the Tuileries, acts as if he is a prophet for this God who is both supreme Reason and a revolutionary spirit. Sieyès is the political philosopher of this Spirit, and he contends that the General Will is expressed in a majority vote and resides in the deputies of the National Assembly.[33] Hegel sees that for the revolutionaries the divine will and "heaven" have come to earth; the will of the god appears in the deputies' vote, and the republic is the one true heaven that stands against the demonic World of the old regime.

Hegel, in evaluating these claims, finds them wanting, or more precisely they are the first real signs of the universal fraud that belongs to the identification of the individual as "citizen." He finds that Sieyès has deliberately misrepresented the General Will as the Will of All. (The distinction that Sieyès is misrepresenting comes from Jean-Jacques Rousseau, who considered the General or Universal Will to be a unifying totality.[34]) For Rousseau the General Will is present in the nation when

---

33. Sieyès writes,"The sole elements of the common will are individual wills. One cannot deny the greatest number the right to play their part, nor decide that these ten wills are equivalent to only one while another ten wills amount to thirty. These are contradictions in terms, pure absurdities. If for the slightest moment one loses sight of **this self-evident principle that the common will is the opinion of the majority** . . . there is no point in carrying on the discussion. One might just as well decide that the will of a single man is to be called the majority and that we no longer need States-General or national will at all. . . . It is a certainty that among the national representatives . . . influence must be proportionate to the number of citizens who have the right to be represented. **If it is to accomplish its task, the representative body must always be the substitute for the nation itself.** It must partake of the same nature, the same proportions and the same rules," Sieyès, *What is the Third Estate?*, trans. by M. Blondel, ed. by S. E. Fines (NY: Praeger Press, 1964), p. 136ff, *passim*. (Emphasis added to the original.) On the meaning of the "General Will," see the next note.

34. Rousseau makes several comments inconsistent with Sieyès, such as, "[The will is general if] it is the will of . . . the people as a whole. . . . In the first case, this declared will is an act of sovereignty and makes law. [If the will is the will of the people as a part, then], it is merely a particular will or an act of magistracy;

the good of the whole takes precedence over private or factional loyalties. The General Will is then a moral concept.[35] It is never decided by a vote, nor does it reside simply in what the legislative assembly believes to be politically popular. The Will of All is, however, factional. It is the spirit of the divided "universal mass," which has to make decisions based on the judgment of the majority. It is a political concept indifferent, at best, to the moral will of the people or, at worst, destructive to such a will, undermining moral sovereignty. By misrepresenting these two distinct notions Sieyès also undercuts Rousseau's idea of national sovereignty. It is not the will of the people whom the deputies must obey; rather, the converse is true. The will of the largest faction determines the course and destiny of the nation; that is presumably the "divine will" on earth. When this occurs, however, we have, by Hegel's analysis, a new tyranny that says it speaks for the people when in fact it speaks only for its own convictions.

This new tyranny must prove to everyone that it is the universal will, and that means it must eradicate those whose will opposes it. Those who are not with this faction are against it; they are immoral, and they corrupt the supreme good sustained by the republic. In this way the distortion of the conceptual identity in the so-called General Will must inevitably lead to the "moral argument" that all those who do not belong to the universal are de facto enemies of the state. In the case of the first French Republic,

---

at most it is a decree," *Du Contract Social*, in *Oeuvres Complètes*, t. 1–4 (Paris: Éditions Gallimard, 1964), T. 3, p. 369. And, "It follows from what has preceded that the General Will is always right and always tends towards public utility; but it does not follow that the deliberations of the people always have the same rectitude. . . . [The General Will] considers only communal interest, whereas [the will of all] considers private interests and is merely the sum of particular wills. . . . For the General Will to be well articulated, it is therefore important that there should be no partial society in the state and that each citizen make up his own mind," p. 371ff. And, "Sovereignty cannot be represented for the same reason that it cannot be alienated. It consists essentially in the General Will, and this Will does not allow of being represented. . . . The deputies of the people, therefore, neither are nor can be representatives; they are merely its agents. . . . [T]he instant a people gives itself representatives, it is no longer free; it is no more," 429–31, *passim*.

It is fairly clear in this context that (a) Sieyès is arguing against Rousseau's theory of the state and (b) Hegel's use of Sieyès is *critical* of the equation between the General Will and the Will of All. It is safe to say that Hegel agrees with Rousseau's contention that a system of representative government that only represents the Will of All would end freedom and disrupt national community as such.

35. This is implied by Rousseau, but is made explicit by Kant. Hegel favors Kant's formulation of the principle, which can be found in Kant's essay, "On the Commonplace: What Is True in Theory Need Not Be True in Practice"(1793), *Akad.*, viii, pp. 273–314.

the defenders of Enlightenment values, particularly the value of liberty, are the leaders of the new tyranny. Their cant is that they represent morality. In their deeds, however, they show that they are evil.

Hegel considers such an eventuality to be inevitable. The purity and simplicity of Jansenist thought, which strove only for an unworldly unity with God, become in turn the secular or worldly authority: first, as a factional consciousness whose intolerance for "free thought" becomes a self-declared "virtue"; and second, as this moral autocracy becomes the secular authority, it shows itself to be an absolute tyranny. Purity and simplicity still remain (self-consciousness retains the "sameness" of the Concept), and liberty is achieved in the absolute will that defines itself in terms of the nation's supreme good. The result of the Concept unifying the purity of religious thought with an absolute will is the Reign of Terror. The Lord of the World, who was first seen as the adolescent beast feasting on all sorts of vices, is now a "pure" moral citizen whose identity is one with the nation's supreme good. The cruelty and savagery are as before; however, the justification for such cruelty is not for egoistic pleasure, nor for the greed and lust of the Prince, but for the supreme moral good of the nation. As with the first Lord of the World, this one will fail too. It will fail in a similar manner. The first Lord is killed by his guards, while this one falls stoically under the blow delivered by the deputies of the assembly. Even Sieyès, who made his appearance on the world stage to argue on behalf of the moral autocracy of the faction, is a party to its demise: having voted for the death of the king, he now votes for the death of "first citizen" Robespierre. The Lord of the World is Death, Hegel tells us, and we should see that this, too, is inevitable, given the rise of moral absolutism identified with political utility.

The connection between the Concept and Sieyès's political cunning seems to be intended by Hegel. We are fully in the "Way of the World," which Hegel has already shown in Chapter 5 to be "artful" and treacherous. The philosophical Concept, as willing to betray all values for personal advantage, is just Reason's Concept as the "Way of the World" playing itself out. The only avenue to subvert the "Way of the World," to transcend state terror but still retain utility, is to betray moral autocracy: to bend the upright will to the popular masses. Sieyès's cunning, which allows him to save himself when so many of his colleagues ended up dead, is seen in his turning from the political identity of the Concept, with its emphasis on public Reason, to one of prudence and self-interest. Such a bending of will, however, destroys the "sameness" of self-consciousness; it cannot remain pure and simple. It enters once more into a tumult, where we see one system of state governance after another rise and fall. The only end to the tumult is the return of princely power.

Hegel alludes to both the political events that brought a demise to the first French Republic and the return of a prince, Napoleon, who, like the emperors of Rome and the Sun King, brings for a time stability and unity to the nation and its people. Once this occurs, the tumult of self-consciousness can also reach stability. Hegel is not, however, arguing that such an occurrence is either "good" or necessary. It is only an eventuality that occurs as a result of the disruption in political and moral identity produced by absolute freedom and terror. This chaos has to end, and it can only end with a return of a forceful state power that reinstates self-conscious unity.[36] Hegel notes that

> Out of this tumult spirit would be hurled back to its starting point, to the ethical and real world of culture that has merely been restored and rejuvenated by the fear of the Lord that has returned to men's minds. If the result were only the complete interpenetration of self-consciousness and substance, spirit would have to run through this cycle of necessity once more, and repeat it over and over again (¶158–594).

In the end, however, history does not repeat itself. There can be no return either to the Roman Imperium or to the spiritual unity of the Estates General, nor even to the absolute moral autocracy of the Jacobin. Such an attempt to return to any of these previous stages is vain and futile. Hegel implies that with Napoleon's ascendancy to the throne, which recalls Augustus' ascendancy to the Imperium, the stage is set for the entire collapse of Culture. Napoleon represents universal self-consciousness in terms of a singular will that presents itself as the universal will. In him the entire stage reaches a climax, where national identity becomes synonymous with the identity that makes the will a pure knowing. Hegel remarks on this form of self-knowledge that

> The *universal will* is rather its *pure knowing* and *willing*, and *it* is universal will, as this pure knowing and willing. It does not lose *itself* therein, for the pure knowing and willing are rather itself as the atom point of consciousness (¶158–594).[37]

---

36. Hegel alludes to the ineptitudes of the Convention, Directory, and Consulate with the line, "Neither does it [Spirit] know the will as revolutionary government or as anarchy striving to constitutionalize anarchy, nor itself as middle point of this faction or its opposite," (¶158–594).

37. Hegel is referring to the state as the Imperiate, the regime initiated is when Napoleon declared himself emperor of France. Napoleon's act of crowning himself before the Pope in 1804 allows Hegel to think of how Clovis took the

Liberty is already dead when the universal will becomes this "atom point of consciousness." The idea of a popular government, whose course is set supposedly by the people, is finished, but the rule of one over the many cannot be sustained without the consent and support of the popular masses. Thus, by the very act of ascending to the throne, and thereby separating himself from the articulated masses, Napoleon has doomed both himself and his nation. We know this to be true because the *universal will is supposed to the moral will,* but in this autocratic Self it is not. The Lord of the World, which Hegel is supposing Napoleon to be, is external to rational self-actualization, which can only occur in true moral self-sufficiency. This is why Hegel contends that this pure willing and knowing self-consciousness cannot remain in the sphere of absolute liberty; it must pass into another land that is defined by moral principles.[38]

Hegel's comment that "The self-estranged spirit, driven to the extreme of its antithesis, in which the pure willing and the pure willed are still differentiated, reduces the antithesis to transparent form, and finds itself therein" looks to be a rebuke on the insufficiency of French culture to sustain itself in universality (¶159–595).[39] Instead, the "other land" is the nordic kingdoms, in which morality, not self-declared liberty, determines the idea of freedom. In moral self-sufficiency, "liberty" becomes the Self's own identity with the moral law and not the national identity of an absolute political consciousness. Public Reason, which maintains the state and its interests, must yield to the dictates of Practical (or Private) Reason, which maintain the individual in and through a commitment to moral perfection. The laws of government, which since

---

imperial Roman mantel. It is *as if* the world-individual is returning to the first moment of Culture. Hegel is, however, discounting such a return. History does not so much repeat itself as imitate the preceding moments.

38. In a letter to Niethammer (29 April 1814), Hegel contends that he predicted Napoleon's defeat at just this point in the text. Hegel says, "I may pride myself, moreover, on having predicted this entire upheaval. In my book [*Phenomenology*], which I completed the night before the battle of Jena, I said on page 547: 'Absolute freedom,' which I had previously described as the purely abstract formal freedom of the French republic, originating, as I showed, in the Enlightenment, 'passes out of its own self-destructive actuality over into *another land*,' I had in mind here a specific *land,* 'of self-conscious spirit, in which, in this unactual form, it passes for truth itself . . .'" (No. 233) Cf. *Hegel: The Letters,* ed. by Clark Butler (Bloomington, IN: Indiana Univ. Press, 1984), p. 307. Hegel likens Napoleon's defeat to a Greek tragedy, one that was brought about by hubris. As with every Lord of the World, this one falls because of an internal flaw produced in his own conceit.

39. I am implying that "French culture" is the culture of liberty defined by the "Rights of Man."

Creon's decrees have had the upper hand, are shown to be weak and in need of counsel. Human positive law must yield to the idea of moral autocracy and its virtues.

Although it may be odd that Hegel would make such claims in 1806, just as Prussia is being defeated by the French and, soon, Hegel's own city of Jena will be destroyed by Napoleon's "march of spirit," it is *necessary* for him to make such a claim, since morality is the universal Concept under which the particularities of political organization become defined. This is clear even in the preceding section "Absolute Freedom and Terror," when the moral code of honoring the universal will becomes articulated in the plan of government. The fact that the "moral argument" had neither honor nor morality in it was, for the political organization, just an inconvenience. Its morality was defined by the instrumental use of Reason, the kind of Reason that Helvétius advocated in his *De l'ésprit*, and it is itself subordinate to utility. But Hegel is making the philosophical point that is implied already in the political cause; it is not that political autocracy defines freedom, the world-historical individual is not one with the "transparent form" of universality that belongs to the Lord of the World. On the contrary, the Self retains its identity and self-determined purpose only when it has *genuine* moral autonomy. French culture, which defined the Enlightenment all along, has placed identity and determinate purpose in the material connection between simple thought and the state's power. It has failed. German culture, which defines moral philosophy and champions self-determination, is where the world-historical individual can attain its *real* character of self-sufficiency. The "simplicity" of self-identity is one with the universal law of Reason, and, at least in the first approximation of this unity, we are back with Reason as the Law Giver and Law Tester (Miller, ¶419ff.)—we are back with what ostensibly began the dialectic of "Spirit."

C. Spirit Certain of Itself. Morality

"Morality" is the third and final phase of "Spirit." In it the unity between the world-historical individual and substance is reestablished. Hegel tells us that "substance" is the simple self-knowing of the world-historical individual in which self-consciousness will maintain its certainty in itself. This substance is the moral law of Reason; the law that originates from within the Self's own self-knowledge, hence it is, following Kant's usage, a "private reason." As such, the substance and the identity of the Self are reconciled, and the impediment to the fulfillment of the law—the problem that was encountered at the end of "Reason"— is now removed. The moral law is self-imposed *and* a law forged from the worldly experiences of self-consciousness. In fact, the moral law as self-consciousness is the divine law itself, but the divine law that is known in and through the Self (and not from some unknown source or submerged desire). It is thus also the human law. Divine law and the human law are one and the same, since such laws are absolutely pure rational laws. This sense of the law is not opposed to the singular will of the individual. Indeed, it is the truth of conscious action belonging to the individual who knows what is right and wills it. Yet, it is also a law that checks absolute freedom—negating the pretense that political autonomy has moral self-sufficiency. Absolute freedom defined under the rational law is tantamount to complete responsibility. The Self as moral certainty is separate from the political individual, and in the concept of the Self qua moral certainty the state and its laws are secondary to the principal rightness of the moral will. The rightness of the moral will makes the individual worthy of happiness or, better, as Kant claimed, worthy of blessedness in the Kingdom of Ends. Thus, the supreme good is established here for the individual in the land of morality.

The moral world-historical individual is only concerned with what is intrinsically right, that is, with what is right in light of Reason's own postulations of right action. The instrumental values, which were determining norms governing the world-historical individual in Culture, are here sublated: they are retained only as tools used to attain the supreme good. In this way the political goals of "Absolute Freedom" are expected to be subservient to the supreme good of moral autonomy.

The substance of the Self is reconciled to the Self's own will, but it is opposed nonetheless to the self-gratification pursued in self-conscious life. Self-conscious life, which is described in Chapter 4, "Self-Certainty," pursues the objects of desire as they are rationally worthy of pursuit, and the attainment of them brings forth self-satisfaction. In order to attain happiness, these yearnings are as essential to the world-historical individual as are the pure will and its object. Within this moral sphere of self-knowledge, then, there develops a fundamental dilemma that will prove destructive to this stage. (The dilemma is based on Kant's Antinomies of Practical Reason.) The dilemma has to be seen as developing throughout this entire section. For if to pursue moral autonomy, or the supreme good, ipso facto denies the goods of self-conscious life, and in this denial these "goods" are seen as "bad," then moral autonomy denies the intrinsic value of self-conscious life. This denial results in self-disruption and the loss of happiness. Or, if to pursue the goods of self-conscious life, even as

Reason seeks them, would mean the sacrifice of moral autonomy—as Kant claims in his so-called solution to the Antinomies, we would be motivated simply by self-love—then this denies us the worthiness to achieve the supreme good. This denial results also in self-disruption and the loss of happiness. So, either way "Morality" will present a logical impasse to the ends of practical Reason.

"Spirit Certain of Itself" has to work through this dilemma, and in order to do that it will first embrace the antecedent alternative, namely, to pursue moral autonomy and to sacrifice the affective life. That course of action will prove to be self-destructive. The first alternative is sublated, even as the principle of moral autonomy is retained. The second alternative will in turn be embraced as the "truth" of moral autonomy in the affective life, but that proves self-contradictory and utterly futile as well. To be even more exact, the second alternative, which identifies morality with the self-sufficient of moral disposition (*Gesinnung*), creates in Hegel's analysis a "beautiful soul." This is an ironic term, since such a sentimental and conceited creature is itself "evil." He means by "evil" that the world-historical individual identifies itself with the extreme of the inner life; it is perplexed because it cannot attain gratification in what it loves, but it also cannot stand to live without this gratification. This Self is a youthful romantic and becomes completely absorbed in its own self-interest and imaginative conceits. It withers and dies because of its own self-absorption. To describe this position, Hegel shows that romanticism and the school of "philosophy" that calls itself *Nichtphilosophie* (nonphilosophy)—the term Eschenmayer uses for "commonsense" practical philosophy—is nothing else than a proponent of "evil."

The dilemma cannot be solved within the scope of the two alternatives. As long as there is a denial of the "true Self" and its object, then the Self remains unhappy, incomplete, and "evil." The attempt to bring about a compromise also fails. Hegel explicitly argues against the view called "syncreticism," which was championed by the "Common Sense" philosophy of W. T. Krug (cf. ¶195–631). That particular attempt simply stated that the affective life itself has the unity and integrity of the "pure Self," thus the dilemma is supposedly resolved. Hegel rejects this view outright, since it denies the true distinctions between the alternatives: it denies the constitution of the essential Self.

We see at the end of this section what Hegel takes to be the solution to the problem at hand. First, the problem itself is none other than the problem of facticity, now seen as having developed throughout "Spirit." Facticity is itself the limitation of our essential being to understand itself as a limited, conceited being; or, better, it understands itself only too well as *no more* than a limited, materially interested being. This fundamental condition is the cause of deception and moral error. Yet, that is how we exist; it is what belongs to the core of self-identity. We cannot overcome that limitation in and of ourselves. The world-historical individual, understanding itself only as a worldly finite being, is doomed to exist within facticity. But there is still another dimension to the Self that transcends its worldly limitations. Transcendence begins to be recognized in the ability of the world-historical individual to accept the "evil" inherent to it. This is what, in effect, morality allows us to do; we do not, by our own means, overcome evil (this is the error of moral autonomy that in theology Pelagius is best known for), but what is within our means is to accept and forgive this evil. "Spirit Certain of Itself" is the agent of acceptance and forgiveness, and it allows us to proceed to the next stage where reconciliation is possible. The world-historical individual must be overcome; it must sublate its own facticity by looking beyond itself. Hegel explains at the very end of the section that once we have acceptance and forgiveness, Spirit is ready to enter into religious consciousness. To transcend the worldliness of finite existence *must* mean that we accept religion as part of our humanity.

The section has three parts: a) the Moral World-View, b) Misrepresentation, and c) Conscience. Each section presents an understanding of rational morality from what might loosely be called the "Kantian" perspective. The positions range from Kant's own understanding of how the postulates of pure practical Reason affect moral and religious values, through Schiller's attempt to reconcile Reason's postulates with sentiment or the "aesthetical sense," to finally the acute form of Romanticism that ultimately surrenders Reason to a law of the heart, which, in turn, recoils upon itself, producing self-conceit and hypocrisy. This third moment is presented through the philosophies of Jacobi and Novalis.

a. The Moral World-View

The first part presents an absolute moral Self: the sort of being who identifies itself with pure, practical Reason and freely imposes categorical duties on itself simply because such duties are "purely rational." This stance belongs to Kant's own doctrine that the Self becomes "good" by the power of her own will to apply the principles of Reason to possible actions, and from this application of Reason in moral judgment to realize all practical actions according to these principles. Hegel relies explicitly on Kant's Postulates of Pure Reason to define this position. There are three postulates, all of which are thought to be necessary in order for there to be such self-certainty. The postulates are "Immortality," "Freedom," and

"God."[40] Kant contends that these postulates are necessary rational concepts under which practical Reason acts and makes moral judgments.
Such judgments determine right from wrong, and when the will follows
such judgments we are led to oppose the radical evil inherent in our own
nature, and simultaneously we become worthy of God's Kingdom of Ends.
Such actions make us worthy, and to attain this state is the supreme good
itself. We *think*, then, that as moral creatures, God, who we presume is the
author of the rational law, will reward us with eternal blessedness.

Kant is usually profiled as a strict deontologist (that is, a rule-oriented
moralist who dismisses consequential considerations from moral judgments), and if we just look at his theory of the Right, he is one. But Hegel
is portraying Kant's philosophy as ultimately a descriptive philosophy of
humanity that embraces ethics, politics, and our true human nature, and
in those terms we do the right in order to obtain the good: this is what
Reason presents to us in its postulates. The moral authority of the Categorical Imperative is completely empty unless we accept the truth value of
these postulates, and if we accept these postulates as true, we are accepting a teleological (and ultimately religious) justification of morality. The
validity of the rational practical judgments lies in the *belief* that we are
free, that we ought to serve God, and that if we do what we ought we may
hope to obtain eternal blessedness. Kant's moral world-view is essentially
a religious one (even though he appears in his writings on religion to justify religious belief only through morality).[41] The argument from the postulates shows that the inverse must also be true: there is no genuine moral
world-view without the rational acceptance of the religious notions of
Immortality, Freedom, and God.

In this position there is an inherent flaw, a vicious circle. If the morally
self-sufficient individual accepts these postulates, then she must accept
the promise of the kingdom of God. To anticipate the kingdom of God,

40. Kant says, "These postulates are those of immortality, of freedom affirma-
tively regarded (as the causality of a being so far as he belongs to the intelligible
world), and of the existence of God. The first derives from the practically necessary condition of a duration adequate to the perfect fulfillment of the moral law.
The second comes from the necessary presupposition of independence from the
world of sense and of the capacity of determining man's will by the law of an intelligible world, i.e., the law of freedom itself; the third arises from the necessary
condition of such an intelligible world by which it may be the highest good,
through the presupposition of the highest good, i.e., the existence of God," *Critique of Practical Reason* (1788), *Akad.*, v, p. 133.

41. Hegel's view on how Kant's philosophy is both religious and confined to
only a moral outlook is due to Kant's treatise, *Religion within the Bounds of Reason
Alone* (1793), *Akad.*, vi. Cf. "The Preface to the First Edition," 3–11.

however, seems to deny the so-called self-sufficiency of the moral world-view. If the postulates pertaining to religious belief are true, however, they are only considered true on the basis of the self-sufficiency of thought to inhere in practical Reason and its subsequent moral judgments. But to say that religious belief is true only in practical judgment denies the religiosity of those beliefs. Kant's view is paradoxical and ultimately self-defeating in this analysis.

One way to step beyond the paradox is to reason that Kant's philosophy, although correct in terms of uniting divine law to human law in practical judgments, fails to unite our human nature with the rational Self. For Kant there is the disruption between human nature and the intrinsic rightness of pure practical Reason. Human nature is, for him, radically evil. His reconciliation between the divine and the human law within us does not encompass our total being. To form a reconciliation within human nature itself might resolve the dilemma of the Kantian ethic. Hegel is aware of this attempt to reach the Kantian unity, but he sees it as contained within the broader spectrum of what belongs to the entirety of our human nature.

b. Misrepresentation

In the second subsection, "Misrepresentation," the attempt is made to overcome the dichotomy and establish the unity of the Self in the whole of human nature. This is still considered a Kantian project. The leading "Kantian" of Hegel's youth who sought such a unity was Friedrich Schiller. He attempts to end the dichotomy between "nature" and rationality by shifting the sphere of moral autonomy away from pure Reason to instead encompass the entire domain of human self-consciousness. Adopting the position of Rousseau, which held that our natural condition is good and Culture makes us evil, Schiller placed moral autonomy in our natural sentiment (*Gesinnung*).[42] The validation of practical judgment does not lie simply and solely in the form of the Categorical Imperative but in the soundness of our *naive* sensibilities. Schiller contends that he has emended Kant, using not the postulates of Reason as his foundation but the idea of beauty that Kant employed in the *Critique of Judgment* (1790).[43] Kant's failure within his system was that he did not employ his

---

42. Schiller opens his essay *Letters on the Aesthetical Education of Man* (1801) with a quotation from Rousseau, "Si c'est la raison qui fait l'homme, c'est le sentiment qui le conduit"—"If it is reason that makes the man, it is feeling that leads him."

43. Kant tells us that the ideal of beauty is a figure of morality. (A representation of the ideal might be some hero or heroine whose countenance is beautiful

own moral paradigm as developed in the Aesthetics.[44] *He* misrepresented the moral sphere by portraying it as exclusively rational instead of seeing morality as the unity between practical Reason and aesthetic sensibility.[45]

Schiller presents what looks to be the solution to the paradox. "Belief," including religious belief, is a subjective judgment rooted in feeling and sentiment, but it is also rooted in the moral direction that pure practical Reason provides. Sound religious belief is itself self-justifying because it presents the elevation, literally the sublimity, of the Self to the level of unity between Reason and sentiment. It is, through its unity with Reason, a perfect representation of moral direction.[46] The

---

but whose soul is moral.) Such an ideal transcends aesthetical judgment, but it belongs to a representation held in the imagination, which artists use in their creative endeavors Cf. *Critique of Judgment*, §17, *Akad.*, v, p. 231ff.

44. The paradigm of morality in the Aesthetics is the "ideal of beauty," concerning which Kant says, "the ideal consists in the expression of the moral, apart from which the object would not please at once universally and positively. . . . The visible expression of moral ideas can only be drawn from experience, but their combination with all that is related to reason connects with the morally good in the idea of the highest purpose—benevolence, purity, strength, or equanimity, etc.—which may be made, as it were, visible in bodily manifestations . . . and this embodiment involves a union of pure ideas of reason and a great imaginative power, in one who would form a judgment of it, not simply one who is the author of it. The correctness of such an ideal of beauty is proven by its disallowance of any sensuous charm to mingle with the delight in its object. . . ." *Critique of Judgment, Akad.*, v, p. 235ff.

45. This is the theme of Schiller's essay "On the Sublime" (1801). Schiller's thesis might be best expressed in his statement, "it is not however simply in humanity's rational nature that there is a moral capacity, which can be developed through the Understanding, but rather rational nature is bound to sensibility; that is, there is present in human nature an *aesthetical* tendency, which is awakened through specific sensible objects and can be cultivated through a refinement of feeling that comes to this idealized ardor of soul. According to the concept and nature of this capacity the idealized tendency, indeed its very reality in life, is placed clearly in the light of day . . ." Schillers *Werke* (Nationalausgabe), Bd. 21: *Philosophische Schriften*, Zweiter Theil, hrsg. von Benno von Wiese (Weimar: Hermann Böhlaus, 1962), p. 40.

46. Schiller contends, "We must therefore be no longer at a loss to find a passage from sensuous dependence to moral freedom, after we have seen, in the case of beauty, that the two can perfectly well subsist together, and that in order to show himself to be Spirit humanity does not need to abandon matter. But if he is free already in an association with sensibility, as the factum of beauty teaches us, and if freedom is something absolute and supersensible . . . there can be no longer any question of how he came to rise from the limited to the absolute and to oppose sensibility in thought and will, since this has already occurred in beauty," *Aesthetical Education*, letter xxv, Schillers *Werke*, Bd. 20, 397ff.

moral paradigm is an aesthetical genius: the person who judges and creates the necessary and sufficient conditions of self-identity in and through creative acts. The prototype for such an individual is the romantic poet, whom Schiller calls the "ideal artist." Schiller in the *Letters on Aesthetical Education* (1801) has in mind Goethe. The "true artist" has a sublime feeling that grants him the privilege of being one with the absolute itself. In this identity all "faults" are cast aside. The "ideal human" is eternally one with God, and in this "endless time" all that is human and all that belongs to the divine law coincide. Schiller describes the moral imperative of such a being:

> Let him look upwards to his own dignity and law, not downwards to fortune and everyday needs. Free alike from the futile activity which would gladly set its mark upon the fleeting moment and from the impatient spirit of extravagance which applies the measure of the absolute to the sorry production of time, let him resign the sphere of the actual to the intellect, whose home it is; but let him strive through the union of the possible with the necessary to produce the ideal. Let him stamp it on illusion and truth, coin it in the play of his imagination and in the gravity of his actions, in every sensible and spiritual form, and quietly launch it into infinite time. (Letter IX, *Schiller's Werke*, Bd. X, 26).

Schiller's overcoming of Kant's one-sided treatment of the moral will places the principle of identity in the creative imagination (what Kant believes belongs to genius alone). He contends that this is the truth of Kant's system as stated in the third Critique. The imagination itself becomes the unifying principle that allies the theoretical faculty of the Understanding (what Hegel simply calls "consciousness") with our sensibilities, which would include both the faculty of sensation and the desires of self-conscious life. This unifying principle identifies the world-historical individual with the divine. Kant seems already to have agreed with the principle when he says, for instance,

> In this faculty [of the imagination] . . . it gives the law to itself in respect to the objects of pure satisfaction, just as Reason does in respect to the faculty of desire. Hence, both on account of this inner possibility in the subject and the external possibility of a nature that agrees with it, it finds itself . . . connected with the supersensible ground of nature. In this supersensible ground,

therefore, the theoretical faculty is bound together in unity with the practical. . . . (*Critique of Judgment*, §59, *Akad.*, v, p. 353).

The "supersensible ground" is the absolute level of Self-Consciousness: the purity of the moral will in complete agreement with the purpose of divine law. The aesthetical genius is himself the Lawgiver, which is the stage of Reason that began this chapter.

This moment of reconciliation within the Self seems to be short-lived, however. The accomplishment of the Self to be the author of the unity between humanity and the divine has to confront the condition of facticity itself. Hegel brings up the point that throughout the history of Self and World there has been a continual recurrence of deception: "*Facticity* has substantiality in general in ethical life, determinate being in culture, self-knowing essentiality of thinking in morality; and in conscience it is the subject that knows these moments in itself " (¶205–641). This is true here as well, but with the difference now that the conscientious individual is the agent who creates the condition of facticity and adopts it for himself: "This *facticity* was [earlier] . . . the *predicate,* but in conscience it is for the first time *subject,* which has posited all the moments of consciousness in it, and for which all these moments—substantiality in general, external being, and the essence of thinking—are contained in this certainty of itself" (¶205–641). The creation occurs initially within what Kant calls the "creative imagination"; that is, in our faculty that imagines plans for future actions. Schiller's attempt at reconciliation will only succeed if the unity within the imagination is maintained by Reason's own purposiveness (*Zweckmässigkeit*). But the determining limitations of our own worldliness oppose such a continuity. The remedy seems to be to allow sentiment itself—a feeling of satisfaction in the good and of remorse in the bad—to act as the guarantor for this practical unity. We call such feeling "conscience" (*Gewissen*). The name itself implies a form of knowledge—*Gewissen* being formed from the past participle of *Wissen,* knowledge.[47] Schiller himself seems to allow that such a state of feeling acts to safeguard Reason's purposiveness by giving a feeling of the unity to the imagination. This "turn" away from rational purposiveness just takes us fully to the second alternative in the original dilemma; namely, to pursue the good by seeking to attain the goods of self-conscious life. "Conscience" desires emotional satisfaction: it seeks completion in and through a "law of the heart."

---

47. *Gewissen,* conscience, is also a play on *Gewißheit,* certainty.

c. Conscience, the Beautiful Soul, Evil and
Its Forgiveness

We are at the final subsection, which is Hegel's account of how the attempt to maintain the moral autonomy and unity of the Self with its substance fails in the aesthetic life. What the aesthetic, or romantic, life presents is an attempt at unifying public and private Reason. If public Reason is understood, following Kant, as obedience to the Universal Will through our own will, and private Reason is our sense of having a disposition to achieve the fulfillment of human yearnings through Morality, then the unity between them is when in the affective life the Self reconciles its affective and imperfect nature with the truth and destiny of Reason. This attempt at self-completion will fail, however. The one who proves its failure is, ironically, Goethe, who ought to depict the paradigm of self-sufficiency and the moral world-view. Goethe as the philosopher-artist makes the important philosophical point against the notion that there can be such an "absolute self." He shows that no man who embraces the unity of facticity can transcend its limitations.

In his written works Goethe presents Faust, Tasso, and young Werther—just to name a few of his characters—as failures of the aesthetic type. While Schiller makes Goethe into the moral paradigm, it takes Goethe to show that no one, not even the artist, has such a standing. This is not to say that conscience plays no role in determining the identity of the Self. Goethe accepts that there are those of "good sentiment" who become moral leaders. In his own work, the knight Götz von Berlichingen is an obvious example of a moral leader. But even such characters have flaws; they suffer from misdirection. Goethe does not contend that they are models of pure practical Reason.

The difficulty with conscience is not in the limited role it plays in securing moral sentiment. That is its "good work." The difficulty lies when one who is striving to be conscientious oversteps the limitations and actually embraces the moral aesthetic as the paradigm. There can be in this elevation a loss of Self, as the Self becomes absorbed in its yearnings. There are several philosophers who attempted to overstep such limitations. For Hegel and Goethe the chief offender was the philosopher Friedrich Jacobi. He was so enamored of the character young Werther that he created his own version of him, one who is supposed to be the "true" spiritual being. This "true absolute self" is the character Woldemar. The actual title of Jacobi's work is *Woldemar: Eine Seltenheit aus der Naturgeschichte* (1779). This novel was written in homage to Goethe and the "spiritual character" of Goethe's aesthetic heroes. Woldemar supposedly represents authentic love, universal friendship, and the yearning for completeness in a sublime feeling of romance. He is supposed to be the ideal of sympathetic union between the heart and mind. This "type" has only one object of love, the "beautiful soul"—following Goethe's name for it in the *Sufferings of Young Werther*. This "beautiful soul" is the best friend, the ideal soul mate to whom the aesthete gives his entire heart. In the novel this is a woman called Henriette.[48] The irony, and outright capriciousness, in the story is that Woldemar actually loves someone else, Allwina (who is married to another), for whom his passions lead him to the point of collapse and apparently death. Right before collapsing he renounces all love and claims that the heart is untrustworthy. Unlike Werther, who kills himself because of his passions, Woldemar fortuitously has a chance at redemption. He expresses in writing what he could not say in person. Henriette finds him passed out, discovers the truth of his feelings, accepts them, and forgives him. Miraculously Woldemar recovers at once from his near death experience, and they go off reconciled and presumably happy. His recantation of love is proven to be untrue and is entirely forgotten in a moment. The reconciliation is supposed to be the triumph of the human heart over all obstacles, the vindication of "feeling" and the "law of the heart" overall.

For Goethe, and later Hegel, Jacobi's character presents the worst form of self-conceit, what in Chapter 5 Hegel calls the "frenzy of self-conceit." Goethe detested Jacobi's novel so much that he wrote a parody of it in which the near death of Woldemar has a cynical and ironic ending.[49] When Henriette enters her room and finds Woldemar passed out, she also finds the devil there. Satan, despite the lovers' attempt to reconcile and to create their own salvation through feeling, carries Woldemar away, but not before he gives a short lecture on the folly of the human heart. Woldemar and Henriette believe mistakenly that love leads to redemption.[50] But this is simply a lie: passion for another

48. Heinz Nicolai notes,"With Henriette, a 'heavenly' maiden brings to him [Woldemar] 'pure' friendship or 'pure' love—what is called in Jacobi's sentimental terminology sublime soul-love. Woldemar finds in her a partner, i.e., the 'beautiful soul,' who becomes his total occupation" (J. B. Metzlersche, 1969), p. 11.

49. Johann von Goethe, *Geheime Nachrichten von den letzten Stunden Woldemars . . .* (1779), rpt. in *Parodie auf Fritz Jacobis "Woldemar,"* hrsg. von Carl Schüddekopf (Weimar: Gesellschaft der Bibliophilen, 1908).

50. The Devil explains to Henriette (the beautiful soul) that "You do not love him as he loves you. . . . Your feelings of friendship are different from his as are mine. His friendship you could let go; you could let him go." She remains indifferent to this reality, but even then the Devil seeks to make her understand Woldemar's unworthiness, trying to make her see things as they really are: "The Devil sprang at her violently, grasping her boldly with both fists, and cried out

requires a check on the sublimity of the Self. There must be an effacing of egoistical conceit in order to have an identity with another. An "absolute ego" cannot, by its own claims to self-sufficiency and to a "free" will, exist as a self-effacing individual. Its false beliefs only show that it is an "evil" being. The devil should understand this claim, since the kind of conceit Woldemar practices is the same sort that the devil himself practices.

At least in the case of Jacobi's *Woldemar* we are dealing with an imaginary character. Jacobi should be seen as advocating a "false type," one that is untrue to the identity of self-consciousness as it pursues genuine self-certainty. One can actually attain the identity of the "beautiful soul." For Hegel the poet-philosopher Friedrich Philipp von Hardenberg, who is known by the pen name Novalis, is an instance of the "true type," since he is the true aesthete philosopher who becomes the prophet for the "beautiful soul." Hardenberg was a student of Schiller's at Jena in 1790–1. He was also a member of the Jena Circle and a close associate of the Schlegels and the playwright Ludwig Tieck. He presents the genuine "moral aesthete," since he centers his own work on the vocation to call forth the unity between the Self, God, and the social World. The soul of humanity is to rise to a divine union in a romantic vision. The outcome of modernity is, for him, nothing other than the cosmopolitan peace that comes to all when we are governed by God's true servants. This is what Kant himself sought to attain in his political writings;[51] it is the accomplishment of moral purpose that is necessary to justify our commitment to the truth of right Reason. Novalis, who adopts Kant's theme, presents the self-effacing love that was lacking in Woldemar's sentiments. In effect he becomes all love in which there is no Self. For instance, in Novalis's third "Hymn to the Night" he recounts his deadly bereavement as he stands over the grave of his true beloved, and in this feeling there is an infinite yearning for eternal love. His feeling is to be one with the "beautiful soul"—namely, Sophie von Kühn, who died of consumption at the ten-

---

'Only ruins! And that is all you have and for that you beg!'. . . . 'I would if I could make his heart as a women holds to the teats of a goat, and from it I would let you drink . . . [but] all you have is this extravagant tumult [of feeling], that is all there is. . . .'" To this Henriette only says, 'Oh, only that: it calls forth! The completeness of his faith; the salvation of my love; the love that I feel and that I have fancied. This is the essential thing [*Wesen*], whose abode is surely eternal, and for it I will depart without complaint; I will be lost to it! She sank down once more. . . ." Goethe, 17–19, *passim*.

51. Novalis is an advocate for Kant's thesis of perpetual peace. Cf. Kant's essay, "Toward Eternal Peace" (1795), *Akad.*, viii, pp. 341–86.

der age of fourteen.[52] (The first mention of the beautiful soul in Hegel's
text speaks of its death.) The beautiful soul is the ideal other, the "better" Self, who redeems the hero from his own wastefulness. It presents a
concord that connects one individual to another in perfect love. Unlike
Woldemar, who seems only to react from confused motivations, Novalis
presents the clarity of romantic sentiment. His love for the other makes
him worthy of being himself a "beautiful soul."[53] This may be why
Hegel picks him to be representative of the true conscience: the sublimity of private Reason. In the text the relation between this "pure aesthetical type" and the other is identified as the relationship between a law
giver and judging consciousness. The "law of the heart" is what is being
posited by the aesthetical consciousness; the judging consciousness is
testing to see if this law is true *and* to see if it can live up to this ideal.
Novalis seems to represent both sides. He posits the law of the heart and
sees in the loss that he suffers that this law fails because life itself is too
limited; our human sentiments are too frail. Yet, he is also the "judging
consciousness" that presents in itself its goal and objective to be the
"beautiful soul," one who is perfectly worthy of love and redeemed
through it. This feeling surmounts all limitations and it becomes the

---

52. Novalis writes, "Once, as I shed bitter tears—in sorrow my hopes
melted away, and I stood lonely by the barren mound, which enclosed the shape
of my life in a narrow dark room; lonely as none before me was ever lonely,
driven by unspeakable dread, bereft of strength, and no more than a thought of
wretchedness—as I gazed about there for help . . . and clung to a fleeting extin-
guishing life with infinite yearning—then, out of blue distances, from the
heights of my old blessedness, there came a twilight seeming, and all at once the
bond of birth broke the fetters of light. Earthly splendor had fled, and with it
my grief. . . . You, night-inspiration, slumber of heaven, did come over me: the
region of gentility rose aloft, and a cloud of dust covered it, and through the
cloud I beheld the transfigured features of my beloved. In her eyes reposed
eternity; I grasped her hands, and my tears became a glittering chain that could
not be wrenched asunder. Millennia passed off into distance, like storms. Upon
her neck I wept ecstatic tears unto the new life. It was my first and only dream,
and since then I have only felt an everlasting, immutable faith in the heaven of
the night and in its sun—the beloved," "Hymns to the Night"(c. 1797–9; publ.
1800) in *Novalis Schriften*, hrsg. von Paul Kluckhohn und Richard Samuel,
Bd. 1: *Das dichterische Werke* 131–57 (Stuttgart: W. Kohlhammer Verlag, 1960),
p. 134.

53. Novalis also died of consumption, when he was twenty-nine. Hegel, in his
Heidelberg Lectures on Political Philosophy (1817–8), names Novalis and
Spinoza (who also died of consumption) as examples of this "type" of moral conscience. Cf. Hegel's *Vorlesungen*, Bd. 1: Naturrecht und Staatswissenschaft, hrsg.
von Otto Pöggeler (Hamburg: Felix Meiner, 1983), p. 80.

symbol for public Reason; in other words, it becomes the "way of the World" and says that the World will be reconciled through it.

Novalis is the genuine prototype for Schiller's aesthetic genius. His philosophical outlook, best known from the essay "Christendom or Europe" (1799), is to be the herald for a new religious reconciliation among all European peoples. He considers Christianity itself to be the model of the triune Concept, which leads to reconciliation and salvation for all:

> Christianity has a threefold form. One is the creative element of religion, the joy of all religion. One is intercession in and of itself, faith in the universal capacity of all earthly things to be the bread and wine of eternal life. One is the faith in Christ, His mother, and the saints. Choose which one you will. Choose all three, it makes no difference. You will thereby become Christians and members of a single, eternal, ineffable community. . . . The other continents await Europe's reconciliation and resurrection in order to join with it and become fellow-citizens of the heavenly kingdom. Should there not be presently once again in Europe a host of truly holy spirits? Should not all those truly related in religion become full of yearning to behold heaven on earth? And should they not gladly join together and begin songs of holy choirs?[54]

Rameau's trinity of a Religion of Man is shown to be an illusion, one that is itself an idol to be cast down. Novalis speaks of the heretics of the Enlightenment as "wayward souls," but with Romanticism, wherein the ideal is made real, the true nature of religious sentiment calls even to them: "Come . . . you lovers of mankind and encyclopedists, into the pacific lodge and receive the fraternal kiss, cast off the gray net, and with youthful love behold the splendors of Nature, of History, and of Mankind. I shall lead you to your brother, and he shall speak with you so that your hearts shall leap up, and so that you shall clothe your dead, beloved institution with a new body, and so that you shall embrace again and recognize what hovered before you and what the sluggish earthly intelligence could not grasp for you" (Novalis, 520ff.). The academy of the Enlightenment, which turns against faith, is here made over into a union between religious vocation and scientific understanding.

Hegel positions Novalis's religious enthusiasm as the apex of the Spirit's interrelationship with the World. In this moment Self and the

---

54. "Die Christenheit oder Europa," in *Novalis Schriften*, Bd. 3: Philosophische Werke II, hrsg. von Richard Samuel (Stuttgart, Berlin: Verlag W. Kohlhammer, 1983): 507–24, p. 523.

society of the estates are realigned, reaffirming the "beautiful concord" that the ancient Greeks held as the connecting knot of their society. What was denied in Absolute Freedom, what was killed by the Terror, now is brought back into the Concept. The singular Self in its passions and yearnings calls forth the motif of reconciliation and, ultimately, of redemption. If this prophetic vision came into the World to heal and bind it, then the ultimate union between Self and its ethical substance would be sustained. The estates, which lost their focal unity in the death of the king, can be reestablished in the spiritual brotherhood that Novalis's vision presents. This vision, although "perfect" in terms of what morality calls for and in what the Self claims to be its self-certainty, will prove itself to be insufficient, however, to gain ascendency in the World and prove itself to the true way.

Hegel in the *Philosophy of Spirit* makes the important point that whenever the inner Self becomes the absolute Self, there must be a mistrust in unity. This mistrust comes necessarily from the Self's own drive to reconcile its imperfect human nature with the "perfected" laws of Reason. Since moral law in the modern age is private Reason, the actual "ethical" bonds that historically held society together are not reconstituted. In fact, quite the contrary, they are dispensed with. There are no bonds other than "my feeling" that ties one to another. So Novalis's vision, which attempts to do so much, actually does nothing. It does not address the "evil" that belongs to the subsumption of the public under the private sphere of Reason. Romantic visions do not speak *for* the World. Novalis's musings, albeit true to the Concept that Spirit seeks to fulfill, is nonetheless only a mystical vision. The Romantics do not have strength of will, of genuine purpose, to bring this hope to fruition. Hegel goes so far to label this position "hypocrisy," because the world-historical individual has sought to demand universal fraternity on *its basis*, not in terms of what the World itself has learned through trials and sacrifices of the Self. The World itself has to present the signs of reconciliation; it must itself bear witness to the truth that the beautiful soul envisions, and, then, the Self must bear witness to what the World proclaims as *its* realizations. Only when the world historical individual humbles itself to acknowledge that it *belongs* to the World as much as the World belongs to it can there be the sufficiency that realizes moral purpose inherent in private Reason. Morality, as the stance of rational self-fulfillment, shows ultimately our inability to attain true autonomy for ourselves. The "self-certainty" belonging to the Concept, in order to maintain the identity of the Self as the autonomous moral Lawgiver, must still learn to humble itself before a "higher" destiny. "Morality" throughout its phases cannot attain the promise of being a true autocratic Self. Indeed, it must declare that even this position is a deception.

Novalis comes close to making these pronouncements himself, first, by accepting that nature has powers of perfection that humanity does not, and second, by accepting that the World reveals the shape of religion that stands above the individual. Hegel has already established the first point in Chapter 5, "Reason," in the sections concerning the "Observations of Nature." It is now time to come to the second point: the World shows that religion has itself created the conditions of Culture and Morality; that religion in its threefold shape marks the completion of the Concept and the obtainment of rational purpose. The three forms of religion, as Novalis presents them, are recognizable to us as belonging to the three stages of Unhappy Consciousness that Hegel developed in Chapter 4 of the *Phenomenology*. There we could see Hegel presenting religious consciousness as (a) the Catholic penitent who knows God as the unchangeable and for whom salvation is only through the mediation of the sacramental life, (b) the Protestant whose singular attestations both declare immediate knowledge of the divine and the worthlessness of human nature, and (c) the *rational spirit* who knows that religion and philosophical certainty are one and the same in "self-certainty." Hegel rejects Novalis's threefold form of religious truth (namely, the Catholic serving the Church, the reforming Protestant and Catholic Counter-Reformer, and finally the ecumenical Romantic) not because it ends with Romanticism, but because for Hegel "true religion" lies not in feeling and the isolated Self, which only has the certainty of sense, but in knowing the absolute, in and through the World's revelations. Novalis presents the heresy in the development of the Concept that we know the absolute Self *in us* and through our sentimental self-affirmations. What we know in us, according to Hegel, are our own triumphs followed by self-deceptions. What we can know from world religion is that "beyond" the limits of facticity and immanent existence is the pathway of Reason reconciled with revelation. Novalis's view of religious Romanticism is only another kind of dogmatism, one that embraces non-philosophy as its ultimate end. This is no better than Jacobi's character, Woldemar. It is not that Hegel is accusing Novalis and the other Romantics of being themselves "evil." He is accusing them of belonging to the dark night of the soul. They aspire to what is true, but they cannot themselves speak it. They are too busy esteeming themselves in their "circles," clubs, and literary societies. They only love what the other gives them. They suffer the evil of privation—the fault of a weak-willed man; they may know the good in general, but they do not have it in their particular acts.

Nonetheless, this spirit reaches the point where imperfection is acknowledged and forgiveness is first posited as *necessary* to reconciliation.

Each Self, since it is aware of its own failings and the failings of others, becomes an agent of forgiveness. If this did not occur, then the central message of revealed religion, which proclaims that the actual redemption has already occurred in the World, would not be recognized as true in the World. So, despite the harsh condemnation that Hegel makes against Novalis and his circle, we are to understand that their dark night of the soul is showing us the truth of the Self. In its forgiveness of fault we will find the truth.

In order for the Self to achieve the "absolute," it must become empty; it must learn the lesson of self-sacrifice; it must become humble; it must be reborn. In terms of religious doctrine, what the Self must accept in itself is the divine *kēnosis*, literally, the *emptying* of the divine into the Self. Once we recognize that the World has come to the point where self-sacrifice is announced, that it bears witness that God is forsaken in any moral self-certainty, then we are ready for the coming of true religion. Hegel's plan from *Faith and Knowledge*, which we now see coming to fruition, is to preach the "speculative Good Friday" which announces the death of the kind of popular philosophies that Jacobi and Eschenmayer (among others) advocated. This is the point that Hegel already made when he said,

> Good Friday must be speculatively re-established in the whole truth and harshness of its Godforsakenness. Only if the serene, less well-based and more individualistically styled dogmatic philosophies as well as natural religions perish, then the highest totality can and must achieve its resurrection solely from this harsh condition of loss . . . (*Faith and Knowledge, GW,* iv, 414).

The fact that Romanticism becomes nonplused, faints, and dies away like the consumptive is the sign that we have reached the place of Spirit's Golgotha. From the beginning of the *Phenomenology*, when Hegel tells us we are on the path of despair (Miller, ¶78), he has been leading us to this eventuality when the "essential Self" perishes, losing its basis in sentiment and self-love, just so that it can be resurrected in the purity of divine Reason.

The thoughtless idea that there is a supremacy of the Self in and of itself is also at an end. We cannot for our own sake turn to any other form of self-conscious life than this moment of death. But it is just at this moment, when self-centered thought dies, that religion comes on the scene to forgive and reconcile. Only religion gives the promise of redemption to humanity, and philosophy acknowledges this too; indeed it has already recognized it in its own condition of Unhappy Consciousness. Looking back at "Spirit," we can now see that this is the promise that faith knew to be true and that the Enlightenment denied in its struggle with faith. In effect, then, the death of the beautiful soul is the point where Self and World unite in the belief that the divine substance is returning and, with it, Spirit will be reborn. With the recognition of our inherent evil, with forgiveness, comes complete reconciliation.

With this expectation—with the promise of the resurrection shown through the shapes of world religion—Hegel's chapter on Spirit ends.

GLOSSARY

(German to English)[1]

Aberglauben	superstition
Absicht	intention
Allgemein	universal
allgemeine Beste	common good
Anerkennen	recognition
Anschauung	intuition
an sich	in itself
Ansich	in–itself; implicit
Ansichsein	being–in–itself
Arbeit	labor
Art	kind
Aufhebung	sublation; overcoming
Aufklärung	Enlightenment
aufopfern	sacrifice
Ausschweifung	orgy
Bedeutung	significance
Begeistung	enlivening; breathed life; is Spirit
Begriff	concept
Beilager	coupling
beleben	quicken
Belebung	give life
bemächtigen sich	takes control; takes possession
Beseelung	animation
Beschränkung	limitation
Bestehen	subsistence, persistence
bestimmen	determine
Bestimmtheit	determinacy
Bestimmung	determination

---

1. German spelling has been modernized.

Betätigung	activity
betätigt	operative
Betrug	deceit
Bewährung	trial; confirmation
Bewegung	movement
Bewußtsein	consciousness
Beziehung	connection
Bild	image
bildet sich	forms itself
Bildung	culture
Böse	evil
Dasein	determinate being; existence
daseinende	existing
Diesseits	this-side
edelmütige	noble
Eigennützig	selfish
Einigkeit	unitedness
Einmütlichkeit	concord; accord
einwandelbare	unalterable
Einsicht	insight
Einzelne	singular
Empörung	rebellion
Entäußerung	externalization
Entgegengesezt	opposite
Entfremdte	estranged
Entfremdung	estrangement, alienation
Entwesung	loss of essence
Entzweiung	division
erkennen	aware of; recognize
Frau	wife
fremde	foreign
für sich	for itself
fürsich	for-itself; for-self; explicitly
Fürsichsein	being-for-itself; being-for-self
Gedankending	*ens rationalis*
Gegensatz	antithesis
Gegenstand	object
Gegenteil	contrary
Geist	spirit
Gelten	status, what counts, in force
geltendte	counted, valued, valid
gemeinte	intended, supposed

Gemeinwesen	communal essence, community, commonweal
Genuß	enjoyment
Gerechtigkeit	justice
Gestalt	shape
Gewalt	violence, dominion
Gewissen	conscience
Glauben	faith; belief
Gleichgewichte	equilibrium
Gleichheit	identity; equality; equivalence
Grösse	quantity
Grund	ground
zum Grund gegangen	perished; gone to ground
Handlung	action
Herr	lord
hervorgegangen	issued forth
Heucheley	hypocrisy
Hinterhalt	reserve
im Hinterhalt	in ambush
Individualität	individuality
Individuum	individual
Jenseits	beyond
Kraft	force; strength
losgebunden	let loose
Lust	pleasure; desire
Macht	power; strength
Männlichkeit	male principle
Mann	man, husband
Maß	measure
Masse	masses; dimensions
Meinung	belief, intention, meaning
Mensch	human (noun)
menschlich	human (adjective)
Mitteilung	share with
Moralität	morality
Nichtigkeit	nullity
niederträchtig	contemptuous
Nützlichkeit	utility
Pflicht	duty
Pietat	devotion

preißgeben	surrender
sich preißgeben	offer at a price; prostitute
Recht	Right, justice
Sache	facticity; fact of the matter
Schein	show
Schlecht	bad
Schicksal	destiny
Schmeicheley	flattery
Selbst	self
Selbstständigkeit	independence
Selbstbewußtsein	self-consciousness
Selbstwesen	essential self
Sein	being
seiende	existent, existing
Sehnsucht	yearning
Sittlichkeit	ethical life
spröde	rigid
Sprache	speech; mode of speech
Stände	estate
Staatmacht	state power
Tat	act
in der Tat	in fact, in the deed
Ton	tone
Trennung	separation
treten gegen über	is faced with
Trieb	drive
Tun	deed
Übermuth	arrogance
Unterdrückung	oppression
Unterschied	distinction, differentiate
Untertan	subject (as in of a state)
unwirklich	ineffectual
Verbindlichkeit	obligation
vergänglich	ephemeral
Verhalten	behavior
Verhältniß	relationship
verkehren	invert; pervert
vermeintlich	intended
Vernunft	reason
Verstand	understanding
Verstellung	dissemblance; misrepresentation
Verworfenheit	rejection

Verwicklung	actualization
Verwüsten	devastation
vollenden	perfect
vollkommen	complete
vorgefunden	already found
Vorstellung	representation
Weib	woman
Weiblichkeit	female principle
Wesen	essence
Widerspruch	contradiction
Willkür	whim
Wirklichkeit	actuality
Wohltat	beneficence
Zerreißen	tearing
Ziel	goal
Zierraten	ornaments
Zufällig	accident, contingent
zusammenschliessen	link together
Zweck	purpose, aim

English to German

accident, –al	*zufällig*
act	*Tat*
action	*Handlung*
activity	*Betätigung*
actuality	*Wirklichkeit*
actualization	*Verwicklichkeit*
aim	*Zweck*
animation	*Beseelung*
arrogance	*Übermut*
aware of	*anerkennen*
bad	*Schlecht*
becoming	*Werden*
being	*Sein*
being-for-itself, -for-self	*Fürsichsein*
belief, -ving	*Meinung; Glauben, glaubende*
beneficence	*Wohltat*
beyond	*Jenseits*
certainty	*Gewißheit*
common good	*allgemeine Beste*
commonweal, -th	*Gemeinwesen*
communal essence	*Gemeinwesen*

community	*Gemeinwesen*
complete	*vollkommen*
concept	*Begriff*
confirmation	*Bewährung*
connection	*Beziehung*
conscience	*Gewissen*
consciousness	*Bewußtsein*
contemptuous	*niederträchtige*
contingent	*zufällige*
contrary	*Gegenteil*
counted	*geltendte*
culture	*Bildung*
deceit; deception	*Betrug*
deed	*Tun*
desire	*Lust*
destiny	*Schicksal*
destruction	*Verlust*
determinate being	*Dasein; bestimmtes Sein*
determine	*bestimmen*
determinacy	*Bestimmtheit*
determination	*Bestimmung*
devastation	*Verwüsten*
devotion	*Pietat*
differentiation	*Unterschied*
dimension	*Mass*
dissemblance	*Verstellung*
distinction	*Unterschied*
division	*Teilung*
drive	*Trieb*
duty	*Pflicht*
enjoyment	*Genuß*
enlivening	*Begeistung*
ens rationalis	*Gedankending*
ephemeral	*vergänglich*
equality	*Gleichheit*
essence	*Wesen*
ethical life	*Sittlichkeit*
existing	*daseinende*
externalization	*Entäußerung*
evil	*Böse*
fact, facticity	*Tatsache; Sache*
faith	*Glauben*
flattery	*Schmeicheley*
for itself	*für sich*

gone to ground	*zum Grund gegangen*
ground	*Grund*
human	*Mensch, -lich*
hypocrisy	*Heucheley*
identity	*Gleichheit*
image	*Bild*
implicit	*ansich*
in fact	*in der Tat*
in itself	*an sich*
in-itself	*Ansich*
individual	*Individuum*
individuality	*Individualität*
insight	*Einsicht*
intention	*Absicht, Meinung*
intuition	*Anschauung*
justice	*Recht, Gerechtigkeit*
kind	*Art*
labor	*Arbeit*
let loose	*losgebunden*
limitation	*Beschränkung*
lord	*Herr*
loss of essence	*Entwesung*
male principle	*Männlichkeit*
man	*Mann*
mass, -es	*Mass, -e*
measure	*Maß*
meaning	*Meinung*
morality	*Moralität*
movement	*Bewegung*
noble	*edelmütige*
nullity	*Nichtigkeit*
object	*Gegenstand*
obligation	*Verbindlichkeit*
operative	*betätigt*
opposite	*Entgegengesetzt*
oppression	*Unterdrückung*
perished	*zum Grund gegangen*
pleasure	*Lust*
power	*Macht*

prostitute (verb)	*sich preißgeben*
purpose	*Zweck*
quicken	*beleben*
reason	*Vernunft*
rebellion	*Empörung*
relation	*Verhältnis*
representation	*Vorstellung*
reserve	*Hinterhalt*
right	*Recht*
sacrifice	*aufopfern*
self	*Selbst*
self-consciousness	*Selbstbewußtsein*
selfish	*Eigennützig*
separation	*Trennung*
share with	*mitteilen*
show	*Schein*
significance	*Bedeutung*
singular	*Einzelne*
speech	*Sprache*
spirit	*Geist*
state power	*Staatmacht*
subject (under the state)	*Untertan*
subsistence	*Bestehen*
surrender	*preißgeben*
tearing	*Zerreißen*
this-side	*Diesseits*
trial	*Bewährung*
understanding	*Verstand*
unity	*Einheit*
universal	*Allgemein*
utility	*Nützlichkeit*
violence	*Gewalt*
wife	*Frau*
whim	*Willkür*
woman	*Weib*
work	*Werk*
yearning	*Sehnsucht*

SELECT BIBLIOGRAPHY

A. Primary Sources Consulted for This Translation

Hegel, Georg Wilhelm Friedrich. *Gesammelte Werke.* Hrsg. von Rheinisch-Westfählischen Akademie der Wissenschaft. Hamburg: Felix Meiner Verlag, 1968ff. Bänden 1–28.

I. Specific works used from the critical edition

Hegel, G. W. F. *Die Phänomenologie des Geistes.* Hrsg. von Wolfgang Bonsiepen und Reinhard Heede. Bd. 9. Hamburg: Felix Meiner, 1980.

————. "Glauben und Wissen" in *Jenaer Kritischen Schriften.* Hrsg. von Hartmut Buchner und Otto Pöggeler. Bd. 4. Hamburg: Felix Meiner, 1968. 313–414.

————. "Logik, Metaphysik, Naturphilosophie" in *Jenaer Systementwürfe II.* Hrsg. von Rolf-Peter Horstmann und Johann Heinrich Trede. Bd. 7. Hamburg: Felix Meiner, 1971.

————. "Philosophie des Geistes" in *Jenaer Systementwürfe III.* Hrsg. von Rolf-Peter Horstmann. Bd. 8. Hamburg: Felix Meiner, 1976.

II. Other works produced by the critical editors that, however,
are not considered reliable enough to be included in the
critical edition

Hegel, G. W. F. *Vorlesungen über Naturrecht und Staatswissenschaft.* Hrsg. von Otto Pöggeler. Hamburg: Felix Meiner, 1983.

III. Other editions of Hegel's work used for this translation

Hegel, G. W. F. *Phänomenologie des Geistes.* Hrsg. von Johannes Hoffmeister. 3rd Auflage: Leipzig: Felix Meiner, 1937.

————. *Theorie-Werkausgabe.* Hrsg. von Eva Moldenhauer und Karl Michel. Frankfurt am Main: Suhrkamp, 1970. Bände 1–20.

B. Other Translations Consulted for This Edition

Baille, J. B., translator. *Hegel's Phenomenology of Mind.* 1903; rpt. NY: Macmillan, 1949.

DeNegri, G., translator. *Fenomenologie dello spirito*. N.d.; rpt. Firenza: LaNuova Italia, 1960.

Hyppolite, Jean, translator. *Phénoménologie de l'Esprit*. Tomes 1–2. Paris: Editions Aubier, 1941.

Miller, Arnold, translator. *Hegel's Phenomenology of Spirit*. New York: Oxford University Press, 1977.

C. Secondary Literature

I. General commentaries on the Phenomenology of Spirit and related works

Crites, Stephen. *Dialectic and Gospel in the Development of Hegel's Thinking*. University Park, PA: Penn State University, 1998. [A developmental account of Hegel's thought from his student days to the completion of the *Phenomenology* in 1806. Crites documents Hegel's theological disagreements with orthodox Christianity but also his commitment to central beliefs of the Christian religion. His thesis in respect to the *Phenomenology* is that it reenacts the Gospel narratives, since it features an account of sin, redemption through God's love, self-sacrifice, and the revelation of the incarnation in human form. Crites underestimates the importance of the "scientific character" of Hegel's philosophy. He considers Hegel's work to be a mythological narrative. Crites's argument, although lengthy and full of textual details, is simpler to follow than H. S. Harris's *Hegel's Ladder*, but Harris's focus on the "scientific" character of the philosophical concept is more accurate to Hegel's position. Nonetheless, Crites's work is very valuable.]

Harris, H. S. *Hegel: Phenomenology and System*. Indianapolis: Hackett Publishing, 1995. [A brief account of Hegel's life and work. It covers in summary fashion all the sections of Hegel's *Phenomenology*. It is clear, but because of its brevity it glosses over much of Hegel's argument. Nonetheless this is a handy reference guide.]

———. *Hegel's Ladder*. Vol. 1: *Pilgrimage of Reason*. Vol. 2: *Odyssey of Spirit*. Indianapolis: Hackett Publishing, 1997. [The only complete commentary on Hegel's *Phenomenology* in English. Harris analyzes each paragraph of the text, as well as gives a defense of Hegel's "scientific" method. He contends that Hegel is presenting the development of the philosophical concept as itself a religious revelation. (This is unlike Crites's position, noted earlier, which simply holds that the life of the god-man, Jesus, is the revelation, and thus the philosophical concept is mythological or representative, not what we would call a "true" philosophical concept.) Harris's interpretation is based on solid evidence and his deep understanding of Hegel's philosophical development throughout his youthful development and early system-building at Jena. This is not a work for beginners, however, who will find Harris's style dense and the commentary full of references to Hegel's lesser known contemporaries, as well as to literature, eighteenth-century science, Greek philosophy, etc. Still, this is the most complete and valuable commentary available today. An extensive bibliography is contained in this work.]

Hyppolite, Jean. *The Genesis and Structure of Hegel's* "Phenomenology of Spirit." Trans. by Samual Cherniak and John Heckman. Evanston, IL: Northwestern University Press, 1974. [One of the best standard commentaries on Hegel's *Phenomenology*. It is more reliable than either Taylor's or Solomon's readings (see later). It is complete and offers good insights into the text. At times, however, Hyppolite tends to underestimate the polemical nature of Hegel's arguments, especially as they are directed against his contemporaries. Harris's *Hegel's Ladder* (see earlier) is more exact on such issues. Nonetheless, Hyppolite's commentary may still be the most useful research tool for the novice to Hegel's great work.]

Kojève, Alexandre. *Introduction to the Reading of Hegel.* Ed. by Allan Bloom. New York: Basic Books, 1969. [This has been the most influential reading on Hegel's work in the twentieth century. It has been most influential in the thinking of "Straussian" commentators, such as Bloom and Stanley Rosen. It inspired Francis Fukuyama in his well-known book, *The End of History and the Last Man* (New York: Free Press, 1992). Kojève's work is an edited translation of his 1930s lectures on Hegel. He tends to blend Hegel, Marx, Heidegger, and Husserl together into what is certainly one of the most imaginative readings of Hegel ever produced. Much should be said in favor of the historical flavor of the commentary, which should remind us that Hegel sees his work as a kind of Universal Philosophical History. Nonetheless, Kojève's treatment of Hegel's work is on the whole inferior to Hyppolite's commentary (Hyppolite was a student of Kojève) and to the other major commentaries selected here.]

Pinkard, Terry. *Hegel's Phenomenology: The Sociality of Reason.* Cambridge, MA: Harvard University Press, 1994. [This interpretation is indebted to Charles Taylor's theory of the modern state, and in spirit it looks back to Kojève's readings of Hegel. Pinkard tends to interpret Hegel as a social critic, and as such he tends to omit or obscure many of Hegel's arguments on the identity of the Self and its relation to Nature and World. For those who wish to see and read Hegel as a precursor to Habermas and, generally, the New Left's critique of social conservatism, this interpretation would be useful.]

Solomon, Robert. *In the Spirit of Hegel.* New York: Oxford University Press, 1983. ["Not in the Spirit of Hegel" might have been a more accurate title for this book. Solomon contends, among other things, that Hegel's work is an epistemology (as opposed to a metaphysical ontology), a subtle defense of atheism, a creation of art rather than a rigorous philosophy rooted in logic, and a social critique. The commentary commits a number of grand blunders, even confusing very specific German terms; e.g., *die Mass, -e,* which we have rendered as "mass" or "masses," (the reference is to a body as a collection of natural elements), he confuses with *das Maß, -e,* which is a "criterion" or "measure" for judging. This leads him to interpret the chapter "Spirit" as a development of "criteria" instead of what Hegel actually says, a development of the spiritual masses, i.e., the body politic and its "natural" associations. There are many other mistakes. This commentary is not recommended.]

Taylor, Charles. *Hegel*. Cambridge: Cambridge University Press, 1977. [Although comprehensive in its scope, this work is flawed in a number of ways, not the least being Taylor's view that Hegel espouses expressionism. Taylor also believes that Hegel's categories are incoherent, which for Taylor is actually a "positive" part of Hegel's philosophy, since modern philosophy should describe the true incoherence of life. The spiritual and historical dimensions of Hegel's arguments are not developed in this work; on the whole Taylor seems to have misunderstood Hegel's objectives. Nonetheless, it is an important work on Hegel. It should be consulted with caution, however.]

II. *Specific commentaries related to "Spirit"*

Jarmos, Daniel, S. J. "'The Appearing God' in Hegel's *Phenomenology of Spirit*," *Clio*, 19:4 (Summer 1990), 353–65. [Jarmos analyzes the final section of "Spirit," the movement of "Conscience." He attempts to identify the meaning of Hegel's term the "appearing God." The essay succeeds in showing that a number of commentators, such as Solomon and Kojève, have misinterpreted "Spirit." The essay is less successful in establishing the meaning of the "beautiful soul," and the interpretation that "God" is a consciousness that thinks universally is too simplistic. Since Hegel clearly identifies the incarnate spirit with "universal self-consciousness," it would be more accurate to say that Spirit, as shaped by its World, is itself the "appearing God."]

Harris, H. S. "Hegel and the French Revolution," *Clio*, 7:1 (Fall 1977), 5–18. [Harris attempts to show that Hegel was sympathetic to the French Revolution as a supporter of the Girondists and that later he was an admirer of Napoleon's legal reforms; however, Harris demonstrates that even at a very early age Hegel was opposed to and horrified at the excesses of the revolution as it guillotined reformers and led to republican tyranny. He also found fault with Napoleon's imperial pretensions. This article is especially important in contesting conventional wisdom that Hegel was an advocate of the revolution. It is more accurate to say that he was an advocate of constitutional reform.]

Knox, T. M. "Hegel's Attitude to Kant's Ethics," *Kant Studien*, 49 (1957–8). [Although Knox's article is old, and there are both more extensive and controversial approaches, it still provides a very useful consideration of Hegel's treatment of Kant's moral philosophy in "Spirit." Knox is subtle enough to know that Hegel is critical of Kant's moral system but that Hegel's own consideration of the "Moral World-View" is indebted to Kant and works within what we might call the "Kantian perspective."]

Robinson, Jonathan. *Duty and Hypocrisy in Hegel's Phenomenology of Mind*. Toronto: University of Toronto, 1977. [Robinson follows Knox's lead, but he does not recognize the subtle textual shifts in Hegel's critique of Romanticism.]

Shannon, Daniel. "Hegel: Modern Philosophy versus Faith," *Philosophy and Theology*, 9, Nos. 3–4 (1996), 351–88. [Shannon attempts to show that Hegel, on the one hand, argues in favor of the scientific idea of the *philosophes*, especially their attempts to create a rational community, for instance, in the national academies of the arts and sciences. Much of the debate between faith and philosophy discussed in Chapter 6 of the *Phenomenology* is decided in favor of establishing a "human right" to know the whole truth, without appeal to the authorities of either Church or State, and to be free of popular superstition. The established Churches, both Catholic and Protestant, are wedded to antirationalistic thought. The value of the Enlightenment is to show the error in such an attitude. On the other hand, Hegel always argues that the *philosophes* deceive themselves about the true value of religion. They failed to grasp the truth of revelation and the human significance of the incarnation. They worship a liberty without communal responsibility. They have faith in a mind filled with amusements and in nature, neither of which are adequate bases for the understanding of the Self and its relation to its World. Only a "true religion" that reflects free, rational values can provide such certainty. Thus, their criticisms against religion ultimately fail.]

Siebert, Rudolf. *Hegel's Concept of Marriage and Family.* Washington, DC: University Press of America, 1979. [Chapters 16 to 20 deal with Hegel's concept of the family in the *Phenomenology of Spirit*. The treatment is brief and superficial but also clear. If the reader is looking for a synopsis of "Ethical Life," this might be a starting point.]

Solomon, Robert. "Hegel's Concept of 'Spirit,'" in *Hegel: A Collection of Critical Essays*. Ed. by Alasdair Macintyre. Notre Dame: University of Notre Dame, 1972. [An interesting introduction to Hegel's Concept. A good place for the Hegel novice to begin.]

Stoliar, Margaret. "The Musician's Madness: Goethe and Hegel on 'Le Neveu de Rameau,'" *Australian Journal of French Studies*, 24 (1987), 309–32. [A solid introduction to the history of *Rameau's Nephew* and how Goethe came to translate it. There is some reasonable conjecture on why Hegel relied on this fairly obscure dialog for his presentation of Culture in the *Phenomenology*. This is an important study. It is recommended to those who are interested in what philosophical works influenced Hegel the most in composing the *Phenomenology*.]

III. Other commentaries of relevant importance

Fackenheim, Emil. *The Religious Dimensions in Hegel's Thought*. Bloomington, IN: University of Indiana, 1967.

Flay, Joseph. *Hegel's Quest for Certainty*. Albany, NY: State University of New York, 1984. [An extensive bibliography is contained in this work.]

Harris, H. S. *Hegel's Development*. Vol. 1: *Toward the Sunlight, 1770–1801* (Oxford: Clarendon Press, 1972). Vol. 2: *Night Thoughts, 1801–1806* (Oxford: Clarendon Press, 1983). [These volumes are required reading for anyone seriously interested in Hegel's development.]

Pippin, Robert. *Hegel's Idealism: The Satisfaction of Self-Consciousness*. New York: Cambridge University Press, 1989. [The importance of the historical reading of Hegel's *Phenomenology* is stressed. Hegel's relation to his idealistic predecessors is developed at some length.]

Rockmore, Tom. *Hegel's Circular Epistemology*. Bloomington, IN: University of Indiana, 1986. [The epistemological problems of Hegel's day are discussed. Hegel's novel "circular" solution is both presented and criticized. Too much emphasis is placed on the *Differenzschrift* though, and not enough on the Jena System projections.]

INDEX

accident, 18n32
Aeschylus, 27n44
Alcestis. See Euripides
Alexander Severus, 176n16, 177
Antigone. See Sophocles
Aristotle: *Nicomachean Ethics*,
    130n244; *Politics*, 28n47
Augustine, 169

Bacchae. See Euripides
beautiful soul, 149–55, 203, 211–3,
    211n48–50, 218
brother and sister, 14f.
Burbidge, John, xiin8, xvii

Concept. *See* Reason
Condé, Prince of France, x, 51n93,
    178n17
conscience, 134–40, 146f., 149f., 209
consciousness: noble-minded, 56ff.;
    contemptuous, 57ff., 154
Creon. See Sophocles
culture, 39–67, 187–9

D'Alembert, Jean, 78n150, 79n152,
    83n162, 98n184, 99n186
Dante, 179
death, 10, n21, 13, 108, 182
Descartes, René, 190; *Discourse on
    Method*, 100n187
destiny, 20, 26
Devil, 154n277, 211n50

D'Holbach, Paul, 77n145–7,
    78n149–50, 79n152, 91n174–5,
    99n186, 193
Diderot, Denis, 62n117, 98n184,
    99n186, 184, 186n26, 188;
    D'Alembert's Dream, 42n78,
    77n148, 181f., 182n23;
    Encyclopédia, 78n151, 79n153;
    Jacques, 190n29; *Rameau's
    Nephew*, 40n73, 40n75, 42n78,
    60n113, 63n119–20, 64n121–4,
    65n126, 66n127, 75n141, 80n154,
    185f., 185n25, 186n26, 193n31
di Giovanni, George, xiin8, xvii
disposition, 114ff.

Elagabalus (Belissus Antonius), x,
    33n58, 173n9, 174f., 174n11–2
Electra. See Euripides
Enlightenment, 37n68, 74ff., 100,
    184, 191ff.
Eschenmayr, Carl, xv–xvii, 130n245,
    135n251, 159
espèce, 40n75, 41n77, 74, 180, 190
estrangement, 35, 38ff., 45, 50, 52,
    177, 183
ethical life, 3–5, 11; demise of, 30ff.
être suprême, 54n101, 105, 182
Euripides: *Alcestis*, 9n19, 18n32;
    Bacchae, 29n49; *Suppliant Women*,
    27n46, 28n48
Evangelical Counsels (poverty,
    chastity, obedience), 87n169–70,
    95n178, 96n181, 191–2, 195

Lares, 10n21, 31n53

law: divine law, 5ff., 27, 28, 37; human law, 5ff., 16, 21, 28

Leibniz, Gottfried (and his school), xii; Hegel's attempt to reconcile Leibniz's system with Kant's in *The Jena System, 1804–5,* xiin8

Lessing, Ephraim, 86n166–7

Louis: XIV, 49n87–8, 50n92, 51n94, 52n98, 55n102, 56n105; XV, 56n103, 57n106, 58n108; XVI, 54n101, 108n201

love, 8n16

luck. *See* accident

Marcus Aurelius, 34n60

mass, -es, 42, 76, 77n147, 83n159, 105

Mettrie, Julien, 101n188, 190n29, 193

Miller, Arnold, viif., xixf., 76n142, 228

misrepresentation, 123ff., 204

Montesquieu, Charles-Louis, 106n192

morality, 112ff., 201ff.

Napoleon: as Lord of the World, 109–11, 199–201; Hegel forecasts demise of, 200n38

Novalis (Philipp von Hardenberg), 204, 212–7; as "beautiful soul," 212; *Christendom or Europe,* 214f.; *Hymns to the Night,* 212, 213n52

Oedipus. See Sophocles

Opera, 186f., 186n26

Origen, 96

Palissot, 65n126

Pascal, Blaise, 66n128, 189

Penates: as Greek household gods, 8ff., 8n14; as guardians of Roman Law and synonymous with households goods, 31n53; as the Furies, 28f. (*see also* Lares)

person, 31f.; as legal personality, 34f.

Plato: *Republic,* 18n32, 22n37; as law tester, 160

pure insight, 67ff.

Rameau, Jean-François, x, 61–6, 61n114–5, 63n119–24, 65n126–7, 184–6, 188n27, 193n31, 214

Reason: antinomies of, 116n214, 123n230, 126n238; as philosophic concept, ix–xi, xivf., 1f, 37, 74n139; as identity of Self and World, 37n67; as Spirit, 1–3; chapter on, 1n2, 3, 20n34, 68n129, 74n139, 161n3, 180n21, 201; dilemma of practical Reason, 116n212; private versus public Reason (in Kant), 198, 200–2, 214f.

reconciliation, 120n227, 156

religion: as faith (*see* faith); as superstition, 192–5; as Hegel's solution to problem of evil, 216f.; Religion of Man, 192, 214

Revolution (French), 38, 107n199

Right, 18, 31–5, 39, 173

Robespierre, Maximilien, 107n198–9, 108n201–2, 166, 196

Robinet, Jacques, 64n125

Rousseau, Jean-Jacques: *Confessions,* 186n26; *Emile,* 74n139, 76n143; *Origin of Inequality,* 39n72, 74n139; *Social Contract,* 106n196, on General Will versus Will of All, 196n34

Sartre, Jean-Paul, viiin2

Schelling, F. W. J., xii–xvii, 147n268

Schiller, Friedrich, 206–9, 206n42, 207n45–6, 210

Schlegel, 149n270, 151n274

self, ix, xvi, 20, 23, 55, 71n134, 83n159, 145n266

self-estrangement. *See* estrangement

self-identity. *See* identity

servant, 35n62, 59n110, 178n18